Lymingtor
War Memorial

Compiled by

John Cockram and Richard Williams

Cover drawn by Gervase A Gregory

Published by the authors in aid of the Royal British Legion Poppy Appeal

BUCKINGHAM PALACE.

I join with my grateful people
in sending you this memorial
of a brave life given for others
in the Great War.

George R.I.

PREFACE

By
Councillor Jane Clarke.

Lymington War Memorial commemorates 159 men from the town who died for their country during the last century.

The sadness is that there is a need for this book at all. There was a time when the stories of all these men were commonplace knowledge. Up to three generations later, however, memories are fading and modern job and social mobility has resulted in many of the families concerned moving away from the town.

I am very grateful to the Lymington Branch of the Royal British Legion, which has encouraged research to be carried out, and to the many local families who have contributed information, which has been integrated with background research and written in its present format by John Cockram and Richard Williams.

The book sets out to explain how the individuals concerned were associated with Lymington and the events that led to their deaths. In this way their lives and their sacrifice can be recorded for future generations.

The creation of the War Memorial itself was the initiative of one of my Mayoral predecessors, Edward Stone. As its maintenance is the Council's responsibility I am delighted to continue the link with this preface.

This book is timely and I commend it to you.

Mayor
Town Hall, Lymington

INTRODUCTION

This book is not intended to be a history of either Lymington or of the two World Wars. After a lapse of up to ninety-one years, the memory of the names recorded on the War Memorial is understandably in danger of becoming dim.   This book is therefore an attempt to reverse this trend.

We have tried, where possible, to establish the individual link with Lymington. An explanation is then offered of where and why the serviceman died. The framework of the appropriate military action is given for clarity, but such scenarios are limited to those relevant to the Lymington men concerned.

One joy has been the discovery of extracts from **Francis Loxton's** diary. It was against Army Regulations for such a record to be kept, but it is pure primary source material and gives an unrivalled snapshot of how those in the trenches viewed their experiences at the time. The letters of **Wilfred Clarke** are of equal value in understanding how soldiers felt about the war, whilst **Henry Foster's** account of being torpedoed is similarly compelling.

Where relatives and friends have come forward the appropriate memorial has been constructed with their help and agreed with them. In other cases Regimental Museums have been involved and have agreed the resultant article. It has not been possible to do this in every case, however, and any mistakes are deeply regretted, but are entirely our own.

The aim is a simple one – it is to record the sacrifice made by these men of Lymington and to ensure they are not forgotten as time passes. It matters not whether they died in action, in Prisoner of War camps, or in hospital of wounds or sickness. **They died whilst in uniform in the service of their country.** We owe them a great debt. The least we can do is to remember them. If this book helps in that task, it will have served its purpose.

July 2005

CONTENTS

THE FIRST WORLD WAR

THE MEMORIAL

THE SECOND WORLD WAR

LATER CONFLICTS

ACKNOWLEDGEMENTS

This has not been an easy book to write as Lymington has experienced a high degree of social mobility since 1945. Nevertheless there has been a rewarding response from a large number of people and organisations, which is evidence that many names on the Memorial are still remembered and cherished.

Help from the families of those who died has come from Jean Smith (Cecil Freeman), Stan Hayward (Earnest Hayward), Peter and Roger Backhurst (Fred Backhurst), Catherine Dashwood (Robert Dashwood), Roger Bygott (Robert Bygott), Ron and Beryl Clark (Stanley Clark), Qwen Tuckerman (Clive Lewington), Ann Witlock and David Hurst (Cyril Hurst), Bob Klitz (Anthony Klitz), David Hayter (George Hayter), John Clarke (WD Clarke), Cliff Stride (Roy Wilson), Bill Clarke (William Clarke), John Hayward (Thomas Hills), Rosemary Voles (Jack Gunnell), Judy Houghton (Robert Rixon), Geoff and Mavis Isted Peter and Bob Isted) and Betty McGregor (Fred Cassey).

We are also very grateful for those people who have spent time and resources in helping to research various aspects of the book. These include Murial Bishop, John Mizzi of Malta, Joan Stephens, Marc Thompson, John Mitchell, David Wilson MBE (PoWs) and James Nunn. Information has also been quarried from the National Archives in Kew, as well as those of Canada and Australia. Medical advice das been given by Dr EriK Eriksson and Dr Perihan Colyer.

Regimental museums have, of course, been very helpful. Whilst it is almost invidious to mention particular ones it must be acknowledged that those of The Royal Hampshires, Devon and Dorsets, Duke of Cornwall's Light Infantry, South Wales Borderers, The Royal Armoured Corps (Bovington), Tank Museum, the Submarine Museum (RNSM) and the Naval Historical Branch at Portsmouth, have been particularly helpful. The New Forest Museum and the St Barbe Museum Lymington, have also generously provided help and material for the project.

Local historians have freely shared information. These include the late Brian Downes, Norman Gannaway, Peggy and Jude James, Dot Jenkinson, Joan Stephens and Shirley Blick (the archivist at St Thomas Church) who rediscovered the 1914-18 Memorial Book. Finally, Les and Pam Stubbs have generously shared their information on Far East Prisoners of War.

Photographs have been kindly provided by Chris Rogers (Singapore), The Commonwealth War Graves Commission (CWGC), National Maritime Museum London (NMM). Imperial War Museum (IWM), Clare Church, The LYMINGTON TIMES, Avril Williams (Somme), Marc Thompson (Flanders), Thelma Stollar, Joan Stephens, various police forces (including Eddie van Driel in Holland), as well as the families concerned. Aircraft artwork has been kindly provided by David Howley. The generosity of Gervase Gregory in providing the cover drawing, free of charge, is also very much appreciated.

Support has been gratefully received from the Lymington Branch of the Royal British Legion, the Town Council (and their very helpful archives section) and not forgetting the encouragement received from Councillor Elizabeth Lewis.

Our proofreaders - Robin Budgett, Don and Ginette Cording, Patricia Hilborne and Gill Cockram, and Peggy and Jude James - have vastly improved the accuracy of the pages. The mistakes that remain, however, are entirely our own.

Hobbs the (Splendid) Printers have once again provided a quality product at a very reasonable price and the cooperation and help of their staff is much appreciated.

Finally we would like to say a very special thank you to Thelma Stollar and Nick Saunders, both of whom have enthusiastically researched extensively - and at their own expense – the more difficult aspects of this book.

In researching material for this book it is evident that minor errors have been made in some of the details on the War Memorial, particularly in respect of rank and initials. Where there is any difference the detail used has been taken from the Commonwealth War Graves Commission – or other official – records.

Published by
John Cockram
of Robin Cottage, Sway Road, Brockenhurst,
Hampshire SO42 7RX.

2005 John Cockram

ISBN No.: 0-9540972-1-1

THE FIRST WORLD WAR

THE WESTERN FRONT
1914-1915

Whilst the casus belli of the First World War was the Serajevo murder of the Crown Prince of Austria, the armed camps of Germany/Austria and France/Russia/Britain ensured, on

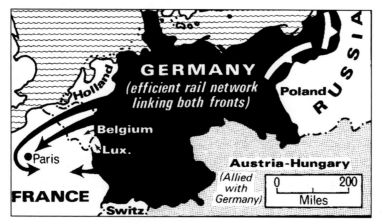

mobilisation, that the main action would immediately be in France and Belgium. Germany had to defeat France within six weeks if she was to win the war. She would then have

time to switch her armies from the western front to the east to defeat Russia, who would take longer to mobilise.

Germany had long prepared for such a war. The Schlieffen Plan, designed in 1905, was a revolving door. As the Germans pushed from the north so the French were propelling themselves into Alsace and Lorraine to the south. This coal rich territory had been lost to the Germans in 1870. The French Plan XVII, to recapture Alsace and Lorraine played into German hands. Schlieffen wanted the French armies to cross the frontier, held, and then destroyed once the rest of France had been occupied.

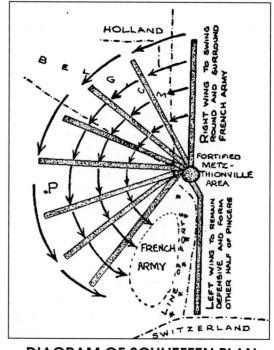

DIAGRAM OF SCHLIEFFEN PLAN

Schlieffen died muttering "**Keep the northern attack strong.**" It was weakened at the last minute, however, with Moltke deploying 7 divisions from the northern hammer blow to stop the Belgian army from breaking out and also despatching 4 divisions to Russia, who was mobilising faster than anticipated.

The German commanders to the south did not allow the French army to penetrate sufficiently to become inextricably enmeshed in the difficult Alsace countryside. These errors, reinforced by the unexpectedly stiff resistance of the small but professional armies of Belgium and Britain in the north, threw the Schlieffen Plan out of kilter. The retreat from Mons, whilst not a victory, was a triumph for the 60,000 British regulars, such as Bertie Kingswell, Bill Lock, Bert Croucher and others and put a brake on the German advance. The halting of the German attack on the Marne and the subsequent allied advance to the Aisne, during which **William Heaste** died, was a decisive moment of the war.

Movement stopped, trench warfare began and with Russian mobilisation completed more rapidly than expected, Germany was faced with its worst nightmare of war on two fronts. In Flanders the "Race for the Sea" began, with the Germans trying unsuccessfully to outflank the allied line northwards. **Harry Hayter** was to lose his life in frustrating this attempt.

Most of the German colonies were quickly captured, although **Arthur Payne** was killed in the capture of Tsingtao, in China.

In Lymington men rushed to join the colours, and the Recruiting Officer, based in Winchester, was kept busy. To

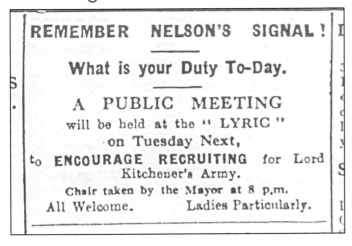

encourage local men THE CHRONICLE published this advert and reported that the Territorial's Drill Hall was now manned by Colonel Apperley, ex-Master Gunner Pocock and ex-Sergeant Major Goodger, who would provide advice to young men anxious to enlist. By the 10th September, 1914, three hundred local men had enlisted in the Army or Royal Navy.

WILLIAM JAMES HEASTE
Private
L/6854
2nd Battalion, Royal Sussex Regiment,
who died on
Monday 14th September 1914, aged 28.

William was the son of Mr and Mrs. W. Heaste, of Winton in Somerset. He was born at 158 Solihull Road in Handsworth, Birmingham and in the 1901 census his father, also William, is described as a carpenter. Sisters Annie and Alethea were also born at this address, although two other sisters – Elizabeth and Ethel - were born in Somerset. William married Beatrice Brown at All Saints Church, Lymington, on the 8th April 1912. At the time he described his profession as that of a wardrobe dealer, although he had followed his father into carpentry. Beatrice's father, George, was a fisherman. They lived in Normandy Lane, Lymington. Beatrice later remarried to become Mrs Gamblin of "Ivel Hurst," New Road, Norton-sub-Hamdon, Stoke-under-Ham, Somerset.

Before the war William enlisted at Poole into the 2nd Battalion the Royal Sussex Regiment and as a regular soldier sailed with the battalion to France on the 21st August 1914. William's regiment was not present at the Battle of Mons, but took part in the retreat back to the south east of Paris.

By early September the First and Second German Armies, on the right of the German advance into France, began to lose close contact with each other. When this was first spotted by a British reconnaissance aircraft on the 5th September, the situation was immediately exploited by the allies - the French sending troops to the front in Paris taxis and the British turning about to threaten the enemy. On the 7th September the Germans rapidly withdrew across the Grand Morin and a day later over the Petit Morin Rivers. William's battalion was the advance guard for the Brigade and came into contact with the German cavalry rearguards.

The British advance was widening the gap between the two German Armies commanded respectively by von Kluck and Bulow. On the 9th September both armies retreated back to the strong natural position overlooking the River Aisne. Despite German rearguard actions the Marne River was soon crossed. The Royal Sussex had advanced 37 miles in three days, over three rivers, in the face of a stronger enemy.

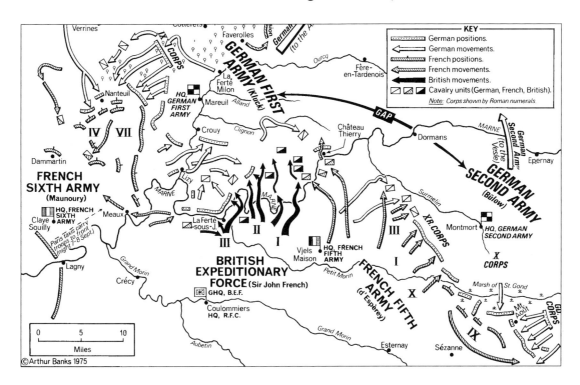

The British continued their advance in cold rainy weather, crossing the river Vesle on the 11th and began crossing the Aisne a day later. By this stage, however, von Kluck had been placed under Bulow's command, a converging retirement had been conducted and two fresh German Army Corps brought up to fill the gap. The German line stabilised and the Germans showed no intention of further retirement.

At 9.00 a.m. on the 12th September the Royal Sussex was advancing near Preiz in heavy rain wearing their waterproof sheets. This movement was observed by our own artillery, which thought the grey-clad figures were Germans and promptly opened fire. This friendly-fire incident cost the Royal Sussex more than 100 casualties, of which William was one. He died of his wounds at St Nazaire and is buried in **St Nazaire (Toutes-Aides) Cemetery**, Loire-Atlantique, France, in:

Grave A. 8.

HARRY CORNELIUS HAYTER

Private,
5563
1st Battalion Scots Guards
who died on
13th November 1914, aged 28.

Harry was born in early 1886 in Milford, where the family lived in Milford Village Cottage. His father, Cornelius, hailed from Dorset and was a bricklayer's labourer – as were his two eldest sons William and James. Harry had a sister, Emily, who was eight years older than himself. He later moved to live in Bath, Somerset.

Harry was a regular soldier who had joined the army before the war. His unit was part of the 1st Guards Brigade in 1 Division. It was amongst the earliest arrivals in France and had taken part in the retreat from Mons and the subsequent advance to the Aisne. By mid October it was moving up to the Ypres area and by the 21st it was holding an extended line on the left flank of the British position.

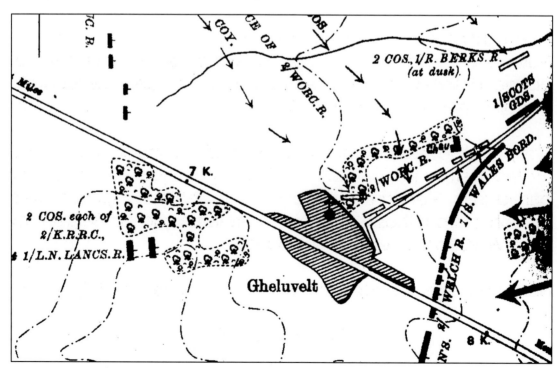

The Germans then commenced an all out attack to break the British/French line and capture Ypres. After a week's fighting the BEF had been pushed back and Harry found himself defending the Chateau on the Gheluvelt plateau.

At 8 a.m. on the 31st October the Chateau was subjected to a violent and searching bombardment. Three hours later the Germans had penetrated the Welch Regiment's positions and were in the Chateau grounds. A charge from the Borders and the Scots Guards restored the position as, in the words of the Official History:

"The Germans in the Chateau grounds showed no desire for cold steel, bolted back pell-mell and were either bayoneted or shot at close quarters, or escaped, dropping arms and equipment in their haste."

Although the position was restored heavy German reinforcements made the plateau untenable. The BEF were slowly pushed back and the battle degenerated into confused engagements in the small woods either side of the Gheluvelt-Ypres Road. The remnants of the Scots Guards and 1 Division fought doggedly in the Nonne Bosschen and Polygon woods.

Their fighting abilities had helped to save Ypres, but by the 11th November, when the division was ordered into reserve at Hooge, Harry's battalion over 900 strong had been reduced to battalion headquarters and 39 men.

Harry was wounded in one of these actions and was captured by the Germans. He died of his wounds, however, and was buried in a German cemetery. In 1924-5 such graves were brought in from their German cemeteries or plots in Belgium by the CWGC for more central reburial.

Harry now rests in **Harlebeke New British Cemetery**, Belgium, in

Grave XIV. C. 9.

ARTHUR GEORGE PAYNE

Sergeant
7235
2nd Battalion, South Wales Borderers,
who died on
Thursday 5th November 1914, aged 33.

Arthur was born in 1881 in Newport, Monmouthshire, to Mr. and Mrs. George Payne, of Brecon. In 1905 he enlisted in Abertillery into the 2nd Battalion the South Wales Borderers.

The battalion returned from the Boer War on 9th June 1904 and settled into Bulford. At the end of 1906 they moved into Oudenarde Barracks, Aldershot, and three years later to Chatham. He married Alice and the couple initially lived in Waterford Lane, Lymington. As Alice was on the strength as an official Regimental wife she accompanied him abroad. On 15th January 1911 the battalion was posted to Pretoria, South Africa, and in October the following year moved to become the garrison battalion of Tientsin, in China.

This British Treaty Port on the coast was 70 miles southeast from Peking and 250 miles northwest from the German Treaty Port of Tsingtau. Germany negotiated her possession of Tsingtau in the aftermath of the Chinese murder of two German Roman Catholic missionaries in 1897. She promptly set about fortifying the area and developing the harbour facilities to make it a base for her Far East Fleet. The German squadron included the modern fast cruiser EMDEN and had been strengthened by the concentration of other German naval ships from the Yangtse River, Shanghai and Chefoo. This mixed squadron posed a threat to Allied commerce in wartime, as British and French warships would be withdrawn closer to home. In the first week of the war the German Pacific Squadron sailed, as planned, to begin its commerce raiding activities. This left the port defended by gunboats and the formidable shore fortifications manned by 4,000 men.

In 1911 an Alliance had been signed between Britain and Japan, which allowed for either party to come to the aid of the other if attacked. Japan declared war on Germany on 23rd August 1914 and immediately proposed a joint Anglo-Japanese force to take Tsingtau by means of a land attack. The Japanese fielded a well-organised force of 22,980 trained soldiers and 142 (mainly siege) guns. The British contribution was mainly naval, with the land component being limited to 910 men of the South Wales Borderers and 450 NCOs and men of the 36th Sikhs. The Japanese forces landed near Tsingtau on 2nd September, but heavy rains limited their advance.

MEN OF THE SOUTH WALES BORDERERS IN TSINGTAU

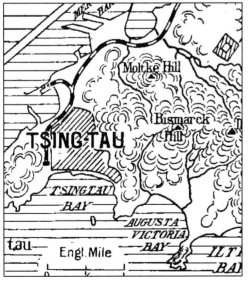

The British force landed on 23rd September and joined their allies before the walls of Tsingtau; they did not play a major part in the campaign. The South Wales Borderers had been moved at such short notice that – as can be seen in the above photograph - they were still in tropical kit and were suffering from the early onset of cold and wet weather. Additionally they had to endure a shortage of rations. Cooperation with the Japanese was also not easy due to different language, tactics and discipline.

The battalion manned its own small section of trenches facing Moltke Hill, to the right of the attacking forces. Arthur was in C Company, the War Diary for which appears to be written in pencil. It tells the story of the final week of Arthur's life.

War Diary "C" Coy 2/KRR.

31-10-14. Two platoons under Capt Johnson were in occupation of the trench in the Artillery covering position on the right of the Regiments line. The other two platoons were in support in the parallel between nos 1 & 2 communication trenches. At night the whole company were employed in completing the 1st attack position & putting up head cover.

1-11-14 Two platoons moved up to 1st attack position & the other two in support in a nullah at end of no 3 Communication trench —

2-11-14 Whole company employed on no 2 attack position at night but this trench was a bad one being full of water

3-11-14 Whole company employed on completing no II attack position. Lt Rawle reconnoitre across the river & found a lot of barbed wire in the ditch on left of bridge. Heavy shell fire on the support during the night

Casualties S/ Briggs Pte Payster & Smith accidentally wounded

& Pte Jones wounded by sharpnels.

4/11/14 Company employed in trenches in the
2 assault position -

5/11/14 The Company were ordered to dig
trench for the 3 attack position on
continuation of Glacis of the 2 Redoubt
from which they were directly enfiladed.
The Company commenced digging after
a German sentry in a look out tower
had been disposed of & his loopholes
blocked -

The whole Company were placed on
the alignment & started digging
when a heavy rifle & machine gun
fire was opened on them left flank
Four men on the left were wounded
one killed I therefore withdrew the
left platoon & continued digging
with the other three - This trench was
completed under heavy fire about
11.30 pm when I retired. Capt
Johnson then volunteered to
take out a rescue party to fetch
in some wounded men of Nº Coy
who were on my left. He took
out Cpl Ward & 4 men of Nº Coy

11

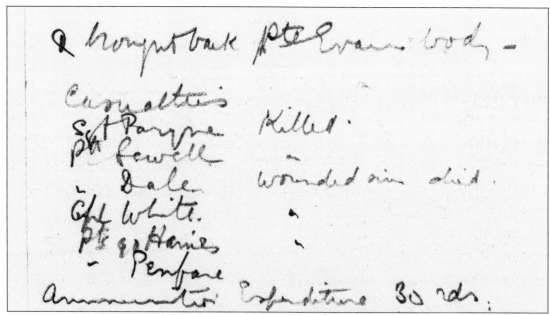

THE SOUTH WALES BORDERERS AND MONMOUTHSHIRE REGIMENTAL MUSEUM

C Company was to lose two more killed and wounded in the final assault on 7th November. It therefore suffered nine of the twelve fatalities incurred by the battalion during the siege. Most of these casualties were caused by artillery and machine gun fire. The Japanese had 1,518 casualties, of whom 236 were killed.

On 16th November the Allies formally occupied Tsingtao and their first act was to hold a memorial service for the dead. On 19th November the Borderers embarked on the battleship TRIUMPH and sailed for Hong Kong, where they boarded troopships for England prior to being sent to Gallipoli.

Sergeant Arthur Payne's name is commemorated on the **Saiwan Memorial**, Hong Kong, on:

Panel 6

When Arthur died his wife returned to England with her family. Sadly his son, Arthur, (see page 225) was to be the first Lymington casualty of the Second World War.

1915

Early 1915 saw the BEF reinforced by Canadian and Indian Divisions as well as by an increasing flow of Territorials. The first New Army Division – the 9th (Scottish) - arrived in May. Equipment deficiencies, however, were not made good until later in the year. **_Anthony Klitz_** was one of the early Territorial casualties of the war.

Ypres. On 22nd April the Germans initiated the Second Battle of Ypres by releasing their new weapon of poison gas.

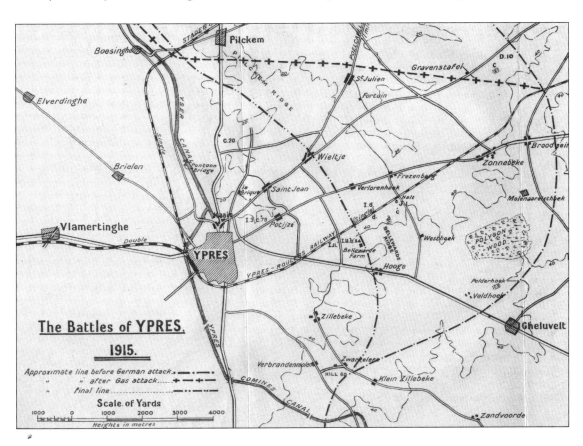

The Battles of YPRES, 1915.

Approximate line before German attack
" " after Gas attack
" " final line

Scale of Yards

Heights in metres

They did not, however, follow up their success and the hole in the line was plugged by the amazing bravery of the Canadians and some British and French Units who, without effective gas masks, frustrated the attack. **_Bertie Kingswell_** of the Hampshires was one such. Whilst the allied line held, the Second Battle of Ypres went a long way towards destroying what was left of the original BEF. The new Kitchener armies were to suffer from the loss of the experience that these pre-war regulars could have brought to their training and operational effectiveness.

The Memorial, (right) commemorates Canadian casualties of this first gas attack incurred at St Julien – amongst whom was **Fred Backhouse**. The trees are deliberately shaped to represent exploding shells.

Cecil Carpenter, Francis Loxton, and *William Lock* all died at Ypres during 1915.

The Western Front. Field Marshal Sir John French, commander of the BEF, tried to improve the line with limited results at Aubers Ridge (March-May), Festubert (15-20th May) and later in the year at Loos (25th September-4th October). The attacks were all to fail due to strong German defences, insufficient artillery ammunition and reserves held too far back to exploit initial gains.

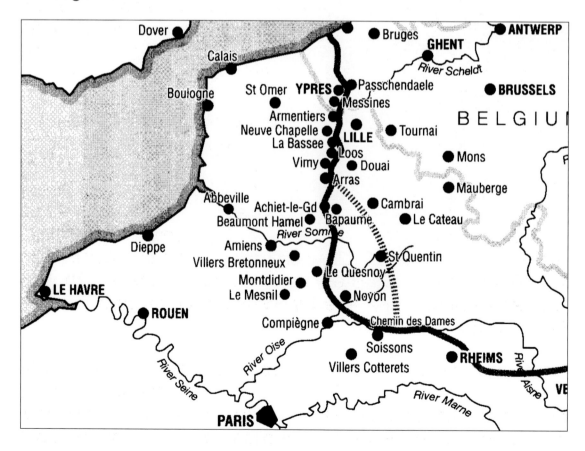

EVELYN ANTHONY KLITZ
Rifleman
9512
5th (City of London) Battalion, London Rifle Brigade,
who died on
Friday 12th March 1915, aged 20.

Evelyn, or Anthony as he was known in the family, was born in Lymington in December 1895, the youngest of eleven children, to William and Ellen Klitz of 88, High Street, Lymington. The family was an integral part of the musical life of Lymington,

William and Ellen being the second generation of the family-run music shop in the High Street. His nephew, Bob Klitz, has kindly provided this family information, photographs and drawings.

Anthony was living in South Norwood when, in early 1914, he enlisted in London into the London Rifle Brigade. On the 19/20th April he took part in a record-breaking march by sixty of his unit from London to Brighton. This they did in fine style in 14 hours and 23 minutes. In a letter to his brother Les, written on the 23rd August 1914, Anthony describes his experiences whilst in P Company marching from Wimbledon to Bisley Camp and writes of the conditions there. Another brother Reginald, who lived in Wimbledon, enlisted into the Royal Engineers.

Anthony's territorial battalion was amongst the earliest of its kind to serve in France. This it did as part of the 4th (Regular) Division, the Londons being incorporated into the 11th Brigade, alongside the 1st (Regular) Battalions of the Somerset Light Infantry, East Lancashires, Hampshires and the Rifle Brigade.

Anthony arrived in France with his battalion on the 4th November 1914 and joined the 11th Brigade – which was recovering from the 1st Battle of Ypres - in trenches at Plug Street. The four companies in the battalion rotated every three days between spells in the trenches, in support just behind the line, in billets in Plug Street and rest in Armentiers.

According to a fellow rifleman, who was in the same area at the same time, the trenches were in muddy ground and were surrounded by thousands of cans and empty tins. Water was everywhere and the water table was high. The front line, therefore, was made up of shallow ditches enhanced by sandbag breastworks. Whilst in the line they observed the German trenches 300 yards away through trench periscopes. There was some shelling, but the real threat was from the ceaseless and accurate German snipers. Everything therefore had to be done doubled up and even at night they couldn't straighten themselves. They cooked bacon and heated tinned food on an improvised brazier, wrote letters, read, kept guard and tried to improve the trenches. In reserve and at "rest," they formed nightly working parties and carried food and defensive stores up to the line.

On the 27th February 1915 Anthony was seriously wounded through the forehead. He was evacuated down the line until he found himself in the Women's Hospital Corps Hospital at Wimereaux, near Boulogne.

An operation was performed and for a time, although his condition was most critical, hopes were entertained that he would recover.

One of his older brothers visited him. But meningitis supervened and he died on 12th March.

ANTHONY'S ORIGINAL GRAVE

PHOTO THELMA STOLLAR

Anthony is buried in **Wimereux Communal Cemetery**, in:

Grave XII. 3.

The family had inscribed on the bottom of the gravestone:

**"TILL THE DAY BREAKS
AND THE SHADOWS FLEE AWAY"**

BERTIE KINGSWELL

Private
5938
1st Battalion, Hampshire Regiment,
who died on
Wednesday 19th May 1915, aged 32.

Bertie was born at Pilley, the son of James, a ship driller, and Augusta Kingswell, of 15, South Street, Lymington.

Clearly of an adventurous turn of mind, Bertie joined the 2nd Battalion, the Hampshire Regiment, and served with them in the Boer War. Indeed, the census of 1901 records him as being a Lance Corporal at the age of 19, resident in Stanhope Lines at Aldershot. Having finished his time with the colours he went on the reserve, and in this category was recalled to the regiment on mobilisation. Bertie was posted, with many other "old soldier" Section D reservists, to the 1st Battalion with the reverted rank of private. This regular battalion landed in France on 23rd August as part of 11 Brigade, 4th Division and entrained for Mons. The retreat from Mons followed, with the subsequent battles of the Marne and the Aisne.

THE DEFENCE OF PLOEGSTEERT WOOD

Bertie arrived in France on 12th September and by the end of the month had joined the Hampshires, on the Aisne. On 12th October they began their advance to the Lys and a week later they were tasked with the defence of Plugstreet Wood. They then settled down to winter trench warfare in this waterlogged area.

On 15th April 1915 the battalion was withdrawn for rest, but a week later the Germans attacked to the north at Ypres and Bertie's unit was warned for a move to the Salient.

Ten days later 11 Brigade was placed under the orders of 28th Division, who were attempting to plug the gap at St Julian created by the German gas attack. By 2nd May, after continuous fighting and shelling, the battalion had suffered 122 all ranks killed or missing and 213 wounded.

After a brief rest the battalion went back into the line, and on 13th May repulsed yet another German attack, incurring a further 169 casualties.

Bertie was severely wounded in this attack and evacuated back to one of the Base Hospitals at Boulogne, where he died.

He is buried in **Boulogne Eastern Cemetery**, Pas de Calais, France in

Grave VIII. D. 23.

FREDERICK JOHN BACKHURST

Private
1624
8ᵗʰ Battalion, Canadian Infantry (Manitoba Regiment),
who died on
Monday 24ᵗʰ May 1915, aged 37.

Fred Backhurst was born in Lymington on 31ˢᵗ May 1877. He had three brothers, William, George and Harry. His father had started a livery business in the Angel Hotel yard and the boys were therefore brought up to be familiar with the care and usage of horses. The Lymington Directory is dated 1891. The Angel Hotel yard

entrance below records

W BACKHURST & SONS
Job-masters & Carriage Proprietors
Posting & Livery Stables

FRED AS POSTILION AT THE CORONATION OF EDWARD VII IN 1902

Fred carried on business in the High Street as a saddler and harness maker, succeeding the late Mr TC Blake, to whom he had served his apprenticeship. Later he gave up the business, going to Canada, where he continued working as a saddler. He made occasional visits home,

"when he always received a joyous welcome, being of such a merry-hearted disposition and well known."

From Service Documents in the possession of Nick Saunders it is recorded that on 13th August 1914 Fred, admitting only to being aged 35, enlisted into the 96th Lake Superior Regiment, being employed as a guard. On the 27th August he was taken

on the strength of the 8th Battalion Canadian Infantry (Winnipeg Rifles), being attested at Valcartier Military Camp in Quebec. He was nearly 5 feet 8 inches in height, a 39-inch chest and of medium complexion with grey eyes and brown hair. He also had a scar inside his left ankle.

Being a saddler by trade it is not surprising that he was classified as a 1st line Driver.

21

The Winnipeg Rifles - nicknamed 'The Little Black Devils' – were part of the 2nd Canadian Infantry Brigade, commanded by Brigadier General AW Currie - who later rose to command the entire Canadian Army in the First World War. The unit sailed on the *Franconia* for France on 3rd October 1914 as part of the first Canadian contingent of 31,250 men. Arriving in England at the end of the month they were promptly sent to camps on Salisbury Plain for intensive training.

In February 1915 the main body of what was now the 1st Canadian Division sailed for France. After equipping for cold weather fighting they took over 7,000 yards of trenches in the Ypres area and endured the next few weeks of trench warfare. By mid April the Division was holding the front line behind Passchendaele with two brigades up and one in reserve. The German gas attack of 22nd April fell on the left of the Canadians' position. Despite the precipitate retreat of units on this flank the Canadians held their ground - although being without gasmasks - and finally stabilised the line at St Julian. The 8th Battalion, under Lieutenant Colonel Lipsett, gained a reputation at this time for holding its trenches firmly, although heavily gassed. According to THE TIMES:

> *"With quick ingenuity the Winnipeg troops transformed their handkerchiefs into respirators and stood their ground."*

One member of the battalion - Colour Sergeant Fredrick Hall - was awarded a posthumous VC for his bravery on 24th April. During the last week of April the battle continued with great bitterness but in spite of their continued use of gas, the Germans were gradually pushed back. On 1st May, just before the Canadians were withdrawn from the Second Battle of Ypres to refit at Bailleul, Fred was struck down by shrapnel and seriously wounded in the abdomen. He was treated at 3 General Hospital in Le Treport.

Fred died of these wounds on the 24th May and he was initially buried in the **Soldiers Cemetery** at Le Treport, in:

Grave 110

After he died his brother George received the following letter:

MILITIA AND DEFENCE
CANADA

MINISTER'S OFFICE

OTTAWA May 28th. 1915.

Personal.

Dear Mr. Backhurst,-

Will you kindly accept my
sincere sympathy and condolence in the decease
of your splendid brother Private Frederick John
Backhurst.

While one cannot too deeply
mourn the loss of such a brave soldier, there is
a consolation in knowing that he did his duty fear-
lessly and well, and gave his life for the cause of
Liberty and the upbuilding of the Empire.

Again extending to you my heart-
felt sympathy,

Faithfully,

Major General,
Minister of Militia and Defence,
for Canada.

George Backhurst, Esq.,
Angel Hotel, Leamington,
Hampshire, England.

Fred's personal effects were also sent to George, at the Angel Hotel in Lymington. After the war his brother also received Fred's memorial medallion and scroll, as well as his medals.

Fred is now buried at **Le Treport Military Cemetery**, Seine-Maritime, France, in:

Plot 2. Row F. Grave 7

He is also commemorated on the family grave in Lymington Cemetery.

CECIL EDMUND CARPENTER
Private
9575
1st Battalion, Hampshire Regiment,
who died on
Sunday 4th July 1915, aged 19.

Cecil was the son of Charles, a mineral water porter, and Ada Carpenter who, in 1901, lived in Church Street, Lymington. In 1915 they were resident at 121, High Street, but the family later moved to 4, Alfred Street, East Cowes, Isle of Wight. Cecil was educated at the Brockenhurst County High School.

When war was declared he enlisted in Winchester into the 1st Battalion, the Hampshire Regiment. This regular Battalion had landed in France on 23rd August as part of 11 Brigade, 4th Division. After taking part in the retreat from Mons and the subsequent battles of the Marne and the Aisne, it had been tasked with the defence of Plugstreet Wood - just to the south of the Ypres Salient. The Hampshires then settled down to winter trench warfare in this waterlogged area.

On 15th April 1915 it was withdrawn for rest, but a week later the Germans attacked to the north at Ypres and the battalion immediately moved to the Salient. On 25th April, 11 Brigade were placed under the orders of 28th Division - which was attempting to plug the gap at St Julian created by the German gas attack. The battalion fought continuously throughout the Second Battle of Ypres, which ended at the end of May. The brunt of this battle had been borne by the old Regular Divisions – the 4th, 5th, 27th and 28th – who had between them incurred over 41,000 of the 59,000 British casualties. This heavy loss of trained soldiers was balanced by the frustration of the German attack, which, if successful, could have led to a breakthrough to the channel ports, a resumption of the German advance into France and arguably the loss of the war by the allies.

Cecil was part of a reinforcement draft arriving in France on 26th May 1915, just as the battalion was transferred to the Sixth Corps under General Keir. The battalion was at rest in "**good Billets**" on the Everdinge - Poperinghe road, and the War Diary also notes that:

"***All the men had a jolly good bath and got well fitted up***".

On 1st July they took over some French trenches to the west of Ypres. It was their third spell in this sector, and they were in reserve behind the Ypres Canal. According to the War Diary, 3rd July was:

"***Very hot – the Bosche included a good many gas shells in their evening "hate." The companies on the banks of the Yser Canal had to put on their respirators.***"

During this time the battalion suffered twenty-five casualties, mainly from shellfire. Cecil was one of 4 other ranks killed on the last day of this period of front line duty.

He had served on the Western Front for less than six weeks.

Cecil is buried in **Talana Farm Cemetery**, Ypres in

Grave II. C. 16.

FRANCIS WILLOUGHBY LOXTON

Corporal
3/7437
6th Battalion, Somerset Light Infantry,
who died on
Wednesday 11th August 1915, aged 32.

Francis was born in Lymington in Trafalgar House, Nelson Place North. His father, Edgar, was a timber merchant and his elder brother, Bertram, worked as clerk to the business. Before the war, Francis married Edith, of Morley House, Yeovil and lived at 54, Upper Tollington Park, Harringay, Middlesex, where he worked as an auctioneer's clerk.

On the outbreak of war Francis enlisted in Yeovil into the Somerset Light Infantry. Clearly an educated man, he kept a private diary of his service, which reflects his feelings in England during that first week of the war:

"On August 6th I signed fresh National Reserve papers, abandoning clause enabling me to resign at any time. This was two days after the declaration of war on Germany, and though I realized the gravity of the war more than many, I at first signed for Home Defence only, as I hardly expected that Great Britain would send a great Army to the Continent, besides the Expeditionary Force of 150,000 men of the Regular Army. During the fortnight which followed, it was brought home to me more and more that the young unmarried men had not yet realized their duty or the extent and thoroughness of the German preparations. Accordingly, upon the National Reserve being given an opportunity of joining the New Army of 100,000 for which Lord Kitchener had asked, I enlisted with other National Reservists at Yeovil, to the total number of 54 (45 of whom were married men) with the approval of my wife.

I was duly attested on 26th August and proceeded next day to Taunton and from there, on 1st September, to North Camp, Aldershot. Here we were duly formed into a platoon of the 6th (Service) Battalion of the Somerset Light Infantry and went through a course of Army reservist training, culminating, after three months, with a course of musketry laid down in peace time for Territorials."

The battalion went to France on 28th May 1915 as part of 43rd Brigade of the 14th (Light) Division. On 11th June the battalion was inducted into trench warfare by being attached for a week to the 5th North Staffordshire Regiment, who were in trenches northeast of Wulverghem. The battalion War Diary records:

"Throughout the whole week the men of the Battalion had been under fire, both artillery and infantry, and their behaviour has been excellent. No complaints at all. The Battalion who were our instructors were full of praise of the bearing and behaviour of the 'Kitcheners,' whom they saw for the first time."

On 24/25th June the 43rd Brigade moved back to the trenches. The Somersets arrived just west of Vlamertinghe at 4 p.m. and there had tea. At 8.30 p.m. the march was continued, though progress was evidently slow, as the battalion did not reach Ypres until 9.15 p.m. Francis records:

"We passed through Ypres, and the memory of this scene of desolation has made the greatest impression on me of anything in the war up to the present. Whole streets of shattered houses, especially around the Cathedral and Cloth Hall, but the builders of the two latter knew their work so well that the outer walls of both mostly remain standing. The Cathedral tower bids defiance to the Huns and the facade of the Cloth Hall is sufficiently intact to show what its original beauty must have been. Modern buildings, however, are smashed to atoms."

Whilst waiting in Ypres to go forward, hostile shells fell frequently, and when at last the battalion got on the move, the relief took a long while to complete, so that it was 2.30 a.m. on 25th before the Somerset men were settled in. One casualty from shellfire and one from rifle fire were suffered by the battalion. The trenches were in a dangerous position. They had been captured from the enemy only a few days previously and occupied the most easterly point of the British position in Belgium, in front of Hooge. The line generally was in a very bad state and under incessant shellfire from the north, east and south. The Battalion War Diary notes:

> *"The Battalion worked very hard in improvement of trenches. The behaviour of all ranks was excellent. Enemy very busy sapping and wiring, but shows no inclination to attack. Heavy shellfire from 11 a.m. to 2 p.m. (28th). High explosive poured upon us."*

Relief came during the night of 29/30th June and the battalion marched back to billets near Vlamertinghe. The total casualties suffered by the battalion during the five days were 43 – including 6 other ranks killed. At 6 p.m. on the 18th, however, the battalion marched out of billets through Ypres and reached the Menin Gate at 9 p.m. Here guides from the 5th KSLI met the Somerset men and conducted the battalion to the front-line trenches, which were only reached after one and three-quarter hours hard walking. This tour lasted until the 22nd and was a difficult one. The enemy's guns were particularly active and on the very first day the casualties of the battalion were heavy - 4 other ranks killed and 29 wounded. The battalion came out of the line on 26th July 1915.

After four days, however, they were sent to Hooge, where the 41st Brigade had fallen back in the face of the first liquid fire attack. Despite an immediate counter-attack they had only re-occupied part of the lost trench line. The Somersets stood to at 5.15 a.m. and finally moved off at 6.35 p.m. arriving in Ypres at 10.15 p.m. At 3.10 a.m. on 31st July, half the battalion moved to reinforce the Durhams in Zouave Wood.

However shelling was so heavy that the wood was not reached until after midday. The rest of the battalion arrived at midnight. Francis, in D Company, was in reserve in Half-way House dugouts. Artillery barrages from both sides swept over the wood for the next five days. On 3rd of August D Company moved out of reserve to relieve A Company. Francis described the scene in his private diary of the time:

> *"Moved up to firing line to-night relieving A Company; worst part of front in the hollow of 'U' facing trench captured by Germans, the space between it and us being open ground covered with long grass, and our position being on edge of Sanctuary Wood, beautifully marked off by German artillery. The whole hollow of the 'U' was covered with dead bodies of K.R.Rs. and R.Bs., killed in original retreat and subsequent counter-attacks, and the stench was awful and outlook appalling. The captured trench was on rising ground and also beautifully ranged by our artillery, who were dropping in shells all day. It is doubtful whether the Germans occupy the trench at all. If they do, or did, then their losses must have been frightful, as our fire from 9'2 and other guns was terrible, practically every shell dropping in trench or parapet. We saw several bodies on parapet in German uniform, a sign that their losses had been heavy, otherwise they would have been recovered and buried."*

The Somersets were relieved on 5th August, but returned to the trenches at Railway Wood on 10th August. The relief was completed just after midnight on the following day. The trenches were in terrible condition, with the parapets blown down, communication trenches blocked and machinegun emplacements destroyed. That afternoon, through German shellfire, Francis and four other Somersets were killed and twelve others wounded

Francis is buried in **Bedford House Cemetery** in Ypres, Belgium, in Enclosure No 2:

Grave II. A. 18

WILLIAM CHARLES LOCK
Rifleman
10338
8th Battalion, King's Royal Rifle Corps,
who died on
Friday 17th September 1915, aged 27.

Bill was born at Crawley, Hampshire in 1888, a son of William Charles and Annie Lock, who later moved to live in St Thomas's Street, Lymington.

Bill lived in Upper Parkstone, Dorset, but enlisted at

Southampton into the King's Royal Rifle Corps. He joined the 1st Battalion In France on 20th December 1914, but, along with many others, was soon evacuated back to England with frostbitten feet.

On recovery he joined the 8th Battalion during its training in England. The 8th Battalion had been formed at the end of August 1914 and with the 7th Battalion and the 7th and 8th Battalions of the Rifle Brigade, formed part of the 41st Brigade of the14th (Light) Division.

This division landed in France in May 1915 and after its initial acclimatisation to trench warfare took over some trenches at Hooge in the Ypres Salient.

Bill's battalion took over forward trenches at Hooge Chateau on the night of 29/30th July. They "stood to" with the 8th Rifle Brigade on their left, half an hour before dawn. At 3.15 a.m. the Germans blew up the stables of the chateau and subjected the British trenches to, what was, the first attack by flame-throwers. Surprise was complete, the 8th Rifle Brigade were overwhelmed and after stiff resistance Bill's battalion, subject to attacks on three sides, was also forced to fall back.

Counter attacks could not regain the lost trenches, so the brigade was withdrawn that night, only to return the next day, when the Germans renewed their attack. This action cost the battalion 190 casualties.

Bill had just been made up to be an acting Lance Corporal, but was never a Sergeant as recorded on the memorial. He was wounded by a single rifle bullet. His Sergeant wrote at the time to the family:

> *"I am afraid it was rather a bad one, but I don't think it will be really serious. We had only been in the trenches about three hours and Lance Corporal Lock was out in front in charge of a small post. It was bad luck, for I was just going out to relieve him when he was hit. He was bandaged at once and got away and the last I saw of him he appeared very bright and cheerful.*
>
> *I was very sorry to lose him for he was a very useful man, appreciated by the officers and liked by the men of his section."*

He was sent to one of the Base Hospitals at Etaples, where he died from his wounds seven weeks later.

He is buried in **Etaples Military Cemetery**, Pas de Calais, France, in:

Grave IV. F. 7A.

THE FIRST WORLD WAR

THE MIDDLE EAST
1915-1917

THE MIDDLE EAST

For centuries the Ottoman Empire had occupied and controlled most of the Middle East. Her influence declined in the 19th century and her position had been further challenged by the Balkan crises of 1908-13. Turkey was not in alliance with Germany, but she had distinct Teutonic leanings, expressed through the Berlin/Baghdad railway project and the import of Krupp arms and German military advisors for her army

In 1914 Turkey was willing to go to war with Russia, which supported the Serbs and Armenians, but was wary of Britain's naval might. In late July 1914 Germany sent two powerful battle cruisers, GOEBEN and BRESLAU, to the Mediterranean. On 1st August these ships sailed past British warships and escaped to Constantinople. Their presence enhanced German prestige and on being "sold" to the Turkish navy gave them enough confidence to join the Central Powers. The immediate effect of this was to block the Gallipoli Straits, thus closing the Black Sea to Russian import of armaments and reducing her fighting capability. It also tied up large British forces in Egypt. Turkey, in turn, had to face war on five fronts:

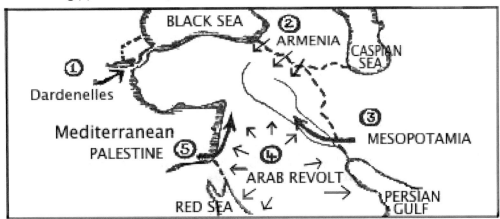

1. The Gallipoli Campaign (see pages 34-40)
2. The Russian advance into Armenia
3. The Mesopotamian Campaign (see pages 41-46)
4. The Arab Revolt
5. The Palestine Campaign (see pages 47-49)

India. Troops from India (see pages 50-55) participated in these British campaigns.

33

GALLIPOLI

The Gallipoli Campaign was conceived by Winston Churchill, with the clear aim was to enable Russia to be supplied with military aid by forcing the Dardanelles and thereby allowing allied ships passage into the Black Sea.

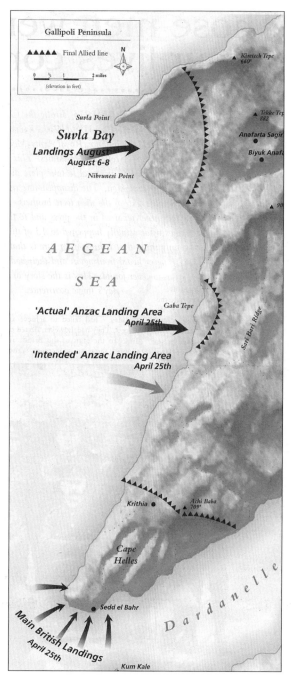

The resultant threat to Constantinople would force Turkey to withdraw from the War, with Bulgaria similarly deterred from co-operating with Germany. Pressure on Russia also thereby be reduced.

Had the initial attack been successful these objectives could arguably have been achieved and the war significantly shortened.

The initial assault by the British and French navies was not successful. In the last week of April 1915, therefore, two ANZAC Divisions, 29th Division, the Royal Naval Division and a French colonial division made a landing at Helles.

The subsequent Battles for Krithia and Achi Baba were not a success.

Turkish reinforcements, freed by Russia's inability to co-ordinate attacks in the Black Sea and helped by German "advisers," frustrated attempts at the Second and Third battles for these locations.

More troops were sent out and on 6th August 1915 landings were made at Sari Bair and Suvla. Confusion, lack of urgency by senior commanders, shortages of water and strong Turkish counter attacks negated early successes. The principal aim of the operation unachieved, the peninsula was finally successfully evacuated on 8th January 1916.

The Hampshire Regiment had three battalions involved in the campaign. The regular 2nd Battalion, part of the 29th ("Immortal") Division, took part in the initial landings on 25th April 1915 and served throughout the entire campaign until the evacuation in December. The 8th Battalion (Territorial Force) landed at Suvla Bay as part of 54th (East Anglian) Division on 9th August and was evacuated early in December. The 10th (Service) Battalion arrived on Gallipoli by taking part in the assault beach landing at Suvla Bay on 7th August as part of 10th (Irish) Division. **Bill Marshman**, who later died on the first day of the Somme, served with them. They were evacuated, a "mere remnant" of a battalion and left the Peninsula at the end of September. Surprisingly the three battalions never served together operationally.

2nd Battalion, the Hampshire Regiment. The War Memorial, however, records the deaths of three soldiers of the 2nd Battalion. After training, 2nd Hampshire (2 HAMPS) left Warwick on 28th March and 993 all ranks, under the command of Lieutenant Colonel Carrington-Smith, embarked on His Majesty's Transports *Aragon* and *Manitou* for Egypt.

Cyril Osborne died of wounds on 6th July. ***Edward Stokes*** was killed on 6th August, and ***Walter Barter*** died of wounds a day later.

As their bodies were either not recovered from the battlefield, or were buried at sea, their names appear on the **Helles Memorial** in Turkey.

CYRIL HARVEY OSBORNE
Private
3/3951
who died on
Tuesday 6th July 1915, aged 19.

EDWARD STOKES
Lance Corporal
14769
who died on
Friday 6th August 1915, aged 32.

WALTER JAMES BARTER
Corporal
7995
who died on
Saturday 7th August 1915, aged 25.

Walter, Cyril and **Edward** had all enlisted into the **Hampshire Regiment** and after basic training were posted to the **2nd Battalion**. Walter was with the 2nd Battalion at Romsey, before it moved to Stratford-on-Avon for brigade training. The others joined it in Gallipoli.

Walter was one of the sons of Frank, a ship's fireman, and Bessie Barter of Quay Street, Lymington. Eliza, Bessie's mother,

lived with the family, which included William, the eldest son, and Walter – both born in Lymington.

He landed with the battalion on 25th April. The initial beach landing at Gallipoli from the *River Clyde* was severely repulsed, with Colonel Carrington-Smith and many others being killed. This photograph was taken from the *River Clyde* bridge just moments before the Hampshire's CO was shot next to the photographer.

The remainder of 88 Brigade, including the remaining two companies of Hampshires, were boated ashore to land at "W" Beach, where they were unopposed. The battalion experienced such a very difficult first five days ashore that its effective strength was reduced to barely 500 men, including Walter. The whole division was reduced to 149 officers and 6,746 men. The beachhead had, however, been successfully established and the division came close to capturing Achi Baba on the 28th.

TAKEN FROM THE SHORE
THE FOLLOWING MORNING
APRIL 26TH 1915.

Cyril arrived with reinforcements and joined the Hampshires when they were withdrawn from the line on 30th April. He had been born in Christchurch in 1896, the son of John Henry and Bessie Osborne, but lived at Quay Hill, Lymington.

The following day the Hampshires relieved the Essex in the front line. They gained 1,200 yards later that day but had to withdraw when other units fell back. Two more days out of the line enabled the remaining 400 men to wash and shave for the first time since the landing.

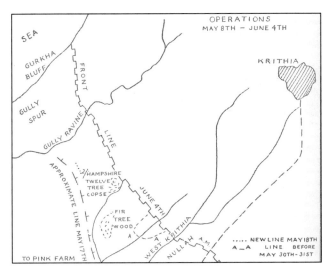

The 2nd Battle of Krithia began on 6th May. The Hampshires, like the other units of 88 Brigade, had lost their battalion commander as well as most of their company, platoon and section leaders. Not a man had had a real night's sleep for a fortnight.

Both attacks on 6th and 7th May were disastrous failures from which the battalion emerged yet further weakened. Over the next month the line was advanced by a number of small local actions combined with sapping forward short distances, until it was relieved from the line on 25th May. Resting at Pink Farm they could, at least, bathe at Gully Beach – although they were never out of the range of Turkish shellfire.

Cyril's Z Company next took part in the attack of 4th June. Whilst the available artillery support for this attack was, in the words of C T Atkinson, historian for the regiment, **"sadly scanty,"** the attack started – as planned - at midday. The company commander, Lieutenant White, was killed almost immediately, but his place was taken by Captain Rosser - who led the company on to capture the Turkish second-line trench H10 until Wounded. The advance continued under Lieutenant Lambert to the final objective

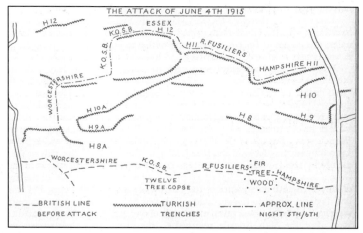

of the enemy's third-line trench, H11. This gain was lost to a Turkish counter-attack the following day, but restored in a VC action by Second Lieutenant Moore, who the following day found himself commanding the battalion as no regular officers remained. Both Walter and Cyril survived this action. The battalion, after a spell in reserve, finally went to rest on Y Beach from 19-24th June, where they were joined by Edward and other reinforcements.

Edward was the second son of Stephen and Mary Jane Stokes, of East End, Lymington. In 1901 the family lived in Little Durnford, Wiltshire, where Stephen worked as a shepherd, Charles, the elder brother, was a domestic groom and Edward an ordinary labourer. Edward married Kathleen Mabel and they lived at Middle Road, Highfield, Lymington. After his death, Kathleen married a Mr. North and moved to Quandialla, New South Wales, Australia.

The battalion moved up to the line in reserve trenches behind Twelve Tree Copse, where they prepared for the next attack on 28th June. The objective this time was H12 in the centre of the line. Repulsing a strong counter-attack they spent the next six days consolidating and strengthening the position. This cost them 28 killed and 74 men wounded. Cyril was badly wounded, being shot in the head on 3rd July. He died of his wounds on 6th July aboard the hospital ship *Sicilia*, and was buried at sea.

Walter and Edward went on with what remained of the battalion to hold trenches in Gully Ravine. But the 29th Division had, after three months continuous fighting, shot its bolt. On 17th July the battalion was withdrawn to the nearby island of Lemnos for a well-earned rest. Here the battalion received 300 reinforcements to bring it up to a strength of 732 other ranks and 24 officers. Although out of the sound of shelling, the "rest camp" had few amenities, was infested with insects and service rations could only be augmented at vast cost from the locals. The fourteen days rest was reduced to eleven when the threat of a Turkish attack sent the division back to Gallipoli on 28th July. The battalion had five days in reserve on Gully Beach, where they were joined by two drafts totalling 4 officers and 126 men – which made the battalion stronger than it had been since the landing.

On 3rd August the battalion moved up to trenches east of Gully Ravine in readiness for the new assault on H 12, H12a and H13, scheduled for 6th August. The aim was to distract Turkish attention from the main attack at Suvla Bay. This, in turn, was designed to link up with - and therefore widen – the Helles bridgehead.

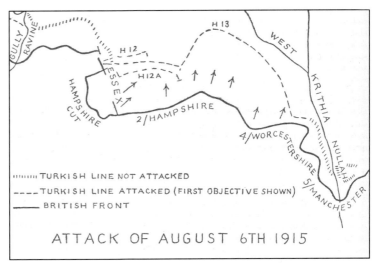

ATTACK OF AUGUST 6TH 1915

The Hampshires attacked in four waves at 3.50 p.m. "supported" by a very inadequate artillery barrage. The attack foundered against Turkish machinegun fire and although some of the attackers reached the enemy trenches, by nightfall the attack had failed. The battalion lost 18 officers and 224 other ranks killed and missing; and 2 officers and 210 men wounded. Nothing had been gained and the battalion was again reduced to about 400 effectives.

Having no marked graves **Cyril Osborne, Edward Stokes** and **Walter Barter** are all commemorated on the **Helles Memorial**, Turkey.

PHOTO CLARE CHURCH

Cyril was buried at sea. His name is on:

Panel 131

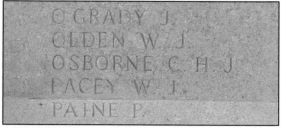

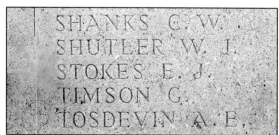

Walter was wounded in the attack, died on HMT *Caledonia* and was buried at sea. His name is on:

Panel 126

Edward was killed in this attack and his body never found. His name is on:

Panel 127

40

MESOPOTAMIA

In November 1914 a brigade, quickly upgraded to the 6th Division, was sent from India to the Persian Gulf with the aim of protecting the Anglo-Persian Oil Company's assets – needed by our oil-burning navy - and to frustrate the German concept of a Berlin-Baghdad railway from having a sea terminus.

The Turks were easily defeated at Sahil and both Basra and Kurna were occupied before the end of the year. The subsequent battle of Shaiba, opened the prospect for the occupation of Baghdad. This was one of the most decisive British victories of the war, but it resulted in an unrealistically low assessment of Turkish capabilities and laid the foundations for subsequent reverses.

The 4th Battalion Hampshire Regiment became the first Territorial battalion in India to be selected for service in the Mesopotamian campaign. On 10th March, 31 officers and 790 men entrained for Karachi and arrived in Basra four days later. It immediately became part of the "Townshend Regatta," as the advance up the Tigris beyond Qurna was called.

A platoon of forty men of the Hampshires in HMS COMET secured Amara and captured several hundred Turks in the process. On 24th July 1915 Nasiriya was successfully attacked.

Meanwhile General Townshend was surprisingly defeated Ctesiphon, 18 miles short of Baghdad. He therefore withdrew to the base at Kut and all troops, (including two companies of Hampshires which were moved to Kut at the end of November) were put to improving its defences. D company of the battalion escorted wounded down the Tigris River – in the process of which **Ronald Ford** was killed. The other company remained to take part in the siege. **Sidney St John** and **James Gates** were both taken prisoner when the town fell on 29th April 1916.

On 31st December 1915 the two companies (364 men) of Hampshires linked up wirh the returned D Company and as part of the 9th Brigade in 7th Division, promptly advanced to relieve Kut.

The subsequent actions at Shaikh Saad and The Wadi cost the Tigris Corps over 6,000 casualties. The Turks next entrenched themselves in a strong position at El Hanna. The 9th Brigade moved up to the position on 19th January and closed to within 300 yards of the Turkish trenches. "H" Hour was set for 6.30 a.m. on 21st January, but a mirage prevented the gunners from seeing their targets. The attack was therefore delayed for 75 minutes, which unfortunately, served to alert the enemy. The attack was a disaster with the Hampshires, alone, losing 13 out of the 16 officers in action and 230 of the 339 men. **Walter Gilmour** was one of those wounded in the battle.

What was left of the Hampshires merged with the 5th Buffs in 35th Brigade of 3 Division and became known as the "Huffs." Given the importance of relieving Kut the brigade moved upcountry. A brilliant night march on 8th March surprised the Turks at El Hanna and made the relief look a reality. However, the opportunity was lost and although the Sanniayat position was reached in April the attack on 21st April failed and Kut had to surrender.

Kut was finally regained on 24th February 1917 and Baghdad occupied on 11th March1917.

RONALD CYRIL FORD
Private
305171
1st/4th (T F) Battalion, Hampshire Regiment,
who died on
Friday 21st January 1916, aged 21.

It has not been possible to find anything about **Ronald's** background, other than the record in *"Soldiers Died"* that he was born and enlisted in Lymington. From the same source he lived, at the time of enlistment, at Goring on Sea, in Sussex. The St Thomas's Memorial Book shows:

✠ Ford Ronald C   Private. 1/7th attached 1/4th Battalions. Hampshire Regiment. India Killed in action in Mesopotamia (in the retreat from Kut).

He enlisted into the 1/7th or 2/7th Hampshires, with the number 7/1241 and was one of the drafts of one officer and fifty men sent to Mesopotamia by both battalions to reinforce the 1/4th Battalion, arriving in theatre on 26th August 1915. He joined the Hampshires probably together with Sidney St John, whose number is very similar. Both soldiers were accorded "long numbers" in March 1917, as neither death had been confirmed at this time.

Ronald was one of the company that had to fight the barges of wounded from Kut, down river through Turkish and Arab ambushes. This involved, when necessary, landing on the riverbank and putting in a quick attack. Ronald was killed in such an action and his body was not recovered. His death certificate therefore records him as

"Presumed Dead."

Ronald is recorded on the **Basra Memorial**, Iraq, on:

Panel 21 and 63

43

SIDNEY St. JOHN
Private
305173
1st/4th (T F) Battalion, Hampshire Regiment,
who died on
Saturday 30th September 1916, aged 22.

Sidney was born and lived in Lymington. His mother, Margaret, died in 1942 and his father, George, five years later. Sidney is recorded on their grave in Lymington cemetery. In 1940, his

brother, Edward St John (a sergeant in the battalion), lived at Colaba, Middle Road, Lymington – Colaba being the barracks in India to which the 1/7th Battalion, including Sidney, were posted in 1914.

Sidney enlisted in Lymington before the war into the 7th (Territorial Force) Battalion of the Hampshire Regiment (number 1243). He sailed to India and was sent to the 1st/4th in Mesopotamia on 31st July 1915.

He was a member of the company that was involved in the defence of Kut until the town surrendered in April 1916. Of 2592 British other ranks that were taken prisoner at Kut 70% died during their captivity and from the 164 strong Hampshire contingent captured only 40 were to survive their experiences in Turkish hands.

According to his death certificate Sidney died from dysentery at some date between 1st and 31st September 1916 whilst a prisoner of war in Turkey. His name is recorded on the **Basra Memorial**, Iraq, on:

Panel 21 and 63

JAMES GATES

Gunner,
66727
Royal Field Artillery
who died on
9th August 1916, aged 36.

James was born in Lymington in 1880, being the son of Edward and Jane Gates, who later lived in the High Street, Merstham, Redhill.

Before the war he enlisted at Woolwich into the Royal Artillery and after training was sent to India to join 76 Battery in 10 Artillery Brigade. His unit, equipped with 18-pounder field guns, was sent to Mesopotamia in December 1914 and became part of Column A of the Tigris Field Force. By October 1915 the brigade was encamped at Kut, operating in support of the advance on Baghdad.

After the defeat at Ctesiphon the brigade took part in the defence of Kut. All through the siege wireless communications had been maintained with Basra, who finally gave authority for Townsend's force to surrender.

James survived the siege and was one of the 2000 British troops that were marched out of Kut, through Baghdad and Mosul, to POW camps in Anatolia. He died in a camp hospital and received a formal burial. His grave was found in Anatolia after the war and his body reburied in **Baghdad (North Gate) Cemetery**, in

Grave XXI. C. 36.

The photograph of the KUT PLOT (Baghdad) was taken in the early 1920s.

WALTER ERNEST GILMOUR
Private
2924
1st/4th (T F) Battalion, Hampshire Regiment,
who died on
Monday, 24th January 1916, aged 27.

Walter was born on 17th April 1888 to Jane, formerly Hampton, and George – a grocer's cellarman. At that time the family lived at 111 Upper Brook Street, in Winchester, but later moved to Abbey Road, Hyde. Although his connection with Lymington is unknown, there is only one Walter E Gilmour who died whilst serving with the Hampshire Regiment.

He enlisted in Bournemouth into the Hampshires and was sent via India to Mesopotamia. He was with his battalion when it set out from Amara to march up the Tigris to help relieve Kut. The progress of these 18 officers and 405 soldiers has been narrated already (see page 43). The attack on 21st January at El Hanna was disastrous. Walter was wounded and evacuated back down the Tigris by barge to Amara. Both medical and transport arrangements were inadequate to meet the needs of the wounded and the conditions were such that the mortality rate for all units was high. Walter apparently survived the experience, but succumbed to his wounds in hospital.

The battle cost the Hampshires 37 men killed or died of wounds, a further 130 men were wounded and 77 were missing. In other words the battalion lost a total of 244 men, nearly 60% of their strength, in this battle. Walter is buried in **Amara War Cemetery**, Iraq, in

Grave I. B. 25.

The battalion War Diary is annotated in manuscript:

"The absolute accuracy of all dates to January 21st cannot be guaranteed as the notes for this period were apparently on the body of Captain A C Brandon (killed in action 21/1/16) and were never recovered"

PALESTINE

The Turks had attacked the Suez Canal in February 1915, but since that time pressure from the Arabs to the South and a positive effort to push the Turks out of Egypt had resulted in a Turkish withdrawal from there to Palestine.

This allowed a water pipeline and a railway to be constructed across the desert and enabled the Egyptian Expeditionary Force to attack Gaza in March 1917. The attack under General Murray failed and **Edwin Elliot** died during this operation.

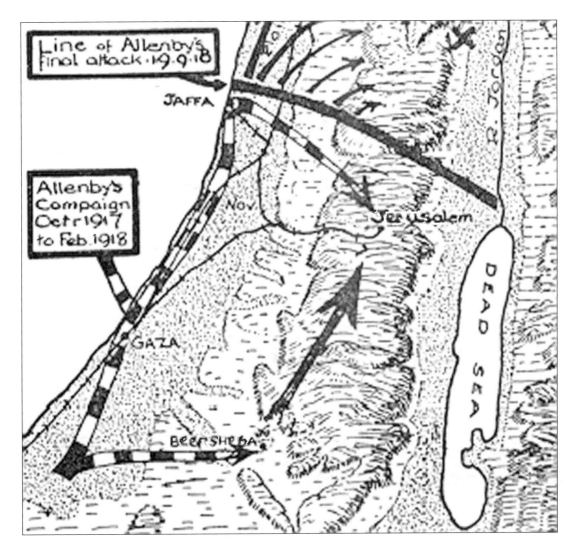

General Allenby took over command, broke through at Beersheba and so opened the way to the capture of Jerusalem later in the year.

EDWIN CHARLES ELLIOTT

Private
331037
1st/8th (T F) Battalion, Hampshire Regiment,
who died on
Thursday 3rd May 1917, aged 18.

John, a fireman, and Sarah Elliott lived in South Street Lymington. When he was 15 years old their eldest son, Albert, was a stable boy. The other children were Florence, Tom, Sydney and Edwin.

Edwin was born and lived in Lymington. He enlisted, under-aged, at Brockenhurst into the Hampshire Regiment. He joined the 8th (Territorial) Battalion in Egypt, where it was serving as part of the 163rd Brigade of the 54th (East Anglian) Division. In 1916 they were tasked with defending the Suez Canal, although the Turkish threat to it steadily diminished. In January 1917 the Hampshires were withdrawn for training, before starting off the following month to join the Desert Column scheduled to take part in the attack on the main Turkish position at Gaza, in Palestine.

The First Battle of Gaza on 27th March was not a success. Although Ali al Muntar, the key to Gaza, was captured the Force Commander, General Murray, responded to the news of strong Turkish reinforcements from the northeast by ordering the withdrawal of the mounted troops screening the attack and warning the 54th Division to fall back to the El Burjabye Ridge. The expected Turkish reinforcement then failed to show. Attempts to recover evacuated positions were unsuccessful and so the battle ended.

Three weeks later Gaza was far more heavily fortified. The plan for the Second Battle of Gaza was for a two-phased attack beginning with the securing of the Sheikh Abbas ridge. 54th Division would then attack the South East of Gaza, with two mounted divisions covering its right flank whilst 52nd and 53rd Divisions operated on its left flank.

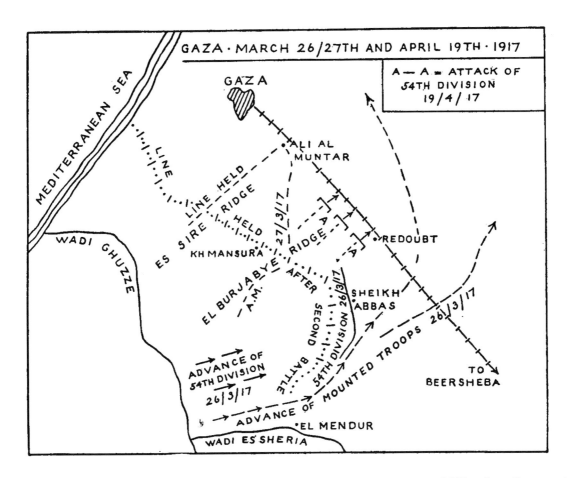

GAZA · MARCH 26/27TH AND APRIL 19TH · 1917

A — A = ATTACK OF 54TH DIVISION 19/4/17

The Hampshires advanced at 4.00 a.m. on 17th April and occupied the Sheikh Abbas ridge at the cost of only two casualties. At 7.30 a.m., two days later, the Hampshires followed the two Norfolk battalions of their brigade towards the Gaza – Beersheba road. They soon came under very heavy fire from the redoubt on their right. This they captured with the help of an elderly tank, but with the attack stalling elsewhere, the redoubt had to be given up, although they made a successful stand from a slight rise nearby. During the night the Hampshires recovered their wounded and dug in along the Sheikh Abbas ridge. They had gone into the battle with 23 officers and 746 other ranks. Of these 3 officers and 28 men had been taken prisoner, 9 officers and 220 men were killed and 9 officers and 298 men were wounded or missing.

Edwin was amongst those missing, but was later found severely wounded. He was evacuated back to hospital, but died of his wounds on 3rd of May. After the war his body was reburied in **Haifa War Cemetery**, Israel, in

Grave B 76

INDIA

Ever since the Mutiny in 1857, British regiments had been sent to India to broaden the British presence and to strengthen its control over the Indian Army. In 1914 most regular British battalions overseas were relieved by Territorial units and sent back to Britain to form the 27th, 28th and 29th Divisions.

The Hampshire 4th, 5th, 6th and 7th Battalions of the Territorial Force had all been at summer camp at Bulford when war was declared. Although recruited for home service, the battalions immediately volunteered for service overseas and on 9th October 1914 all four battalions sailed for India.

Territorials, like the two sergeants of the 1/7th Hampshires pictured here, rapidly acclimatised to the conditions and acquired the smartness and efficiency to perform the routine garrison and internal security duties required. They also trained for war and were put through challenging "Kitchener tests" to determine fitness for active service.

In 1915 the 1st/4th Hampshires were sent to Mesopotamia and fed trained reinforcement drafts by the remaining units of the Hampshire Territorial Brigade in India. The latter, in turn, had to make up their own numbers with a continuous supply of fresh reinforcements from the United Kingdom. They also had to cope with the traditional problems of the Indian climate, animals, accidents, sickness, disease and - particularly - the regular epidemics of polio and cholera. The annual routine of duties included rotating men through the cooler hill stations during the hot season to mitigate these problems.

Despite such precautions **Thomas Pelfrey** was to succumb to cholera in May 1915. **Charles Gates** died from bronchiectasis in Deolali in September 1917 and **Ernest Hart** died from dysentery two months later.

THOMAS WILLIAM PELFREY

Lance Corporal
1972
1st/7th Battalion, Hampshire Regiment,
who died on
Sunday 16th May 1915, aged 40.

Thomas was the son of Thomas and Jane Pelfrey of Westfield Road, Lymington. He was an educated man and worked as a County Court clerk. His wife, Florence, was also born in Lymington. In 1901 the family, consisting of two daughters – Florence and Dorothy – also lived in Westfield Road. They later moved to Holly Cottage, Spring Road, Waterford, Lymington.

Before the war Thomas had enlisted into the 7th (Territorial) Battalion of the Hampshire Regiment and went with them to India. They were initially in Bombay, but later moved north to Kasauli, with two companies at Chakrata. It was here that Tom died in a cholera epidemic. He was buried in Chakrata Cemetery, India, with due military honours.

His name is recorded on his wife's grave in Lymington Cemetery. It also appears on the **Madras War Memorial**, Chennai, India, on:

Face 16.

The LYMINGTON TIMES of 3rd June 1915 reported his Memorial Service:

"The general regret felt throughout the town in the death of Mr Thomas William Pelfrey, who succumbed to an attack of cholera whilst serving with the Hampshire Regiment (Territorial) in India, found expression in the large and representative attendance which assembled in the Lymington Congregational Church on Thursday afternoon when an impressive memorial service was held, conducted by the Pastor, the Rev. W Vine BA, whilst the address was given by the Rev. H New, a personal friend of the deceased. Mr Palfrey had been a prominent member of the Town Council, a valued Assistant Clerk of the Rural District Council and held an important position in the firm of Messrs. Moore, Rawlins and Vicary, solicitors. He was also an officer of the Powney Lodge of Freemasons, Assistant Hon. Secretary of the Literary Institute, one of the leaders of the Town Improvement Association and held other honourable positions in the town and members of each of these and other bodies attended to pay a tribute to his memory and to show sympathy with the bereaved widow.

In the course of a feeling address the Rev New paid full recognition to the life and character of the deceased and the intense earnestness with which he set about doing everything and his thoroughness in all he attempted. Though they might have differed from him, all had learnt to admire his courage: never was he frightened to stand alone if he was convinced that he was right. The only question he asked himself is it right and ought it to be done? He had always been absolutely sincere in what he did. In his public life their departed friend had travelled faster than many of them. He could grasp great subjects in a way others could not; we should arrive there presently and then discover many things he had advocated were right and we should wonder why we did not see their utility and force sooner. In time he would come into his own. His one great passionate desire was the betterment of his native town and such an ambition they must admire and imitate as much as possible."

CHARLES HENRY GATES

Private
306137
2nd/7th (T F) Battalion, Hampshire Regiment,
who died on
Sunday 14th October 1917, aged 27.

Charles was the eldest son of Charles and Amy Gates of Western Road, Lymington. There were three other children also born in Lymington. Their father was, recorded in the 1901 Census, as a whitesmith. At the beginning of the war he enlisted into the Royal Army Medical Corps and served as a private. The family later moved to 6, Maple Terrace, Western Road.

 Charles Henry enlisted in Lymington into the 7th (Territorial) Battalion the Hampshire Regiment with the number 2485. He went to India with the 1/7th Battalion but was later transferred into the 2/7th Battalion, serving in A Company. He acquired a new regimental number early in 1917 when all Territorial soldiers were given "long numbers" of six figures.

Charles reported sick and was sent to the 34th Welsh General Hospital at Deolali, where officers, sisters and orderlies all remarked to Bandsman Roland Brenton, a fellow Lymingtonian, that Charles was a bright, happy and cheerful patient to the very last. He died there on 14th October 1917 of bronchiectasis. THE CHRONICLE noted that

"He was well known in Lymington and made many friends, by whom he will be sadly missed."

His name is recorded on the **Kirkee 1914-1918 Memorial**, India, on:

Face 6

ERNEST HART

Lance Corporal
305060
1st/7th (T F) Battalion, Hampshire Regiment,
who died on
Thursday 25th October 1917, aged 28.

Ernest was born in Sway in 1889. His parents, Robert and Mary, both came from Hordle, his father working as a domestic coachman. It was a large family living in St Rose Cottage, Sway Road, as there were six children – Percy, Beatrice, Ernest, Wallace, Blanche and Ethel.

In 1908 Ernest enlisted in Lymington as a private, number G/7/544, into the Territorial Army and was at Summer Camp on Salisbury Plain when war was declared. He sailed with the 1/7th Battalion to Colaba in India and settled down to garrison duties.

Ernest, by now a Corporal, was part of a reinforcements draft (including Ronald Ford – see page 43), which arrived in Mesopotamia on 25th August 1915 to take part in the campaign.

Ernest may have been ill or wounded, as he rejoined his battalion in India in 1916. The battalion later moved up-country to provide the garrison for Ambala, in the North of India, between Delhi and Simla. In the hot weather two companies were deployed on rotation to the cooler hill station of Chakrata.

Ernest died on 25th October 1917.

305060	L/Cpl. 1/7th	HART Ernest	28	England	25-10-1917	Basra 40 Brit. Gen. Hos.	Died of Dysentry

According to his death certificate (above) Ernest died of dysentery in the 40th British General Hospital at Basra, in Mesopotamia.

54

This is somewhat of a mystery. As he apparently died in Basra, he must have been part of another reinforcement draft for the 1/4th Hampshires in Mesopotamia. But dying in hospital would have resulted in a burial - and the recording of such by the Graves Registration Commission. Yet no such grave is recorded and his name does not appear on the Basra Memorial.

The Hampshire Territorial Force Association for the 1/7th Hampshires records him as dying at Kasauli, in India, on 25th October 1917.

Ernest's name is therefore commemorated on the **Kirkee 1914-1918 Memorial**, India, on:

Face 6

His name is also remembered on the Sway War Memorial.

THE FIRST WORLD WAR

THE WESTERN FRONT
1916-1918

1916

!916 was the year in which the Allies believed they were going to win the war.

On 19th December 1915 Field Marshal Sir Douglas Haig took command of the BEF and in so doing inherited the plans agreed for 1916 by Sir John French with the French Army. These centred on a major assault on the Somme where the two armies joined. Joint planning took place between Britain, France and Russia to co-ordinate offensives on all fronts. This was, to some extent, successful.

Unfortunately it was also the year in which Germany was going to win the war and she kicked off with an assault in February on Verdun. This battle went on until the end of the year and succeeded in its aim of drawing French reserves into the killing ground of Verdun, where they could be destroyed by heavy artillery and poison gas.

For Britain, this was the year when the new Kitchener armies came on stream. However, the destruction of the old regular BEF in 1914/15 at Ypres had limited the training the new armies had received and there were still some shortages in equipment and munitions. Despite this, planning went on for the main thrust of the Somme battle, in which we would play a minor part to the French. As the casualties at Verdun mounted the British were forced to agree to taking over significantly more of the French trench line on the Somme.

It is interesting to note that despite the carnage of the First and Second battles of Ypres there were still "old soldiers" in the ranks, like **Bert Croucher** (see page 70). There were to be fewer of them in 1917.

Meanwhile routine trench warfare continued and *Walter Shuttler* was killed near Armentiers and *Allen Clark* was killed in the Loos salient. Later in the year *George Mutter* was killed in the trenches at Ypres.

WALTER HENRY SHUTTLER

Corporal
29150
51st Trench Mortar Battery, Royal Garrison Artillery,
who died on
Monday, 24th January 1916, aged 25.

Walter was born in Spring Road, Pennington to George and Julia Shuttler. The family later lived in Quay Street, Lymington. Walter's father, George, born in Milford, was a master mariner working on his own account. Walter had two older sisters, Maggie and Emile and two older brothers – Frank, who joined the Royal Navy and George, who enlisted into the 1/5th Hampshires.

Walter became associated with military life as a cadet when the Lymington Corps first started. After leaving school he joined the Royal Garrison Artillery for eight years, five of which were spent in South Africa. On returning to England he married Dorothy, who later moved to Newbury, Berkshire.

At the beginning of the war Walter enlisted in Lymington into the Royal Artillery and went to France on 18th November 1915 to join the 51st Division's Mortar Battery.

When the war began the British Army had no mortars in service, but light, medium and heavy mortars were quickly introduced by April 1915 – manned by mixed teams of infantrymen and gunners. Mortars were not liked by the infantry as they had to be fired from the front line because of their short range. The enemy quickly located such firing positions and retaliated heavily - usually on the resident infantry, as the mortars operated a "shoot and scoot" policy.

On 24th January 1916, in the Font Ballot salient near Armentieres manned by the 62nd Brigade, Walter fired fifteen bombs from his 2-inch mortar, one of which blew up a small ammunition dump in the German trenches. After the last bomb the enemy hit Walter's gun destroying it and killing Walter and two other soldiers.

January 27th, 1916,
H Co.,
62 Infantry Brigade.
B. E. F., France.

Dear Mrs. Shuttler,—I am very sorry indeed to have to tell you that your husband, Corpl. W. H. Shuttler, 29150, R.G.A., was killed here at his gun on Monday by a German shell. He died instantly and without suffering, and I buried him with a comrade in the presence of his friends yesterday. The cemetery is some way from the firing line, and his grave will be carefully tended to, and a cross put to his memory. This will be a sad shock to you, I fear, but it will console you to know that he died at his post and duty, and that he bore the highest possible reputation among all who knew him. I trust you will accept my warmest sympathy with you in your sorrow, and that God will give you strength to bear it bravely.—Believe me,
Sincerely yours,

KENNETH E. KIRK (Chaplain).

The widow has also received other letters expressing sympathy from the officers and friends of the deceased's regiment.

Walter is buried in the **Cite Bonjean Military Cemetery**, Armentieres, Nord, France, in:

Grave IX. E. 73.

ALLEN CLARK
Private
14336
11th (Service) Battalion, Hampshire Regiment,
who died on
Friday 16th June 1916, aged 32.

Allen was a son of Mr and Mrs Clark of Quay Street, Lymington. He enlisted in Lymington into the Hampshire Regiment.

The 11th Battalion was raised in Dublin and attached to the 16th (Irish) Division as pioneers. On 18th December 1915 Allen sailed with his battalion for France, arriving at Noeux les Mines in the Loos sector, where it erected huts for the division, bored wells and was involved with the inevitable road making. Allen's unit also went up to the line and helped the 47th Division in wiring and entrenching, as well as helping to consolidate a new mine-crater near the Double Crassier, south east of Loos. As soon as the mine exploded the pioneers went forward to dig in. This was done under heavy fire with the pioneers showing up clearly against the white chalk of the explosion. The divisional General praised the battalion for its steadiness under fire, its good discipline and its hard work.

Early in April 1916 the 16th Division took over the northern part of the Loos Salient. The work was varied, with some in the front line, others working on communication trenches or in the rear area.

Allen was in D Company. Their major task was to rebuild Railway Alley, a communication trench to the front near Chalk Pit Wood. They also, at the end of April, had to repair the latter trenches under fire when the Germans attacked using gas. The pioneers repulsed Germans who penetrated our trenches and, two days later, repeated the action whilst they were repairing the wire in front of our lines. Casualties were also frequent from German barrages, but not heavy.

The battalion was still there in June. The Trench Diary entry for 16th June reads:

The Boyaus mentioned in the War Diary was one of the defensive strong points surrounding Loos. The weather was a problem at this time, with thunderstorms and heavy rain, which turned trenches in the Boyaus area into streams. The mud made it difficult to effect repairs on the collapsed trench line and living conditions were grim, with poor food and no respite from the wearing of wet clothing.

Allen was killed in this attritional trench warfare. His company officer Lieutenant Wire, who lived in Blake's Lodge, Walhampton, wrote to Mrs Clark:

PHOTOGRAPH AVRIL WILLIAMS

"I am writing to express my sympathy in the sad loss you have sustained in the death of your son. He was killed by a rifle grenade whilst working in the front line and died almost immediately, so that I feel sure he cannot have suffered much. He was a good soldier and always did well. I feel a personal sorrow in that I knew him about Lymington before the war. I attended his funeral, which took place in the English Cemetery, and his grave is marked with a cross. I should like to add that he will be missed by all his friends and that he died doing his duty for King and Country."

He is buried in **St Patrick's Cemetery**, Loos, in:

Grave III. C. 40.

GEORGE W MUTTER
Private
18278
2nd Battalion, Hampshire Regiment,
who died on
Wednesday 9th August 1916, aged 34.

George was born in Portsmouth. His parents, William and Margaret Mutter, lived in Woodside Lane, Lymington. George later married and lived with his wife at 155 Squires Lane, Finchley, London.

He enlisted in Holloway, London into the 2nd Battalion, the Hampshire Regiment as Walter Barter, Cyril Osborne and many of his other friends had also done. He joined the battalion at Gallipoli on 5th December 1915, just before the evacuation five weeks later.

They returned to France, still part of 88 Brigade in the 29th Division and on the first day of the Somme battle had taken a heavy part in trying to capture Beaumont Hamel. They remained there until, on 27 July, they were rotated to the quieter Ypres section to recover before returning to the Somme in early October.

Whilst there were no set piece battles at Ypres at this time, the Salient continued to be an area of heavy attritional trench warfare. The battalion had gone into trenches by Potijze, near Ypres, on 30th July. The support line was really only a series of shell-holes on the Pilkem Ridge and the Hampshires had spent the time improving the trenches and consolidating a new mine crater into the position.

On the night of 8/9th August 1916 the enemy released gas on nearly the whole Ypres front. The slowly moving, mainly phosgene, gas cloud descended on the trenches. As the troops were donning their respirators and manning the fire step of the trenches a heavy German artillery barrage descended. The War Diary relates:

On the night of 8th/9th the gas alarm was sounded by horn on our left. The wind was from the NE and very light and as soon as the gas cloud was observed to be approaching our line the alarm was taken up and due precautions made. The cloud took about an hour to pass and came in two waves. During this time our supporting artillery opened a barrage of shrapnel fire and the enemy made no attempt to leave his trenches. The enemy at the same time opened a fairly heavy shrapnel fire on to our front line system and main communications a few large howitzer shells being directed at our reserves. The gas seemed to be of a particularly deadly kind and penetrated a considerable distance, the effect being felt some distance in rear. It was noticeable that the gas corroded all metal it came in contact with and killed many rats and birds. Casualties: Capt P.S.B. Hall, Lieut E.W.C. Turner, 2/Lt H.C. Scoggin, 2/Lt J. McCurdy (killed), 6 officers wounded. O.Rs. 125 killed (and died of wounds), 100 wounded. On the night of 9th/10th Bn. was relieved by the 1st Essex Regiment.

The excessive number of killed alarmed the Division, who set up an enquiry. Brigadier Cayley, Commanding George's Brigade, advised that:

1. The helmets did not give complete protection, owing to the gas cloud being stronger than hitherto experienced. Probably the proportions of the Chlorine and Phosgene were different, there being more of the latter gas.

2. It is of the utmost importance that men should keep quiet long after the gas has gone over. No men should be allowed to walk back to the dressing stations.

George Mutter was one of the 125 soldiers killed in this action. He is buried alongside 44 other Hampshire casualties of this attack in **Potijze Chateau Wood Cemetery** Ypres, in:

Grave A. 27.

THE SOMME

The bulk of the assault was originally planned to be carried out by the French, with the British in support. As, however, the German attack at Verdun in early 1916 drew in all available French reserves, so French involvement was scaled down. British participation therefore increased, with additional French-manned trenches being taken over up to a month before the battle. Objectives and tactics therefore changed significantly as the date of the battle approached and the British finally had to accept that they would carry the major part of the battle.

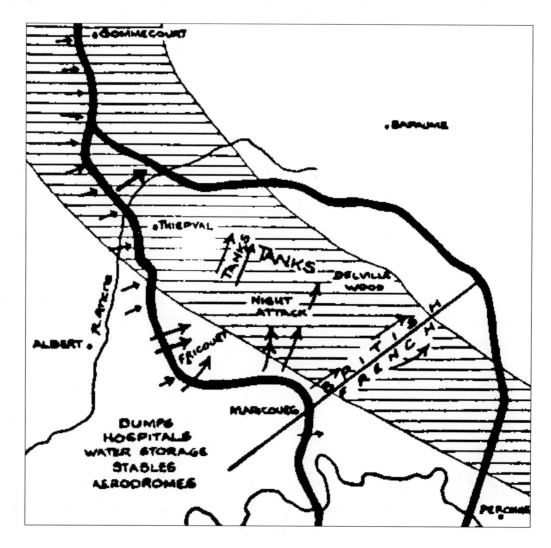

By 1916, the British army had learnt some hard lessons. Equipment and ammunition provision had been reorganised and railways now allowed the rapid concentration of large bodies of troops.

The Kitchener armies were arriving in France in large numbers but their training, perforce, had been rushed. Progress on the battlefield was still dictated by the pace of the Infantryman or the horse. These factors led, on the Somme, to the policy of a simple assault after a seven-day artillery barrage against limited objectives. The more difficult objectives were given to the better-trained Regular Divisions e.g. the assault on Beaumont Hamel, which was entrusted to the 4th and 29th Divisions.

Medical and Engineering services – including the provision of water on the battlefield - were well thought out and the prospects for success were considered good. Surprise, however, had been sacrificed during the pre-battle preparations and the first day of the Somme (1st July) resulted in nearly 20,000 men being killed and 40,000 wounded.

Five battalions of the county regiment, the Hampshires, were involved in the battle at various times.

The 1st Battalion, as part of 11th Brigade, 4th Division, advanced at "H-hour," 7.30 a.m., against the Redan Ridge. This small feature covered the northern approach to Beaumont Hamel – one of the key objectives of the day. The Ridge, however, was swept by flanking machine gun fire and very few Hampshires reached the wire. The battalion incurred over 500 casualties, of which 320 were killed. **William Marshman** was killed in this attack and **Frank Holloway** died of wounds the following day. The battalion remained in action until 23rd July, when they returned to the Ypres Salient. They returned to the Somme in mid September and remained until early November. The 2nd Battalion, and the 11th, 14th and 15th (Service) Battalions all played their parts in this battle.

Herbert Croucher of the Dorsetshire Regiment was also killed on the first day and **Oswald Perry**, of the Royal Fusiliers, was killed on 27th July. **Edward Frampton**, a sapper, was killed the following day and **William Wild** was killed in August when the Australians were advancing up the Bapaume Road. Other Lymington men – **George Lewis** and **Joseph Frampton,** both Royal Fusiliers - were killed towards the end of the battle.

WILLIAM MARSHMAN
Private
9984
1st Battalion, Hampshire Regiment,
who died on
Saturday 1st July 1916, aged 24.
and
FRANK H HOLLOWAY
Private
15255
1st Battalion, Hampshire Regiment,
who died on
Sunday 2nd July 1916.

Bill was born at Poole, to parents William and Alice Marshman. Later mother and son lived at 24, Gosport Street Lymington. He enlisted in Lymington into the Hampshire Regiment at the very beginning of the war, responding to Kitchener's call for the "First Hundred Thousand" volunteers. He served with the 10th Battalion in Gallipoli, landing with them on 5th August. Bill, was one of the many battle casualties of that day as he was admitted to the University Western Hospital, Southampton, on 23rd August 1915, suffering from a shrapnel wound to the right shoulder.

 **Frank** was born in Lymore Lane, Milford, a son of Mr and Mrs Mark Holloway of Lymington. In August 1916 it was reported that five of his brothers were on active service and a sixth had been invalided out. One brother, Gunner Fred Holloway, was later awarded the Military Medal for rescuing wounded under heavy fire. Frank was the first husband of Mrs. J. Lane, of Dover Cottage, Woodside, Lymington. He enlisted into the Hampshires shortly after the outbreak of war but did not move to France until early 1916.

Both soldiers joined in the 1st Battalion of the Hampshire Regiment, which was part of the 10th Division in 4 Division. This regular battalion had had a difficult war, having been involved on the Western Front since Mons. They had also suffered badly in the Second Battle of Ypres.

In July 1915, the division was transferred to the newly created 3rd Army and took over trenches on the Ancre. These had been taken over from the French and for nearly a year the battalion had a relatively quiet time. This enabled the unit to recover from the losses of the Second Battle of Ypres and to absorb new drafts of men and train for the battles ahead. The battalion was described at this time as being near to their 1914 standard.

In 1916 the battalion moved to the Somme and spent the first ten days of June 1916 digging assembly trenches for the forthcoming battle. They then had two weeks rest in Beauval and Beaussart, during which time they were used at night to widen the assembly trenches. They moved back to their trenches on 26th June.

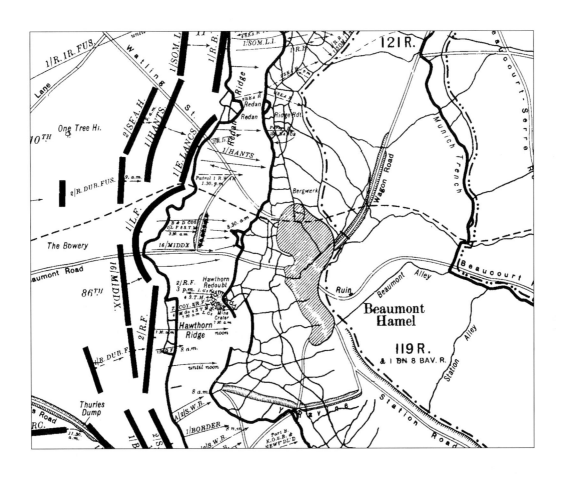

The battle of the Somme opened on 1st July with the exploding of the Hawthorne Ridge mine at 7.20 a.m., ten minutes before the attack began. Whilst this enabled the position, which dominated the southern flank of the Hampshire attack, to be taken, it also ensured - along with a ten-minute pause of the barrage - that the Germans could come up from their deep dugouts and prepare to defend their line. Both Bill and Frank were about 400 yards away from this explosion and would have felt the ground shake in their trenches.

At 7.30 a.m. the 1st East Lancashires led the brigade attack against the northern defences of Beaumont Hamel, with the objective of reaching Munich Trench 1,000 yards behind the front line. This lodgement could then be used by follow-up troops to exploit the situation. This initial attack was destroyed within minutes by machinegun fire from Redan Redoubt and the Quadrilateral to the north, neither of which had yet been captured.

The Hampshires attacked ten minutes later. Their War Diary records:

> *"We had A company, half of B and C Coys in the front line – half of C Coy to look after an enemy trench on right flank and D Coy in reserve. As soon as our troops left their trenches heavy machine gun fire was brought to bear on them from all directions and it was impossible even to reach the German front line.*
>
> *Our casualties in officers amounted to 100% and was also very heavy in other ranks. After lying about in shell holes all day the men came back to their original front line. That night the remains of the 11th Brigade were relieved by the 10th Brigade and went back to billets in Mailly."*

With all the officers killed or wounded the author of the War Diary is unknown, but could be accused of understatement. The Hampshires incurred total casualties of 586 all ranks of whom 11 officers and 310 men were killed or missing.

PHOTO AVRIL WILLIAMS

Bill was killed in the attack and his body later recovered for burial.

From his entry on his Medal Roll, he is shown as having been killed in Gallipoli. This is clearly wrong as he recovered from his Gallipoli wound and joined the 2nd Battalion before being transferred to the 1st Battalion.

He is buried in 10th Brigade Cemetery, now called the **Sucrerie Military Cemetery**, Colincamps, Somme, in:

Grave 1. D. 79

Frank was wounded in the attack. He was evacuated successfully back to the Casualty Clearing Station at Mailly-Maillet. This CCS was, not surprisingly, swamped with the influx of casualties from the failed attacks on Beaumont Hamel.

He died from his wounds the following day.

Frank is buried in **Mailly Wood Cemetery**, Somme, France, in

Grave I. P. 7.

PHOTO AVRIL WILLIAMS

HERBERT HENRY CROUCHER

Private
7242
1st Battalion, Dorsetshire Regiment,
who died on
Saturday 1st July 1916, aged 32.

Bert was the son of Sarah and Henry Croucher, of 16, Southampton Buildings, Lymington. Henry was born in Lymington and later worked there as a coachman. After leaving school he worked as an ironmonger's assistant. There was also a daughter, Ada.

Bert enlisted in Poole as a regular soldier into the Dorsetshire Regiment at Colchester on 11th May 1904. Clearly a good soldier, he was granted a Good Conduct badge two years later and permitted to complete five years with the Colours. On 10th October he embarked on the *SS Plassy* for the Orient reporting to the 2nd Battalion in India twenty-two days later. Almost immediately he was hospitalised at Calicut with ague. On 5th September 1907 he was admitted back to the same hospital for twenty-nine days with a contusion to a shoulder caused by a fall. On 28th March 1911 he was in hospital in Poona for ten days with a sprained ankle. After nearly nine years service he decided to soldier no more and left India on 10th January 1913. He transferred to the Reserve on 9th March 1913

He was mobilised at Dorchester on 5th August 1914 and immediately sent with 246 other reservists to Belfast, to join the 1st Battalion. This group was described as

> *"A very fine party and the appearance of the men made a great impression as they marched through the main streets to Victoria Barracks."*

They landed at Le Havre five days later in the heat of summer, and were showered by the locals with drinks, smokes and eatables.

By 21st August they were digging in at Mons, but on the 24th, orders were received to withdraw and the Dorsets conducted a successful rearguard action in contact with the enemy. By 9.00 a.m. the sun was exceedingly hot and the way was crowded with refugees. With the Germans close behind it proved impossible to break contact, so General Smith-Dorrien decided to stand and fight. The resultant battle of Le Cateau saved the BEF, buying time for Haig's Corps to recover and to continue the retreat in good order.

The Dorsets retired to Gagny, turned, and on 6th September, became the advance guard for 15th Division as it moved forward to the Aisne. This it crossed on the night of the 13th by means of two rafts. The local situation then became static, whilst both armies began to extend northwards in what became known as the "race to the sea." By 10th October the battalion was in trenches near Givenchy, incurring 400 casualties, but blocking a serious effort by the Germans to break through their line. At the end of the month Bert and his unit moved north in London buses and were immediately thrown into battle at Plugstreet Wood, remaining there for the next seven weeks. In a letter written to a friend on 5th November, Bert reports

"We are keeping up Bonfire night in reality this time, shells bursting all over the place, - not a very comfortable position to be in, I give you my word, but I am glad to be back again – that's the main thing."

The winter was a severe one and on 6th December Bert was sent back to a hospital in England with frost bitten feet.

Bert returned to France on 13th May 1915. He rejoined the 1st Battalion, just after they had suffered badly in the German gas attack at the 2nd battle of Ypres. The

> Private Croucher, of the "Dorsets," a Lymingtonian, who has been with the Expeditionary Force since the fighting at Mons, now returned home suffering from frostbite in the feet, the result of service in the trenches, said he could endorse every word the Captain had said in regard to experience in the firing line (applause).
> After a spirited rendering of "Tipperary," song and chorus (with a repeat) splendidly sung by Mr. James Bradford, of Brockenhurst,

battalion had gone into action two weeks earlier over 800 strong and came out of action 173 all ranks.

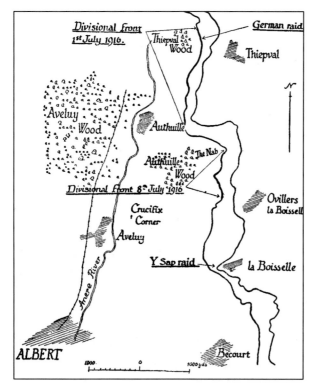

In early 1916 the Dorsets were posted to the 14th Brigade in 32nd Division. They moved to the Somme and in March took part in an unsuccessful trench raid on Y-Sap at La Boisselle. At 6.30 a.m. on 1st July they ate breakfast and entered Authuille Wood. They attacked at 07.45 behind the 11th Border Regiment, going for the Leipzig Redoubt, but they had to exit the Wood at a place targeted by the Germans. Half the total casualties of the day occurred while passing over the narrow stretch of country to the front line. They were encouraged by Drum-Major Kerr, who played the Regimental March on his flute until his arm was shattered by a bullet. Twenty-one men got to the enemy trenches, but had to withdraw.

PHOTO AVRIL WILLIAMS

Bert was one of the 500 casualties incurred by the battalion that day. Initially reported as missing, his records show that a burial detail from the 10th Cheshire Regiment reported that his body was

"buried in the neighbourhood of Authuille Wood."

After the war Bert was re-buried in **Serre Road Cemetery No 2,** Somme, in:

Grave XII. H. 1/14

On 9th September 1916 his mother, Sarah, received his personal effects and in 1921 received his medals, service scroll and plaque. She annotated the receipt of these items

"With Thanks."

OSWALD PERRY

Private
SPTS/807
23rd Battalion, Royal Fusiliers,
who died on
Thursday 27th July 1916, aged 38.

Oswald was the only son of Jane Perry and B. S. Perry. He was born in Lymington. By 1901 he was working as a drapery warehousman in London. His mother, Jane, was then living in Clovelly, Southampton Buildings, Lymington. She lived on her own means and the family, which also included a daughter Ella, was looked after by a young servant, Charlotte Winkworth. Jane later moved to Highfield, Lymington

THE LATE

LORD ROBERTS'
STIRRING WORDS
TO LONDON'S SPECIAL SERVICE BATTALION:

"I respect and honour you more than I can say. My feeling towards you is one of intense "admiration.

"**HOW VERY DIFFERENT IS YOUR**
"**ACTION TO THAT OF THE MEN**
"**WHO CAN STILL GO ON WITH**
"**THEIR CRICKET AND FOOTBALL**

"as if the very existence of the country were not "at stake!

"THIS IS NOT THE TIME TO PLAY GAMES
"We are engaged in a life and death struggle, "and you are showing your determination to do "your duty as soldiers, and, by all means in your "power, to bring this War to a successful result. "GOD BLESS AND WATCH OVER YOU ALL."

CAN YOU READ THIS UNMOVED?

Oswald enlisted in London into the Royal Fusiliers and served in the 23rd (Service) Battalion (1st Sportsman's) and went to France with them on 16th November 1915. Before the end of the year, as part of 99 Brigade in 2nd Division, it had been in the trenches at Bethune and Cambrin.

1916 saw Oswald in the front line at Festubert, Givenchy and Souchez, before moving to the Somme. On 20th July they went into camp at Morlancourt. Three days later they moved to Sandpit Valley, and then on to Bernafay Wood and Montauban Alley.

73

They were then warned off for an attack to clear Devil's Wood and on 26th July they moved up in preparation to occupy their start line of the western side of Campbell Street. At 6.10 a.m. the following day a heavy barrage was put down on Devil's Wood. An hour later it lifted and 1 KRRC and Oswald's Battalion followed it forward until their objective, just inside the northern edge, was reached.

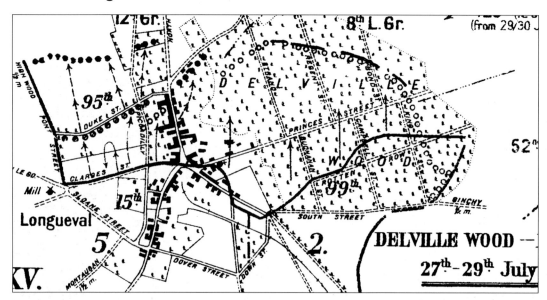

The Fusiliers' regimental history records the battalion coming out of the action smoking German cigars. The advance had 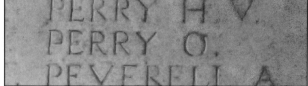 cost the battalion, however, 288 casualties – one of whom was Oswald. As his body was never recovered, his name is recorded on the **Thiepval Memorial**, Somme, France, on:

Pier and Face **8 C 9 A and 16 A**

Mrs Cunliffe-Owen raised both the 23rd and the 24th, known as the "Sportsman's Battalions." She raised, quartered and fed the 1,500 men concerned and then sent Lord Kitchener the following telegraph:

> *Will you accept complete battalion of upper and middle class men, physically fit, able to shoot and ride, up to the age of forty-five?"*

Lord Kitchener accepted gratefully. Mrs Cunliffe-Owen was very particular about her recruits. She measured their chests and had them doing physical training in Savoy Street every day.

EDWARD WILLIAM FRAMPTON

Sapper
49118
Royal Engineers
who died on
Friday, 28th July 1916, aged 21.

Edward was born in Quay Street Lymington and lived with his parents Thomas, a hairdresser, and Sarah in Key Street North. Edward was the second youngest boy of the family, having three elder brothers – Thomas, Alban, and Harry, whilst Joseph (see page 80) was the youngest. There were three elder sisters.

Before the war Edward worked for the local boat builders Courtney and Co. On 4th September 1914 he enlisted in Lymington into the Royal Engineers. Serving initially as a pioneer, he arrived in France on 30th May 1915 and was posted to 69th Field Company as a sapper.

On 22nd July 1916 Edward was at work building deep dugouts in the front line at Maily Mailet, on the Somme. Three days later they handed over to 123 Coy RE and moved to Bouzincourt, where they took over working on improving strong points in the line. Edward was killed instantly at 11 o'clock at night whilst on this work, being struck on the head by a piece of shrapnel. One of his section wrote that he *"was liked by all."* His comrades carried him back to the **Blighty Valley Cemetery** near their billets in Authuile Wood. Edward is buried in:

Grave I. B. 21.

WILLIAM EDWARD WILD

Private
3290
4th Battalion, Australian Infantry, A.I.F.
who died on
Tuesday 15th August 1916, aged 28.

Ed was born in Florence Villa, Western Road, Lymington. His father, Frederick, was a tinsmith, and he and his wife Caroline were parents of not only William, but also of Gertrude, Walter and Alfred. Ed emigrated to Australia in 1911 and became a farmer.

He enlisted into the Australian Imperial Force at Harwick Farm in New South Wales on 11th August 1915, passed his medical in Sydney and by 16th November was in the 7th Reinforcement Company of the 19th Infantry Battalion. On 14th February 1916 he was transferred to the 4th Battalion and joined it at Tel-el-Kebir, Egypt. Ed's Battalion embarked on the Transport **Simla** at Alexandria on 23rd March and arrived at Marseilles at the end of the month.

Ed was a member of A Company of the 4th Battalion, which was part of the 1st Brigade of the 1st Australian Division. On 23rd July this division was thrown into the Somme battle when it attacked Pozieres. The initial attack was successful and the village taken by 26th July. The advance then pushed forward until it settled on the Pozieres windmill/Mouquet Farm line. This latter position was only half taken and the Germans used their tunnels, to what had previously been their front line, to raid behind the Australian positions. In this confused fighting his unit records him as being killed in action between 15th and 17th August and

__"Buried between Poziers and Mouquet Farm, probably in Cemetery SL57 SE R 34 C."__

His effects, of a wrist watch, knife, razor in case, diary and a wallet were sent to his father in package 6954, who acknowledged receipt:

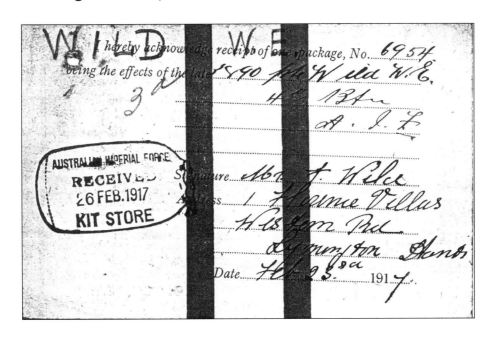

After the war his body could not be found.

His name therefore appears on the **Villers Bretonneux Memorial,** Somme, France.

GEORGE EDWARD LEWIS

Private
5563
1st/3rd (City of London) Battalion (Royal Fusiliers)
who died on
Sunday 8th October 1916, aged 21.

George was born in Lymington in 1895. Although the family originally came from Pennington, by 1901 they had moved to Priestlands Place. At that time his mother, Augusta, was a widow with four children. The eldest son Fred, 17, worked as an assistant in a furniture shop, whilst the other children were Nellie, 8 and twins George and Charles, 5. Two lodgers also shared the home.

In 1914 George enlisted in Trafalgar Square, London, into the London Regiment of the Territorial Force. As an early recruit he went with the battalion to France in January 1915. The following month they found themselves with the Garhwal Brigade of the Meerut Division and on 10th Mach attacked with them at Neuve Chapelle. The battalion went forward in the snow and successfully attacked the PORT ARTHUR trenches – although at a cost of 348 casualties.

They remained in the area after the battle and on 16th May took part in an abortive attack east of Festubert. They continued to remain in this sector and had their headquarters on the Rue de Bois.

By 1916 George's battalion was part of 167th Brigade in 56th (1st London) Division. It had moved to the Somme early in the year to help with the preparations for the forthcoming battle. On the opening day it was part of the two divisional diversionary attack on Gommecourt, in the north, that was designed to draw enemy reserves away from the main assault further south. This it singularly failed to do and the battalion suffered 123 casualties.

At the end of August it moved south to Lousy Wood, near Guillemont. Here in September George took part in the intense fighting for Wedge Wood, Angle Wood Valley, Trones Wood and Flers.

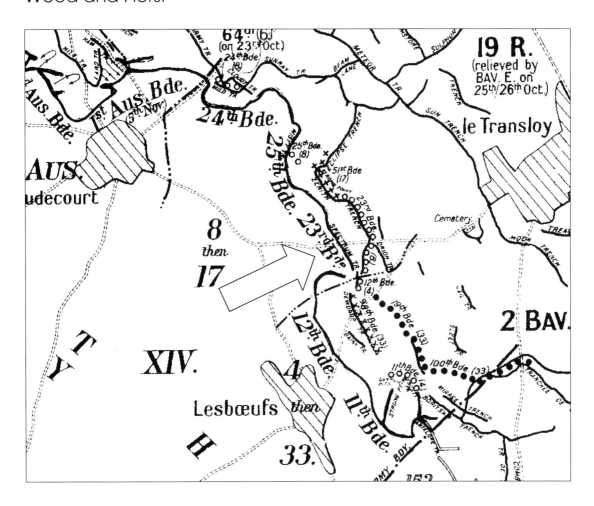

He was killed, however, in the attack on Spectrum Trench. The map above shows its location, but reflects the situation nearly three weeks later – by which time his formation had been replaced by the 23rd Brigade.

His body was lost, so George's name is recorded on the **Thiepval Memorial**, France, on:

Pier and Face 9D and 16B

JOSEPH FRAMPTON

Private
C/13945

17th Battalion, Royal Fusiliers,

who died on
Monday 13th November 1916, aged 19.

Joe was the younger brother of Edward Frampton (see page 75) and was also born and brought up in Lymington.

He enlisted in Dover into the Royal Fusiliers and after training

joined the 17th (Service) Battalion (Empire). This battalion had been raised by "The British Empire Committee" in ten days and went into camp at Warlingham in Surrey on 12th September 1914. Joe sailed with the battalion to France on 17th August 1915, where it formed part of the 99th Brigade of the 33rd Division. They then gained experience of trench warfare in the area about the La Basee Canal. By the end of the year Joe's battalion had become part of 5 Brigade in 2 Division, as a result of the policy to mix new and regular battalions.

This division moved to the Somme on 21st July 1916. Joseph and his fellow soldiers were in support positions between Trones Wood and Longueval Alley four days later. They took part in the clearance of Devil's Wood on 27th July, incurring 118 casualties (see Oswald Perry page 73). Joe incurred a shell wound to the chest and was in hospital in France. He returned to the battalion in time to take part in what was to be the last throw of the Battle of the Somme, before winter closed it down.

The Battle of the Ancre was designed to capture the fortified ruined village of Beaumont Hamel and to clear the enemy from their positions along the River Ancre to the north.

The 2nd Division was tasked with capturing the Redan Ridge, which covered the north side of Beaumont Hamel. This 200-yard feature had almost been captured, on 1st July. At 6.15 a.m. on 13th November, 5th Brigade formed up in the open and advanced under the cover of a rolling barrage to take the German front line. The two leading battalions then carried on to take Beaumont Trench. Meanwhile Joe's battalion, which had been in the second wave of the attack, was tasked to attack FRANKFURT TRENCH.

PHOTO BY AVRIL WILLIAMS

This attack began at 7.30 a.m. and although the trench was partially taken the remnants of both the 2nd Ox and Bucks and Joe's battalion were forced to gradually fall back, in the face of a determined enemy counter-attack.

They withdrew to MUNICH TRENCH and then gradually fell back to Wagon Road, until finally stabilising the line when they reached Crater Lane. Here they stood until relieved.

Joseph was killed in action in this attack.

He is buried in **Redan Ridge Cemetery No 1**, Beaumont-Hamel, Somme, France in:

Grave C. 19.

1917

1917 was to prove a year of significant change.

Europe was entering its third year of war and the strain was showing. From the Allies point of view France, who had so far carried the main burden of the war on the Western Front, had been bled at Verdun (see map below) to such an extent that her offensive capability had been blunted.

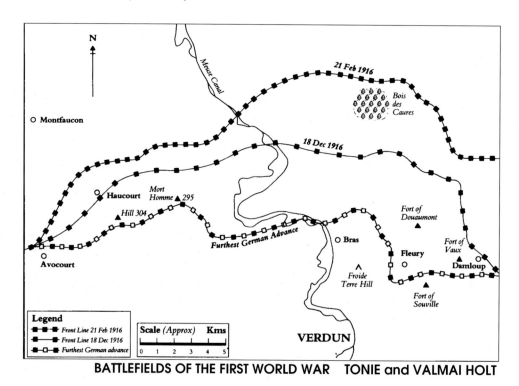

BATTLEFIELDS OF THE FIRST WORLD WAR   TONIE and VALMAI HOLT

The battle lasted from February to December 1916 and the French incurred 540,000 casualties defending Verdun.

Britain, despite the Somme experience, was reaching the peak of her military capacity and was playing a leading role in the war. She was having to introduce conscription, however, and future manpower increases would be limited. The entry of America on 6th April into the war boosted Allied morale, although it was realised that her army in France would not be effective for another year. More pressing was the effective withdrawal of Russia from the war in July due to war-weariness and revolution. This was to tilt the balance of power on the Western front in favour of the Triple Alliance later in the year.

The Germans, however, were also reaching the peak of their military resources. They had effectively lost the war on the sea at Jutland and the Allied blockade was biting - hence the German concentration on submarine warfare. The ethnic fault-lines within the Austro Hungarian Empire were becoming more prominent and reducing the effectiveness of her armed forces. The Turkish Empire was beginning to buckle and the effect was showing in her gradual withdrawal from Palestine and Mesopotamia. Increasing demands were therefore being made on German material, manpower and leadership in support of her own allies. The effectiveness of such support had been seen in Gallipoli in 1915, on the Eastern Front in 1916 and was to be seen again in Italy in the coming year.

The Western Front. After the Battle of the Somme the Germans gave slightly, and the Allies seized the chance to mount the Arras offensive, which lasted until May 1917. Then the battle of Messines led into the third battle of Ypres, in July 1917. In November, the slow progress of the war shifted on to Cambrai, where tanks made their first effective contribution to the art of war.

Trench warfare, however, continued to take its toll around the planned set piece battles.

MAP FROM CHEERFUL SACRIFICE BY JONATHAN NICHOLLS
PUBLISHED BY PEN AND SWORD BOOKS LTD

Edgar Darlington and *William Tilley* died on the Somme, *Sydney Jones* in the Ypres Salient, *Douglas Kindersley* in the Arras trenches, *Walter King* near Vimy, *Ben Broomfield* in the Armentieres sector and *George Smith* at St Quentin.

EDGAR ROBERT DARLINGTON

Private
23423
2nd Battalion, Hampshire Regiment,
who died on
Wednesday 21st February 1917, aged 20.

Edgar was a son of William Henry and Mary Darlington of 8, Emsworth Road, Lymington. He was born in Market Drayton, but was brought up in Lymington and enlisted there into the Hampshire Regiment.

Edgar joined the 2nd Battalion in 1916. The battalion went through the winter without heavy casualties. Although the 29th Division had twice been involved in minor offensives over the winter, 88th Brigade was in reserve on both occasions. In November and early December the battalion was in the line near Les Boeufs on the Somme. Heavy rain had turned this old battlefield into a

"*deplorable state*"

and nearly 400 admissions to hospital occurred in this period. In the four months from November the battalion only suffered 24 killed and 79 wounded, directly caused by trench warfare.

On 11th January 1917 the battalion entrained for Corbie and nine days rest. The train was six hours late because of the snow and slush.

They then took over trenches 2 miles North East of Morval. The line was a chain of isolated posts that could not be linked together because of the frozen ground. Movement in the support trenches was difficult because of the ice-coated duckboards. Fifteen men were admitted to hospital with hypothermia during this period. The sector was quiet, however, as the Germans were no better off.

Two further spells in this sector incurred eleven and thirteen casualties respectively. On 20th February the battalion returned to the trenches at Saillesel.

Edgar was wounded at some stage of these operations. He was evacuated back to No 1 General Hospital in Etretat, one of the earliest base hospitals, located 26 kilometres north of Le Havre. Despite the care and attention available in such a hospital, Edgar succumbed to his wounds and died on 21st February 1917.

He is buried in **Etretat Churchyard Extension**, Seine-Maritime France in:

Grave I. C. 3.

WILLIAM TILLEY

Private
267137
1st/6th Battalion, Gloucestershire Regiment,
who died on
Tuesday 24th April 1917, aged 32.

Bill Tilley was born in Lymington in 1885. In the 1901 Census the family is recorded as living at Pitmore Pond in Sway. William's father Henry worked from home as a boot and shoemaker, whilst his mother Mary took in washing. William himself worked as a bricklayer.

He enlisted in Winchester into the Gloucestershire Regiment, and served in the 1st/6th (Territorial Force) Battalion. This battalion arrived in France at the end of March 1915 as part of the 144th Brigade of the 48th (South Midland) Division. During the year they occupied trenches in Plugstreet, Messines, Loos and Arras. They began 1916 on the Somme at Hebuterne and played an almost continuous part in the battle.

Bill was amongst the large drafts of reinforcements that joined them on the Somme over the winter. The conditions were particularly vile and the troops were continuously sodden, living and operating in a sea of mud and perpetually cold. They spent all of January 1917 in training south of Peronne and the following six weeks in a quiet sector of trenches north of Barleux. On 16th March the Germans began to withdraw to the Hindenburg Line. The first the battalion knew of this was on the previous day, when their War Diary states:

> *"Information received from Brigade at 9 p.m. that a deserter had come in on our left stating that the enemy were withdrawing on our front and had only left twenty men per company in trenches. Orders were issued to C Company ordering a fighting patrol to be sent out."*

The patrol reported empty trenches, and the division began to follow up the retreating Germans, who laid waste and booby-trapped the area as they left. At the end of March the battalion went into rest billets in Peronne

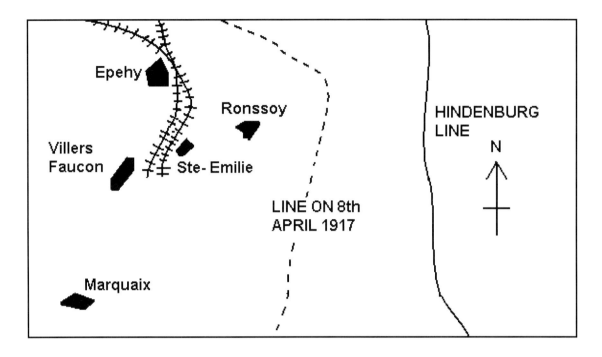

The German withdrawal ended on 5th April, by which date Bill and his battalion were in Marquaix. The weather continued to alternate between rain and snow and the enemy continued to be active.

On 18th April Bill's battalion lost all its command staff when the cellar they were in at Villers Faucon blew up at 3.55 a.m., when a delayed-action booby trap detonated. Despite this the battalion was ordered to attack the enemy on the Knoll to their front. At 3.45 a.m. the following day two companies attacked, the first line of which initially gained the objective. They were forced back, however, when the second line was broken up by machinegun fire and so failed to arrive in support on the objective. The battalion suffered a total of 91 casualties.

Bill was one of the three men killed in this attack. As his body was lost in the German trenches his name is therefore recorded on the **Thiepval Memorial**, Somme, France, on

Pier and Face 5 A and 5 B

SYDNEY GEORGE ELLIS JONES MC

Warrant Officer 2nd Class
320461
6th Battalion, City of London Rifles,

who died on

Wednesday 1st March 1917, aged 29.

According to *Soldiers Died*, **Sydney** was born and lived in Hammersmith and enlisted in London. Whilst no connection with Lymington has yet been discovered there can be no other combination of personal details for any other soldier.

He joined the Territorials before the war, enlisting into the 6th Londons with the regimental number of 2035. Sydney was a Lance Sergeant with his battalion when it sailed for France on 17th March 1915. After the usual induction and service in the Ypres Salient, 1916 found them further south. On 21st March 1916 they took over trenches on Vimy Ridge.

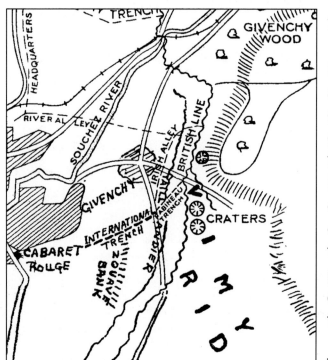

On the 29th they were subject to heavy fire from guns, mortars and rifle grenades. At 6.45 p.m. the Germans fired two large mines under the centre Company. This demolished the front line trenches and was so powerful that only one officer and three men of the Company survived.

The Germans immediately attacked to occupy the craters, but Vickers machineguns at the junction of RABINEAU and INTERNATIONAL TRENCHES stemmed the attack, until all but one were put out of action.

Sydney, as Company Sergeant Major, organised some wounded men from B Company to fill belts for the gun, rallied his men and reoccupied the line. The LONDON GAZETTE for 24th June 1916, awarding him the Military Cross, reads:

> 2035 Coy. S./M. Sydney Jones, 6th Bn., Lond. R., T.F.
>
> For conspicuous courage and coolness, coupled with the very skilful handling of his platoon, during an attack. His inspiriting example materially assisted the advance under very heavy fire.

The Londons remained in the trenches at Vimy for a further three months before being withdrawn. In August they moved down to the Somme and on 15th September took part in an attack on High Wood. They suffered heavily in the advance, but captured and consolidated COUGH DROP TRENCH before assaulting the Flers line with tanks. In early October they took part in operations around the Butte de Warlencourt, before being moved on 14th October to the Ypres sector.

On 9th November the battalion took over trenches around Hill 60. They returned for a third tour on 27th February. The War Diary reports that an intense bombardment:

Summary of Events and Information

developed over the sector held by this Battalion. At 10.45 P.M. the bombardment ceased.

Battalion H.Q was hit and 2nd Lt. G B Martin was slightly wounded. 2nd Lt. A.T.S. Smith of the 7th Batt London Regt who had only reported half an hour previous to the bombardment was severely wounded. In all, 2 officers and 24 other ranks were wounded, and 2 other ranks, including C.S.M. Jones, killed. Much damage was done to the trenches.

G.H. Neely
Major.
Commanding 6th Bn London Regt

TNA (PRO) WO95/2729

Sydney is buried in **Railway Dugouts Burial Ground (Transport Farm)**, Ypres, in:

Grave VII. E. 10.

DOUGLAS CUMMING PAGET KINDERSLEY DSO
Captain
3rd Battalion, Highland Light Infantry,
who died on
Friday 22nd June 1917, aged 45.

Douglas was born on 8th August 1873, the youngest of three sons born to Captain Henry W. Kindersley. Henry had served with the 29th Regiment and lived in Tranmere, Stanley Road, Lymington. He sent all the boys to be educated at The Edinburgh Academy and all three were to serve in the Highland Light Infantry (HLI).

Douglas's eldest brother, Archibald, was born in South Africa in 1869. He attended the Academy from 1881 to 1887, leaving to be commissioned into the 4th Battalion HLI. He served in the Brass River Expedition of 1895 and the Boer War. He was then seconded to the Transvaal Government in the Department of Native Affairs before being appointed Honorary Attaché, in 1911, to His Britannic Majesty's Embassy to Japan. In the First World War he served in Salonica. He later retired to the Isle of Wight.

In 1893 his other brother Ronald, who was born in 1870, had gone to Selangor, Malaya, as a rubber planter. He later became the General Manager of several rubber estates. Ronald returned from Malaya in 1935 and settled in the Old Ferry house at Walhampton, Lymington.

Douglas had left school in 1887. In 1893 he applied to take the entrance exam for the Military Academy at Sandhurst. This he passed, but failed to take up the offered place. At some later stage he joined Ronald as a rubber planter in Malaya. In 1904 he joined the Malay States Volunteer Rifles and served as a Sergeant until 1910, when he resigned. By 1914 he had become the General Manager of the Glenshiel Rubber Estates Company in Kajang, Selangor. In that year Douglas married Ivy, the only daughter of William Tyler.

The First World War brought Douglas back to England and he was commissioned in September 1914 as a Second Lieutenant into the Third Battalion of the Highland Light Infantry. In February 1915 he was promoted Captain.

He went to France on 27th April 1915 as one of a draft of officers to be sent to the 2nd Battalion, Kings Own Scottish Borderers and was appointed adjutant. By 1917 he had been promoted to temporary Major, twice mentioned in despatches (15th June 1916 and 15th May 1917) and was second in command of the battalion. In the LONDON GAZETTE of 4th June 1917 he was admitted into the Distinguished Service Order

> *"For gallantry on 9th April 1917, on VIMY RIDGE. Capt. Kindersley who was acting as Adjutant of the Battalion organised the defence of the captured position under heavy rifle and M.G. fire. The line of resistance to be taken up was at right angles to the direction of the attack and it was largely owing to this officer's indefatigable efforts this manoeuvre was carried out. Capt. Kindersley has previously been recommended for the Military Cross.*

PHOTO RICHARD WILLIAMS

He was killed in the line on 22nd June 1917. A month later he was awarded the Croix de Guerre. His name is recorded on the family grave in **Lymington Cemetery**, but he is buried in **Roclincourt Military Cemetery**, Pas de Calais, France, in:

Grave II. C. 10.

WALTER NIKE KING

Private
80191
31st Battalion, Canadian Infantry (Alberta Regiment),
who died on
Tuesday 14th August 1917, aged 41.

Walter was a son of John Charles Nike and Mary E King of Wisteria, St Thomas Street, Lymington. John later became a Justice of the Peace.

At some stage Walter emigrated to Canada where, according to THE CHRONICLE, he held *"a good appointment."* He enlisted into the Canadian Army on 16th March 1915.

After basic training at Calgary his draft embarked on the *SS Northland* on 29th May 1915 for England. After further training

on Salisbury Plain the 31st Battalion sailed for France on 18th September. He then trained as an observer and on 10th February 1916 was attached to 6 Canadian Brigade HQ as a brigade observer. At the beginning of April he was granted ten days leave in France, but the next six months was mainly spent in hospital with knee and ankle problems.

He rejoined his unit on 10th August and soldiered with them until, on 14th May 1917, he was admitted to No 3 Canadian General Hospital at Boulogne suffering from myalgia and pleurisy. After a spell in the convalescent depot and No 3 Large Rest Camp he returned to active soldiering, being attached to the 2nd Support Battalion on 8th June. He was killed in action on 4th August. At the time of his death his army records show him to be 41 years old. The family grave states that he was aged 45.

PHOTO RICHARD WILLIAMS

Thomas was originally buried in Gohelle Military Cemetery. He has now been reburied, by the War Graves Commission, in **Fosse No 10 Communal Cemetery Extension**, Sains-en-Gohelle, Pas de Calais, France, in:

Grave II. C. 24.

Walter is also remembered on his father's grave in Pennington.

BEN BROOMFIELD

Private
45527
2nd Battalion, Devonshire Regiment,

who died on

Tuesday 30th October 1917, aged 41.

According to his documents, **Ben Broomfield** was born in Boldre, lived in Waterloo Road and worked as a bricklayer. He was well known as a prominent player of the Lymington League. Married, with six children, he is more likely to have died aged 41 – as reported in THE CHRONICLE of 10th January 1918 – than aged 27, as preserved in his documents.

He enlisted in Brockenhurst in 1915 into the Devonshire Regiment. By 1917 he was serving in A Company of the 2nd Battalion on the Western Front. This battalion, in 23 Brigade, 8 Division, had been in the Army Reserve for the successful Battle of Messines.

The last two weeks of July saw a barrage of 4 million shells fired to preface the opening of the Passchendaele offensive on 31st July.

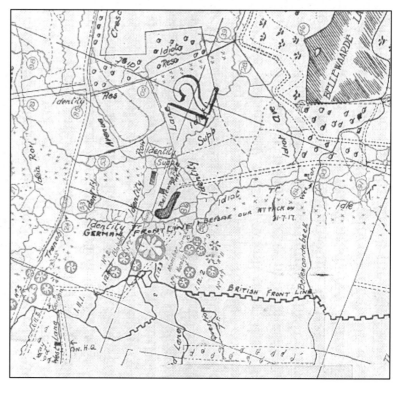

The objective for the 23rd Brigade was two lines, separated by 400 yards of ground that had extensive German trench systems. At 3.50 a.m. the Devons and West Yorkshires advanced. Aided by a "*splendid barrage*" the first objective was taken within the hour. The Middlesex and the Scottish Rifles then passed through to attack the second line. This was captured but the failure of the flanking division to keep up made its retention difficult. An order for the whole brigade to halt was issued, but was not received by the Devons. They therefore followed orders and advanced beyond the second line in short rushes, until increasing casualties prevented further movement forward. On 16th August the 8th Division tried again, but with no further success.

At the end of the month the Devons were rotated out of the Ypres sector and took over trenches in a quiet sector of the Douve valley, to the south of Plugstreet. On 7th October Ben was granted seven days leave.

PHOTO MARC THOMPSON

Two weeks after returning to the front Ben was killed instantaneously when the roof of his dugout was penetrated by an "*aerial torpedo.*" In this seven-day period of "normal" attrition of trench warfare he was one of only four soldiers killed. Another four were wounded. He was described as having been

"a fine soldier, liked and respected by not only his comrades but also by his officers."

He is buried in the nearby **Lancashire Cottage Cemetery**, Comines-Warneton, Hainaut, Belgium, in:

Grave II. F. 4.

GEORGE ALBERT SMITH

Private
242441
2nd/6th Battalion, Royal Warwickshire Regiment
who died on
Sunday, 1st July 1917, aged 36.

George was born and brought up in Lymington, the son of Joseph, a Royal Marine, and his wife who lived in Lower Buckland Road. By trade George was a painter, living in Cannon Street. He married Rosina, the daughter of Alfred Andrews, a labourer of Buckland, on 11th June 1906. They lived at 7, Rosetta Place, Lower Buckland Road, Lymington.

He enlisted at Brockenhurst into the Royal Warwickshire Regiment. He served in the 2nd/6th Battalion, which was raised in 1915 and completed its training on Salisbury Plain early the following year. All the four (2nd Line) territorial battalions were formed into the 182nd Brigade. This brigade left for France in May 1916 and completed its formation training near Bethune.

The battalion then manned trenches at Fauquissart, in the Laventie sector where, on 19th July 1916, it took part in an extensive attack, which penetrated to the enemy trench line. In the attack George's battalion came under heavy shellfire, which killed or wounded all its officers and 163 men. Nevertheless the men held on and two platoons reached the enemy trenches. They could not, however, proceed further and the attack was eventually abandoned.

This gallant effort, aimed at keeping German troops from re-enforcing the Somme battle, cost the battalion 242 casualties. They remained in this area until the end of October.

The battalion then moved down to the Somme for the very last weeks of the battle and stayed there over the winter.

In the early part of April 1917 the brigade took over the line at Marteville, six miles from St Quentin. On 9th April they attacked Hill 120, only to find that the enemy had hastily retreated. They consolidated the position and remained there for the next six weeks, being withdrawn on 13th May for rest and training. In this period of time the battalion lost 54 casualties.

George was one such and was evacuated back to a base hospital at Rouen, where he died from his wounds.

PHOTO CWGC

George is buried in **St. Sever Cemetery Extension**, Rouen, Seine-Maritime, France, in:

Grave P. II. I. 13B.

1917 ARRAS

Over the winter of 1916/17 Lloyd George had become Prime Minister in England, whilst in France the French Army had

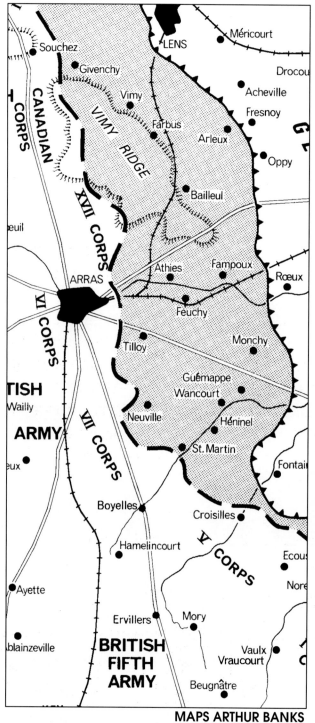

replaced General Joffre with General Niville. The latter spoke perfect English and with his ideas for a quick end to the war, soon persuaded Lloyd George to virtually subordinate the British Armies in France to Niville's control.

This resulted in us taking over yet more parts of the French line to free French troops for Niville's planned Spring offensive, thus reducing our own offensive capabilities.

On the southern part of the line the Germans had withdrawn to the impregnable Hindenburg Line of well-sited concrete gun and machine gun posts that provided defence in depth. This barely affected the Arras front, where preparations were complete for an attack, agreed with Joffre before his demise.

MAPS ARTHUR BANKS

The battle began on 4th April and ended on 17th May. **Harry King** was killed in its early stages, **John Lydford** died accidentally, whilst **Samuel Hurford** later died of wounds.

HARRY KING

Lance Corporal
24863
1st Battalion, Hampshire Regiment,
who died on
Thursday 12th April 1917.

Harry was born in Kingston, Ringwood, in 1890. In 1901 his father, George, was a carter on a local farm and Harry's older brother, Albert, worked as a farm labourer. In the Lymington Local Directory for 1916 a Mr and Mrs H King are shown as living at 10 Nelson Place.

Harry enlisted in Brockenhurst in 1916 into the Hampshire Regiment and joined them in France at the turn of the year.

The battalion was out of the line in November 1916, took over French trenches in the Combles sector in December, and in reserve again for the first three weeks of the 1917 New Year. It then manned trenches three miles north of Peronne until the 22nd of February. It then marched to near Doullens, where it trained for the forthcoming Arras battle. This included rehearsing over ground marked out to represent the battalion's intended objective.

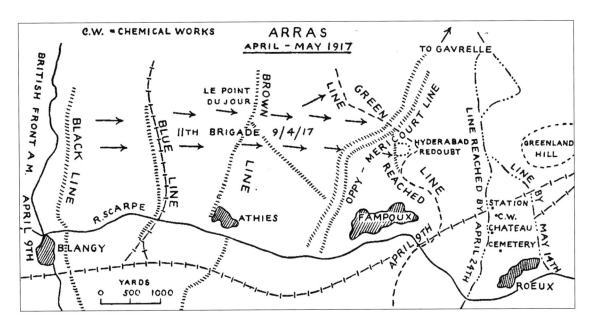

On 7th April Harry and his battalion moved towards Arras. Early on 9th April they filed into their assembly area ready for the attack. The battle of Arras began in a heavy snowstorm on Easter Monday, 9th April 1917. After a preliminary bombardment from nearly 3,000 guns, thirteen British and four Canadian divisions captured most of Vimy Ridge within a day, taking many prisoners and guns. The Hampshires' role was to move through the 9th Scottish Division, when they had taken their objectives of the BLACK, BLUE and BROWN LINES, assault the Oppy-Mericourt Line and then to move on beyond Fampoux and capture the GREEN LINE.

The Scottish Division captured all its objectives on time. The Hampshires, waiting in the snow, were heartened both by a hot meal and the sight of German prisoners streaming past them. At 10.00 a.m. they moved up in column until the BLUE LINE was reached, after which they shook out into artillery formation. They then advanced to the BROWN LINE and paused for an hour, to wait for the covering barrage. They advanced at 3.00 p.m. to the wire, cut their way through it and secured the Oppy-Mericourt Line at a cost of 60 casualties. The Rifle Brigade then passed through them and captured the Hyderabad Redoubt. This advance was the greatest success achieved on the Western Front in a single day.

The snow and sleet, however, hindered the forward movement of the guns, impeded communications and caused hardship to the troops. The Hampshires beat off a counter-attack that evening and patrolled aggressively overnight. The following day opposition stiffened and although further counter-attacks were driven off, the GREEN LINE remained in German hands.

On 12th April the battalion attempted to bomb their way forward, in order to continue the advance, but with little success. The Hampshires suffered a further 27 casualties, of whom Harry was one of the 11 killed. His body was lost in the subsequent fighting. Harry's name is therefore recorded on the **Arras Memorial**, Pas de Calais, France, on

Bay 6

JOHN STANLEY LYDFORD

Rifleman
C/4725
1st Battalion, King's Royal Rifle Corps,
who died on
Saturday 21st April 1917, aged 32.

John was born in Quay Street Lymington in 1884. His father, George, came from Dorset and worked as a general labourer. His mother, from Somerset, does not feature in the 1901 census, but the family is shown as including three younger children – Francis, William and Ernest. From a later Next-of-Kin form there were two other elder sisters who had already left home by 1901. John, at the age of sixteen, is shown as working as a shopkeeper grocer and this is also the calling declared at his attestation (Form B2505) completed on 21st December 1915.

By this time John was living at 33 Bassinbury Road in Islington, London. He enlisted at Andover, initially into the 19th Battalion, Kings Royal Rifle Corps. After basic training at Winchester he embarked for France on 17th May 1916, but was immediately admitted to 20 General Hospital at Etaples with scabies. On 14th June he was returned to England where he underwent further infantry training.

On 2nd August John returned to France and joined the 1st Battalion in the field. Three days later he was admitted to hospital again – this time with flat feet. He rejoined his battalion on 30th August, but five days later was sent sick to 100 Field Ambulance in 2 Division. On 9th September he joined 205 Divisional Employment Company in 2 Division and settled down to soldiering under front-line trench warfare conditions.

Having survived six months of trench life, one of those unpredictable accidents occurred, which was to cost John his life. The record of the Court of Enquiry held on 29th July 1917 tells it all.

C O P Y.   Army Form A.

PROCEEDINGS of a Court of Enquiry.
assembled at In the Field.
on the Twenty ninth day of July 1917.
by order of M. G. C. 2nd Division.

for the purpose of investigating the circumstances under which
No.G/50283 L/Cpl J.L.OLDING Royal Fusiliers and No.C/4725
Rfn J.LYDFORD 1st K.R.R.C. were accidentally Killed on 21-4-17.

P R E S I D E N T.

Captain R.G. HILLCOAT, 23 Roy. Fus.

M E M B E R S.

Captain H.S.JOHNSON. 22 Roy. Fus.
2/Lt E.B. JACKSON, 205 Divl Employ. Coy. 2nd Division.

I N   A T T E N D A N C E.

The COURT having duly assembled pursuant to order, proceed to
take evidence.

1st Witness. No.8173 L/Cpl Richardson, 1st King's Regt states:- at about
1 a.m. on the morning of the 21st April 1917 I was lying in a
dugout at ROCLINCOURT. Most of the men of the Divl Coy were in
this dugout. It was a very deep long dugout. It was wide enough
to allow of one man sleeping on each side lying at right angles
to the sides. On my right was lying Pte LYDFORD and beyond him
L/Cpl OLDING and then Sgt KYTE. At the time above stated I had
a candle burning and was not asleep. I heard a crack then I saw
the chalk from the roof rolling up towards me. I jumped up
warned the men on my left and ran for the exit. I shouted for
the men to get shovels etc and went and told the Coy Sergt Major.
We all got to work at once to get the stuff cleared. The dugout
had a number of entrances. Sergt KYTE was got out very soon
after the fall by men working from one of the other entrances.
No progress could be made for a long time in getting the other two
men out as the chalk was constantly sliding down. It was only
after about 5 hours work that the body of L/Cpl OLDING was got
out. A party of men under an officer from one of the tunnelling
Coys came over and gave every assistance and it was on the
advice of the Tunnelling Officer that the further work necessary
to get Pte LYDFORD'S body out was not got on with as it was xxxxxxx
xxx considered dangerous. I think that death in the case of
L/Cpl Olding and Pte Lydford must have been instantaneous as the
whole weight of the fall came directly on to them. There had
been troops occupying this dugout previously. Just a day or two
after we occupied it a Battery of Heavy Guns came into position
close by. When these guns fired it shook the whole dugout

                                   (Sd) J.Richardson, L/Cpl
                                              1/.King's.

102

2nd Witness. No.8906 C.S.M. WOOLDRIDGE. The Cameronians attached 205
Divisional Employment Coy 2nd Divn states:- About 1-10 a.m.
on the morning of the 21st April 1917 at Roclincourt I was
wakened by L/Cpl Richardson who told me that part of the
dugout in which the Coy was sleeping had fallen in. I went at
once to the dugout and found that a part of the roof had
collapsed. I sent for the Coy Officer and the Doctor. Word was
also sent across to an R.E.Tunnelling Coy billeted near. We
started work at once to dig the fall clear. No.18539 Sergt
KYTE.E. 1st King's Regt was got out almost at once. He was
badly shaken and taken to Hospital. The fall had not come down
directly on top of him but had just covered him. We had just
got Sergt KYTE out when the R.E's came over. Work was gone on with
until the body of L/Cpl Olding (No.50283 of the 23 Roy Fus) was
got out. This took about 5 or 6 hours. Meanwhile a roll had been
called and it was found that one other man No.C/4725 Pte
Lydford J. 1st K.R.R.C. was beneath the fall. The Coy officer
then stopped the work on the advice of the R.E.Officer as it was
considered likely that a further fall might take place. This dugou
t had been occupied by troops just before we went in. It appeared
a good dugout of French construction. Shortly after we went in
a Battery of Heavy Guns took up position quite close. I think
the shock from their fire helped to bring about this fall.
During the process of digging a large unexploded shell was dugout
This appeared to have broken up the chalk just over where the
fall took place. As a result of this accident all the troops
were removed from the dugout the entrances were wired up and
marked dangerous. The body of Pte LYDFORD was left buried and
the place marked on the top with a cross and wired round.
I think death in the case of both L/Cpl Olding and Pte Lydford
must have been almost instantaneous.

                        (Sd) G.J.Wooldridge C.S.M.
                             1st Cameronians S.R.

The Court having considered the evidence are of opinion that the
two deaths above mentioned were the result of an accident.

              (Sd) R.G.Hillcoat, Capt. President.

              (Sd) H.S.Johnson, Capt. Member.

              (Sd) Edward B.Jackson. 2/Lt. Member.

In the Field.
29-7-17.

              CERTIFIED TRUE COPY.

                                        Captain for Major.
G.H.Q. 3rd Echelon.

11th August 1917.   Officer i/c Regular Infantry Section No.2.

TNA(PRO)WO95

After the war the Graves Commission could not find his body.
His name is therefore commemorated on the **Arras Memorial**,
Pas de Calais, France, on

Bay 7

SAMUEL MAURICE HURFORD
Private
27660
2nd Battalion, Hampshire Regiment,
who died on
Saturday 26th May 1917, aged 30.

Sam was born in Lymington to Maurice, a painter, and Annie Hurford, who lived at 7, Church Street, Lymington. In 1905 Sam had been appointed Sacristan and Parish Clerk at St Thomas's Church. On 26th December 1907, at St Thomas's Church, he married Ida Florence, daughter of Samuel Bowyer, civil assistant, of Ashtree Road Bitterne, Southampton and the couple moved into their home in Belmore Lane. He worked hard at his job. As the Vicar was to write in the Parish Magazine in 1917:

"His work brought him into contact with large numbers of parishioners and his reverent spirit, his devotion to duty and his whole-hearted love of his Church work have shown themselves consistently in the care which he expended on the Parish Church and in the orderliness which characterised all his labours."

In 1916, he enlisted into the Hampshire Regiment and after training was posted to the 2nd Battalion, part of the 88th Brigade in the 29th Division. This unit moved from Beauval on 1st April 1917 and was held in reserve west of Arras. On the 12th it struggled up the congested road to Orange Hill, a mile west of the village of Monchy-le-Preux, which was in a salient of the line and had a good view of the plain of Douai.

The battalion provided a small force to hold the village and helped dig an assembly trench east of the village for the other battalions of the brigade who were to attack Infantry Hill. This hill was gained but then lost again to a sharp counter-attack by a fresh Bavarian Division, which then went on to attack Monchy. This latter attack was, however, thwarted by the Hampshires who, later, were credited as

"The means of saving Monchy,"

although at the cost of fifty casualties, including eight killed.

The need to take the pressure off the collapsing French Army led to the offensive being prolonged. On 23rd April the 2nd Hampshires therefore continued to attack Infantry Hill and, indeed, even pushed on beyond it. The failure of the division

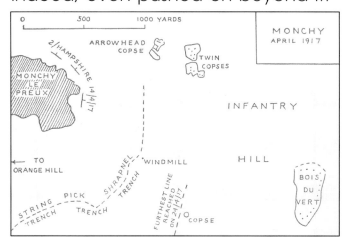

on the right, however, made its retention untenable and it could not be recaptured. Half a mile of ground had been taken and 2,500 prisoners had been captured at a cost of half of those in action.

Sam was wounded at some stage of these operations. He was evacuated to the 8th Casualty Clearing Station at Duisans, but died of his wounds on 26th May 1917. He is buried in **Duisans British Cemetery,** Etrun, Pas de Calais, France, in

Grave IV. M. 5.

PHOTOGRAPH RICHARD WILLIAMS

His wife set up this headstone in **Lymington Cemetery.**

1917 THE THIRD BATTLE OF YPRES: MESSINES

The aim of the Third Battle of Ypres was to breach the German Line and then to break out across the Plain of Flanders and capture the Channel ports of Dunkirk and Zeebrugge - from which the Germans were operating their all too successful submarine campaign against our shipping in the Atlantic.

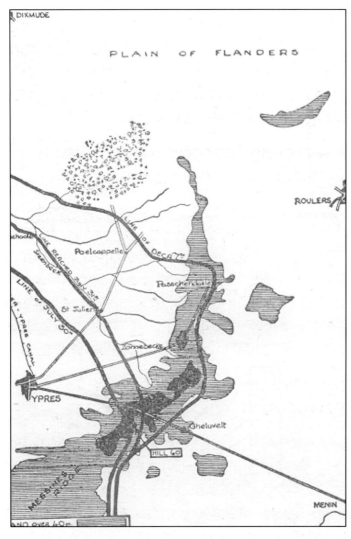

The battle was in two phases, with the aim of capturing the Messines Ridge. The Germans had occupied this ridge in 1914 and from it had an unimpeded view of the Ypres salient.

The capture of the southern part of the ridge would ease the capture of the northern part by Passchendaele, which in turn would open the way to the Plain of Flanders and the taking of the desired channel ports.

The first phase started very successfully with the Battle of Messines. There was a preliminary bombardment by over 3 million shells augmented by the simultaneous explosion of nineteen mines, many of which had been laid during 1916. This onslaught shocked the Germans, destroyed some of their main defensive positions and enabled the occupation of the ridge at small cost in life - although at the expense of the lives of **Charles Sainsbury** and **Thomas MacGreggor**

CHARLES SAINSBURY MC

Lieutenant
1st Battalion, Wiltshire Regiment,
who died on
Thursday 7th June 1917, aged 27.

Charles was the eldest son of Herbert, a corn and coal merchant, and Margaret Fanny Sainsbury, of Greystone House, Devizes. There was also a younger brother, Ronald, and a sister, Doris. Charles's connection with Lymington is not known, other than an entry in the electoral roll for 1915, which records him living in the Anglesea Hotel, renting a

*"sitting room on the ground floor and a bedroom
on the first floor furnished, for 8 shillings a week. "*

Charles arrived in France on 18th November 1915. On 3rd May 1916 the battalion was in the trenches at La Targette, in the Vimy sector, when – at 8 p.m. – the Germans fired two mines - one of which, to the north of Birkin Communication Trench, blew up a bombing post, killing its three occupants. Both sides tried to occupy the overlapping craters, and the near lips were successfully occupied. The War Diary states:

*"The consolidating of the Birkin crater was under
the direction of Capt Austin and 2nd Lieut Sainsbury."*

The following evening another mine was detonated near Grange Communication Trench, burying two men and Second Lieutenant Clark, a brother subaltern in Charles's D Company. The near edge of the crater was again consolidated and it was noted that Charles, again, did good work.

In mid June he was awarded the Military Cross

"For conspicuous gallantry in the trenches NE of NEUVILLE St VAAST on the 3rd, 4th and 8th May when hostile mines were exploded in front of the trench held by C Coy."

On the night of 6/7th June 1917 the battalion moved into assembly trenches in the Wulverghem Sector prior to taking part in the opening phase of the Battle of Messines Ridge.

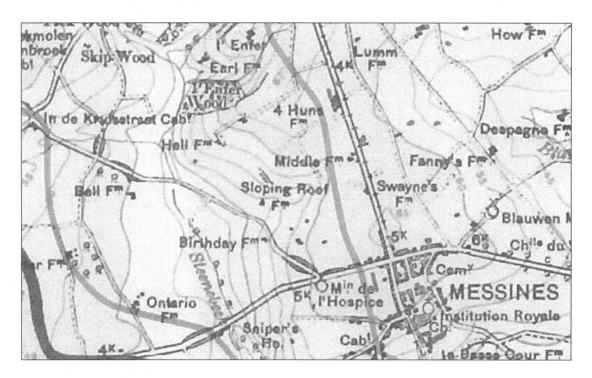

At 3.10 a.m., an hour before dawn, the attack was prefaced by the explosion of 19 mines under the main enemy positions. The Germans were taken completely by surprise and Charles's battalion advanced rapidly down the slope, through the mine-wrecked Ontario Farm and over the dried-up Steenbeek. The War diary tells the story:

"After the STEENBECQUE had been crossed the Div operating on the left bore away to the left slightly, and it was necessary to keep in touch with them. This however, was soon corrected and the Battn now that it had passed through the other Battns continued its advance in accordance with the Barrage timetable. At Zero plus 100 minutes the Battn charged its first objective OCTOBER TRENCH. Some resistance was encountered in strong concrete dugouts, but was successfully dealt with and in each case the garrison were either killed or taken prisoner The attack on 4 HUNS FARM and OCTOBER SUPPORT, the Battn's second objective was delayed for some time on account of the standing artillery barrage not lifting at the correct time and at this juncture several casualties occurred.

Eventually this objective fell and prisoners and two machine guns were taken. A gap was however left in existence, which threatened the left flank and a hostile machine gun was active in LUMMS FARM and was causing casualties. An immediate attack was made upon this strong point and the garrison of 40 were killed or captured. Although the Battn had now reached its final objective the advance was continued, this being necessitated by the fact that the Division's left flank was still exposed."

Between 7th and 11th June the Wiltshires captured 148 prisoners and 7 machine guns - at a cost of 2 officers and 19 men killed and 2 officers and 98 men wounded. Charles and 7 other men died of wounds received in this battle.

PHOTO CWGC

Charles is buried in **St Quentin Cabaret Military Cemetery**, Heuvelland, West-Vlaanderen, Belgium in:

Grave II. N. I.

The Cabaret was an inn, on the south side of Wulvergem, that was sometimes used as a battalion headquarters.

THOMAS CHARLES STUART MACGREGOR
Second Lieutenant
53rd Squadron, Royal Flying Corps,
and Highland Light Infantry
who died on
Friday 8th June 1917, aged 20.

William and Mary MacGregor lived for fifty years in Ranchi, India and then retired to Rudley, Pennington. Their eldest son, Raymond, was born in 1889 and educated at Wellington and Sandhurst. He was commissioned into the Indian Army and in 1935 was Commanding Officer of the Poona Horse. Raymond retired to Ringwood in 1939. **Thomas,** their younger son, was educated at Malvern and Sandhurst and also joined the army.

Tom joined the Royal Flying Corps on 30th October 1916 as an aviation cadet at No 1 School of Military Aviation and spent the next three months learning to fly. On 18th January 1917 he moved to 27 Reserve Squadron for four months advanced training. On completion on 8th May 1917 he was commissioned as a temporary Second Lieutenant in the Highland Light Infantry. He was then posted to 20 Reserve Squadron for a day before being sent on to join 53 Squadron in France.

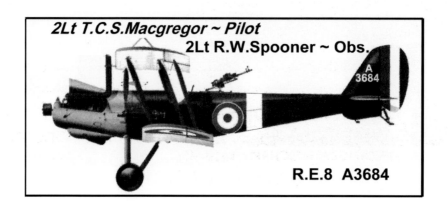

2Lt T.C.S.Macgregor ~ Pilot
2Lt R.W.Spooner ~ Obs.
A 3684
R.E.8 A3684

53 Squadron was formed in May 1916 as a Reconnaissance and Army Cooperation Squadron, flying BE2c's, attached to IX Army Corps. In April 1917 they were re-equipped with RE8's, known to the troops as "Harry Tates" - after the music hall comedian.

On 7th June General Plummer, the Army commander, opened his very successful battle of Messines by exploding nineteen mines under the German trenches southeast of Ypres. Aircraft were used at low level to report the advance and to provide tactical bombing support.

Tom was killed on 8th of June 1917, having only been with his squadron a bare month. He was flying an RE 8 aircraft serial number A3684, on a contact patrol on the second day of the attack during the battle for Messines Ridge. His observer, Second Lieutenant R.W. Spooner, also died in this incident.

They had taken off at 5.45 a.m. and were shot down by anti-aircraft fire. The aircraft crashed and was a wreck near or about the Oosttaverne Line.

In the confusion of battle their bodies were not recovered.

Thomas MacGregor is commemorated on the Arras **Flying Services Memorial.**

Thomas is also commemorated on a plaque in **St Mark's Church**, Pennington.

PHOTOGRAPH RICHARD WILLIAMS

111

1917 THIRD BATTLE OF YPRES: PASSCHENDAELE

The second phase, to the north of the Ypres-Menin road, was not so successful. The attack started in rain on 31ˢᵗ July, after over 4 million shells had been fired in the preliminary bombardment. The clay ground rapidly turned into a swamp and the Germans, on the higher ground, were able to control the battle by artillery fire.

Nevertheless by November Passchendaele had been taken, although at a cost of nearly 300,000 casualties. The prolonged offensive had, however, worn the allies down and the attack over the Plain had to be abandoned. From the German point of view, after seventy-eight divisions were thrown into the battle, the German commander, Ludendorff, believed that this battle was disastrous for the morale of the German army.

PHOTO CWGC

In the morass of the battlefield men disappeared in shell holes, wounded could not always be evacuated and those who were buried in the line often had their graves destroyed by subsequent shellfire. The Tyne Cot cemetery contains the graves of 11,500 men who were killed nearby. The associated Memorial on the wall records the names of 33,707 British soldiers who were lost in Flanders from 16ᵗʰ August 1917 until the end of the war and have no known grave.

Frederick Mansfield died of wounds received in this battle and **Robert Rixon** was killed at Broodseinde.

FREDERICK MANSFIELD
Gunner
43223
Royal Field Artillery
who died on
Saturday 18th August 1917, aged 28.

Fred was born in East Stour, Gillingham, Dorset, a son of Charles, a livery stables groom and Alice Mansfield. Before the war Fred lived with his wife, Maggie Ethel, at 2, The Priory, Hardway, Gosport, Hampshire. Although his link with Lymington is unknown his name is recorded in the Memorial Book in St Thomas Church.

He enlisted at Weymouth into the Royal Artillery and served with the 83rd Battery in the 11th Brigade. This brigade had arrived in France in 1914 with the two Indian divisions and moved into the Ypres sector, taking part in the First and Second Battles of Ypres.

When the Indian divisions went to Egypt in late 1915, Frederick's brigade became an Army Field Artillery Brigade, remaining equipped with 18 pdr field guns and 4.5-inch howitzers. It therefore went where it was needed and - as such - fired its guns in support of operations on the Somme in 1916 and Vimy in April 1917.

11th Brigade was also in support at Passchendaele. In the course of this battle Frederick was wounded and sent back to the Casualty Clearing Station complex at Dozinghem ("Dosing them" to the troops), where he died of his wounds on 18th August 1917. He is buried in **Dozinghem Militery Cemetery**, Poperinge, West-Vlaanderen, Belgium.

Grave IV. B. 9.

ROBERT JAMES RIXON

Private
18386
1st Battalion, Hampshire Regiment,
who died on
Thursday 4th October 1917, aged 29.

Bob was a son of James and Maria Rixon. The 1901 Census reports that he was born in Plough Lane, Boldre, Lymington, but was working as a domestic page in Beddington, near Wimbledon. The census also records that he was, at the time, visiting his sister, Maria, who lived in South Baddesley and worked as a washerwoman.

PHOTOGRAPH JUDY HOUGHTON

In 1912/13 Robert married Christine Cooper and initially lived in Waterford. He was well known on the Pylewell estate where he worked as an electrician. They later moved to live at 9, Latimer Road, Godalming, Surrey. A daughter, Lydia, was born on 14th November 1915. This family information has been kindly provided by Judy Houghton, a granddaughter of Christine's sister, Lydia, who is standing on the left of the above picture, holding a toddler.

Bob enlisted in Brockenhurst in 1916 into the Hampshire Regiment and was posted to the 1st Battalion. This battalion had been transferred to the 11th Brigade, 4th Division, in March 1917, as part of reinforcements to the 3rd Army for its planned spring attack at Arras. After rehearsing for this offensive the unit arrived in the Arras area on 7th April **"strong and fit."**

The opening attack on 9th April, in which the Hampshires played a leading role, was brilliantly successful. Its exploitation of the gains was limited by snow, which impeded the forward movement of the supporting guns. The failure of the Nivelle  offensive on the Aisne and the subsequent unrest in the French army meant that for the remainder of 1917 the British Expeditionary Force had to continue the attack. Although the objectives of the Arras attack had been achieved within a week, the attacks were therefore continued on a broader front. This involved the 1st Battalion in further attacks on 11th and 12th May. Both attacks were successful, but the battalion was now below 250 effectives and therefore was relieved from the line.

Bob was sent to hospital in France at this time suffering from shell-shock. The battalion remained in the Arras sector until the end of August before moving to Flanders, where they trained for the new German methods of defence to be encountered in the battles of Passchendale.

By 4th October Bob had rejoined the battalion, which was back to a strength of 1000 all ranks. Allowing for those sick, men on leave, carrying parties, divisional employment, courses, transport, and the battle nucleus, only 540 men of the battalion were involved in the attack that day at Broodseinde.

Their initial objective was beyond KANGAROO TRENCH, with exploitation on to Tragique Farm. The battalion attacked at 6.10 a.m. and forty minutes later had captured Beek Villa. It then pushed on but was checked by its own barrage and forced to dig in short of the final objective.

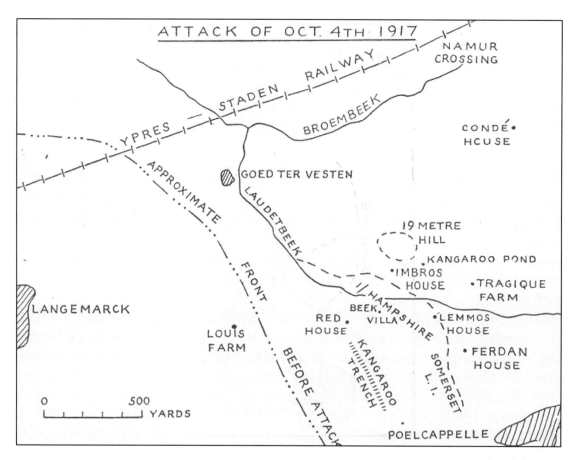

The battalion report written on 11th October describes the action in great detail but, curiously, does not mention anything about casualties. The casualties were half of those in action and Robert was amongst the 80 men missing or killed in action that day. As late as February 1919 his mother was still hopeful that Bob would be found alive and well as a prisoner of war.

As his body was never recovered, Robert's name is recorded on the **Tyne Cote Memorial,** Zonnebeke, Belgium, on:

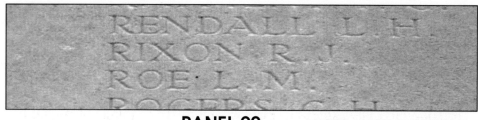

PANEL 90   **PHOTO MARC THOMPSON**

His name is also commemorated on the War Memorial at **Stoke Road, Guildford**, where his parents were living and on the memorial at **Busbridge Church, Godaming**, Surrey, where Robert lived with his wife.

1917 BATTLE OF CAMBRAI

The aim of the battle was to break through the HINDENBURG LINE – a series concrete emplacements with interlocking fields of fire, wire and ditches in depth well supported by artillery firing on pre-ranged targets. The crossings over the canals at Masnieres and Marcoing could then be secured and the Masnieres – Beaurevoir defensive position captured. Finally the Cambrai – Sensee river – Canal du Nord position would be captured, thus allowing the cavalry to pass through and exploit the open warfare situation to defeat the Germans.

The battle was the first time that tanks, infantry, artillery and airpower were married together effectively. To keep the element of surprise, the guns of the artillery were "surveyed in" by the Royal Engineers and the grid references of their targets placed on the same grid of the operations map. This enabled accurate predicted fire to be given at the moment of attack, without previous registration. The opening barrage on 20th November therefore caught the enemy totally by surprise and the enemy's front trenches were captured even before the appearance of the tanks. The whole HINDENBURG LINE in the battle area was breached and the Cambrai – Bapaume road reached, whilst the canal was crossed at Marcoing.

But the momentum of the attack could not be kept going. The German defence of Flesquieres Ridge checked part of the advance, tank crews needed rest and the tanks themselves needed repair and maintenance. The enemy gained time and quickly organised a powerful counterattack. – on the first day of which **Edward Rickman** was killed. By the end of the month much of the ground gained in the first few days of the battle was lost.

The battle did, however, prove that the HINDENBURG LINE – and similar fixed defences – was vulnerable. It also showed the way ahead for the tactical use of tanks, ground/air cooperation and the use of artillery that ultimately led to the dramatic defeat of the German Army in the last three months of the war.

EDWARD GEORGE RICKMAN

Private
28878
7th Battalion, Somerset Light Infantry
who died on
Friday, 30th November 1917, aged 34.

Edward was born and lived in Lymington. After leaving school he joined the Royal Navy and served for ten years. He later married, fathered two children and lived in Cannon Street. He enlisted at Brockenhurst into the Royal Field Artillery (no. 223563) and later transferred into the Somerset Light Infantry, serving in its 7th Battalion in 61st Brigade in 20th Division.

After a difficult time at Passchendaele this division was moved to the Cambrai front, where it started training with tanks in preparation for the Battle of Cambrai. 20th Division was to attack northeast across the HINDENBURG MAIN and SUPPORT LINES Edward's battalion had been tasked with the capture of La Vacquerie, a strong point in the enemy's defences.

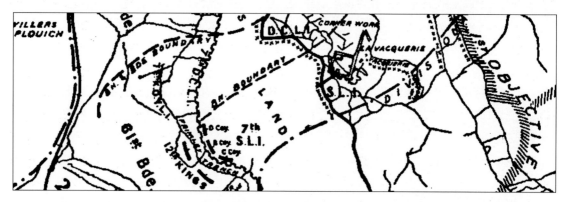

At 6.20 a.m. on 20th November the advance began and the troops could see La Vacquerie covered with shellfire. The attack went to plan and by 7.30 a.m. the village had been captured and the position began to be consolidated. At 11.00 a.m. the Somersets were sent north east to reinforce the 88th Brigade in 29th Division, which had just captured Masnieres. They reached this town at 6 p.m. after a difficult cross-country march. It was now raining and Edward and his friends had a very uncomfortable night before consolidating Masnieres.

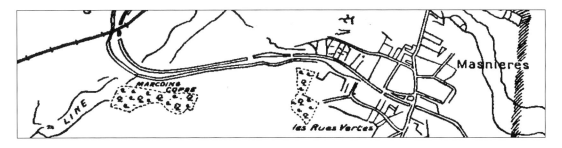

The General commanding 88 Brigade reported:

> *"I wish to tell you how much I appreciate the excellent work done by the 7th Somerset L I in Masnieres in clearing the houses of snipers and exploring the many underground passages. The place is quite quiet now with a Somerset on guard at each hole."*

The battalion rejoined the 61st Brigade on 25th November and went back into the line to the north east of Lateau Wood. The following day was quiet – as was the night of 29/30th November. At 7.00 a.m. the Germans attacked under the cover of heavy mist. The forward positions of the Somersets were destroyed although, happily, they had been withdrawn from them the previous night. Edward's battalion fired at the

PHOTO NICK SAUNDERS

massed waves of the enemy to such effect that they ran low on ammunition. When the battalion on their right flank gave way, the Somersets withdrew to the HINDENBURG LINEThey held this line, but in so doing were practically wiped out. At Roll Call the following day only 2 officers and 62 men answered. 12 officers and 332 men were lost.

Edward was reported as missing and six months later was officially presumed dead. His name is therefore recorded on the **Cambrai Memorial,** Louverval, Nord, France, on:

Panel 4 and 5

119

1918

1918 was a year of contradictions. In eleven months the Allies in France moved from defence, through defeat, to victory.

For Britain, it began with the heritage of failure to break German resistance at Passchendaele and even at Cambrai. The British and French armies had both passed their apogee of effectiveness and the pool of manpower was becoming very shallow. Women were increasingly filling men's jobs at home. Margaret Croucher and other local girls made shells in the South Coast Garage in Lymington.

Lloyd George's refusal to replace the losses in manpower of Third Ypres led, in February, to Haig having to reorganise divisional strength from twelve, down to nine, battalions. At the same time he had to take over yet more French trenches to cover the war-weariness of our Gallic allies. This precluded any form of offensive action. Yet "normal" trench warfare was to take the lives of **Herbert Haines** and **Arthur Clarke**.

The collapse of Russia enabled Germany to reallocate divisions to France. An impending German offensive in France was therefore both recognised and feared as American forces were not yet ready for action. The Germans' opening attack on the Somme, on 21st March 1918, was devastating. Subsequent attacks on other parts of the line threatened the Channel ports - our lifeline for the supply of men and materials – as well as putting Paris in danger.

The attacks, however, were finally held. In July the Allies moved towards a counterstroke, which turned into an all-out offensive (see page 144) and forced Germany to sue for an armistice.

HERBERT SIDNEY HAINES

Private
21594
2nd Battalion, Devonshire Regiment,
who died on
Friday 15th February 1918, aged 29.

Bert was the second son of William and Kate Haines of 1 Bridge Road, Lymington. He was a keen footballer. When he enlisted in Yeovil into the Devonshire Regiment, he was living in West Coker, Somerset, where he worked as a gardener at the Hall.

He was the husband of Alice Nellie Haines of 50, Gosport Street, Lymington. There was one child to the marriage.

Bert served in D Company of the 2nd Battalion the Devonshire Regiment. This regular battalion had gone to France from Egypt in early November 1914 as part of the 23rd Brigade of 8 Division and had played a full part in the 1915 battles as well as the Somme in 1916.

Bert joined them in March 1917, when the battalion was operating against the HINDENBURG LINE, before it moved to the Ypres Salient and Passchendaele. From September to November 1917 the battalion operated in the Plugstreet area, where the line was long and mainly consisted of detached posts. However, by vigorous patrolling and some sharp encounters, the Devons enjoyed complete ascendancy over the opposing Germans and casualties were not heavy.

On 18th November they relieved a Canadian division in the northeastern extremity of the salient, north of Passchendaele village. The line was both difficult to reach and to defend because of the mud and slime.

Bringing up rations and back-loading casualties was precarious and costly, as the enemy had registered its guns on the wooden roads and tracks of the battlefield. The battalion, however, was tasked with active patrolling to locate the enemy's positions and to see if the line could be advanced.

The patrols found the area alive with Germans in shell-holes and identified a machine-gun post and a strongpoint. These were attacked on 25th November and taken, with a resultant 400-yard forward movement of the front line. The battalion was immediately relieved, but returned three days later just in time to beat off a counter attack.

The battalion was out of the line for a month, but returned to the trenches at Bellevue, north west of Passchendaele at the end of January 1918, with a fighting strength of 655 all ranks. The rain had stopped, but it was still cold and the ground was beginning to dry out. In mid January, however, they were visited by a storm, which washed away the plank roads and duckboards. The light railway then broke down under the increased traffic. The enemy was more active and there were several minor encounters and small raids.

February was an active month, with the German artillery more prominent and its infantry raiding more penetrative. The main attack on the Devons was on 13th February, when a strong party tried to rush them at Vat cottages. This was repulsed.

On the 15th they attacked again and captured three Devons. Although the Germans were dislodged by an immediate counter attack Bert was killed in this incident. The Regimental padre wrote to explain that Bert had been in an advanced post on the front line with an officer and two others when a shell burst inside the post killing them all instantaneously. He was buried by his comrades near where he died.

The grave was lost in the subsequent fighting, however, and his name is therefore recorded on the **Tyne Cote Memorial**, on:

Panel 38-40

ARTHUR CLARKE
Sapper
143720
Royal Engineers
who died on
Sunday 17th February 1918, aged 30.

Arthur was the son of William and Mary Clarke of Ashley Arnewood, Milton. The family included his elder sisters and a younger brother Bertie, Louisa, a domestic cook, and Ellen, a housemaid. In 1917 they were living in Broad Lane, Lymington. At some stage he married Rosalie, who later lived in Salisbury.

Arthur enlisted in Brockenhurst into the Royal Engineers and by 1918 was serving with the 93rd Field Company Royal Engineers on the Western Front. On 16th February his Field Company was located in
forward billets in Railway West Camp at Lechelle, midway between Peronne and Bapaume, on the Somme. Here it was tasked with building light railways, preparing gun positions and repairing and improving the trench line in anticipation of the expected German spring offensive. Working parties were continuous by day and night, with the sappers providing the directional expertise to the labouring infantry and gunners. The War Diary for the unit, at this time, notes:

16. 02.18. Work as usual. 15 O.Rs .wounded shellfire (gas). Strength 7 officers, 180 O.Rs., 72 animals.

Arthur and the other gas casualties had been evacuated back to the 21st Casualty Clearing Station at Ytres, for treatment. Both he and another sapper were to die from the effects of this gassing the following day.

Arthur is buried at **Rocquigny-Equancourt Road, British Cemetery**, Manancourt, Somme, France, in:

Grave X. B. 16

1918 THE GERMAN OFFENSIVE

After Cambrai, the winter cooled the ardour of both sides. The armies took stock of their fortunes. Time and numbers were running against Germany. Its submarine campaign to starve Britain into submission had failed. Germany's allies, Turkey and Austro-Hungary, were beginning to lose their enthusiasm for the war, whilst the American armies were streaming into Europe. The release of fifty-two divisions of trained and battle-hardened troops from the Eastern Front gave Ludendorff a window of opportunity within which to attack on the Western front, before America tilted the balance back in favour of the Allies. In the early months of 1918 they prepared for their last, make or break, offensive.

When the Germans began their five-phased spring offensive on 21st March they started with OPERATION MICHAEL, over the old Somme battlefield. Storm Troops had been specially trained to rapidly penetrate the Allied lines, bypassing any resistance – which was mopped up by more conventional troops later, if required. The German artillery had also developed new skills in hitting a target without previous registration and could take on targets of opportunity quickly with their Forward Observation Officers. Integrated aerial reconnaissance and artillery observation also helped the rapid gains achieved.

The British braced themselves for the inevitable attack. Though a faint hint of ultimate victory was in the damp March air, the battalions of the front line were sore and weary. There had been too much death. Battalions were now largely made up of quickly trained young conscripts, or soldiers fresh out of hospital with bodies mended from wounds but minds perhaps still confused. Many battalions were not ready, in numbers or condition, to withstand the severity of the German onslaught. Colonel Edmund Malone recorded that in his last draft he had found seven Russians dressed as Fusiliers. They could not speak English -having enlisted in Chicago and been drilled at Dover without being spotted. Operationally his Royal Fusilier battalion was in a bad way:

> *"Our salient at Flesquieres was about the nearest point to Berlin. We had a frightful gassing the week before. The G.O.C. asked if we were fit to go back to the line. I pointed out that we had only 300 survivors and 100 recruits just joined. 'Our own side are damn dangerous,' he added; 'the Hun is quite innocuous.'"*

When the attacks came, and the Allies were forced back, the front-line troops regarded their plight with an almost ironic disinterest. Colonel Malone cast his detached eye over the events of March 21, and wrote a letter in these terms:

> *"I sat in the dugout with pages of orders before me as to how to behave when attacked; still ready to die to the last man. As soon as a Hun was sighted we fired off the S.O.S. signal, at the same time releasing a poor pigeon who had been bottled up in the dugout. I then told the battalion in support to make a counterattack as per orders. They flatly declined. Not that I minded very much, but it would have been interesting to have watched them. After all, orders are orders.*
>
> *I was much struck by the lack of interest shown in this great battle. The mess waiter - a bishop's butler in private life - insisted on serving dinner as usual, quite unperturbed. We got a grand view of the Fifth Army on our right, running like hares. Our Army (the Third) was slouching along the road like a crowd leaving a Cup Final - no hurry, all regiments mixed up, some of them singing, some of them looting chocs from abandoned canteens, but no one taking the slightest interest in the War except ourselves. We more or less had to, as we were still a unit.*
>
> *Whenever we got a bit scattered I made Jack Forster blow his hunting horn. He was a rum fellow: had lost his tin hat, wore a girl's silk stocking around his neck as a mascot and carried a small dog under his arm."*

Aided by heavy morning mist seeded with gas and smoke shells, deep penetration of our Fifth Army - newly created to take over French trenches - was achieved. British troops reeled back in confusion and chaos at all levels was evident. **Alfred Wearn, Charles Warder** and **Charles White** were all killed in this period.

After two weeks the Germans repeated the dose, in OPERATION GEORGETTE, against Armentieres and followed it up against the French line from the end of May to Mid July.

Edward Miller, Jesse Tregunna, Thomas Banks, Walter Pearce and **William Jenvey** all died at this time, helping to stem enemy advances.

ALFRED GEORGE WEARN
Gunner
184388
Royal Field Artillery
who died on
Thursday, 21st March 1918, aged 27.

Alfred was a son of Henry and Ann Amelia Wearn, of 12, Gosport Street, Lymington.

Before the war he "went for a soldier" and joined the 11th Hussars as Trooper number 5071, serving with them for seven years. Four of his brothers also served in the Great War – one in Mesopotamia, another went to India with the Territorials in December1914 and a third, the family believed, served with the American troops. A fourth brother was discharged.

Alfred was called back to the colours in 1914, but this time into the Royal Field Artillery. By 1918 he was serving with A Battery, 331st Brigade, attached to the 66th Division.

18 Pdr FIELD GUN

The Somme battles showed that the practice of withdrawing infantry divisions for rest, but leaving their artillery in action, created acute strain on gunners. A reorganisation therefore took place whereby each division was supported by two artillery brigades. Each brigade comprised three batteries of six 18-pounder field guns and one battery of six 4.5-inch Howitzers. This dedicated artillery support - 330th and 331st Brigades in the case of 66 Division - moved as an integral part of the division.

Alfred was a gunner in A Battery, of 331st Brigade. This was an 18-Pounder horse-drawn battery. These 3.3-inch calibre guns could fire an 18.5-lb shell over 9,000 yards. Initially they were capable of firing high explosive or shrapnel shells, but later in the war gas and smoke shells were also developed. It was such an effective weapon that the 25-Pdr field gun of the Second World War was developed from it.

AN 18-Pdr GUN IN ACTION   **PHOTO IWM**

When the Germans opened their attacks on 21st March, the 66th Division – as part of the 19th Corps in the Fifth Army – was holding 12,000 yards of the line at Roisel, 7 miles east of Peronne. The 330th Brigade was in direct support in the Battle Zone and the 331st Brigade in reserve in the Rear Zone.

Forty-three German divisions attacked the fourteen divisions of the Fifth Army. At 4.40 a.m. the Germans opened up an accurate barrage by 6,473 guns over a fifty mile front. The barrage concentrated on the Forward Zone, the belts of wire and artillery locations. The heavy mist prevented any aerial reconnaissance and so there was no intelligence of German movements. The fog of war was so intense that some infantry positions and battery sites did not realise an enemy assault was underway until they were overrun.

In the 66th Divisional area the Manchesters had been attacked in Brosse Wood. Close fire from a battery of 330 Brigade had kept the Germans at bay until the evening, when they were surrounded and remnants captured. 331 Brigade galloped forward to help save the division, but the situation was very fluid.

The War Diary for the 331 Brigade for the period shows:

The War Diary, on line 13 above, records the capture of Alfred's A battery about 10 a.m., being used at this time in the anti-tank role. Alfred was killed in the confused fighting of the day in what was to become known as the Battle of Saint Quentin. The brigade's total casualties were 102 all ranks, of whom 26 were killed and 36 missing.

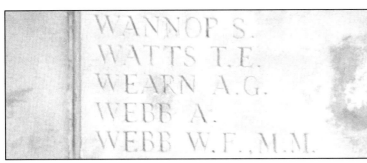

PHOTO AVRIL WILLIAMS

His body was never recovered and so Alfred's name appears on the **Poziers Memorial**, Somme, France, on:

Panels 7-10.

CHARLES EVERARD WARDER

Private
31581
1st Battalion,
Wiltshire Regiment
who died on
Sunday 24th March 1918, aged 35.

The Warders were a very large family who lived at the Brickyard, Walhampton. Harry Warder came from Yarmouth on the Isle of Wight, and was an estate carpenter. By 1901, he and his wife Mary had ten children: Ketty, **Charles** – who was a bricklayer's apprentice – Sissy, Arnold (a plumbers apprentice), Dorothy, Elsie, Daisy, Clifford, Godfrey and May. They later moved to Union Hill, Lymington.

Charles enlisted in Lymington into the Wiltshire Regiment. At the outbreak of war the 1st Battalion was part of 10 Brigade in the 4th Division. On 22nd August it proceeded to France and it remained on the Western Front continuously until the end of the war.

The battalion took part in the retreat from Mons and stood at Le Cateau. It then experienced constant trench warfare until the Battle of the Somme, when it was part of the opening attack and had a prolonged second tour in October. 1917 saw it taking part in the Battle of Arras in April. It remained there until September, when it moved to Ypres and fought in the later Passchendaele battles. It then returned to the Arras trenches before moving to the Lys sector in April, where it occupied trenches at Hinges. The 1st Battalion remained in the trenches before Arras until 8th September 1917.

After training it then went back into the line at Ypres. For the early part of 1918 the 1st Battalion remained in the trenches at Hinges, in the northern part of the line. In his last spell in the line here Charles is recorded as having been

"shot by a sniper, but stayed on duty in the trenches."

When the German attack began the battalion was in reserve at ACHIET - LE - GRAND. At 11.30 a.m. the battalion moved to the area NW of FREMICOURT and the same evening proceeded to the Army Line occupying the central position in the Brigade on a line running from the E of BEUGNATRE and FREMICOURT. The enemy attacked strongly and by the evening had carried the line by assault. The following morning the enemy twice attacked the battalion front, but was completely repulsed, sustaining very heavy casualties. The night of the 23rd/24th was somewhat lively owing to the enemy continuously trying to creep up and cut the wire. The War Diary for 24th March records:

"In the morning the enemy shelled the whole of the Battn Trench System, fire being directed by hostile aeroplanes. The absence of our planes was noticeable. Our guns retaliated but unfortunately there was a considerable amount of short shooting causing several casualties. In the afternoon there was an intensive bombardment by the enemy and about 4 p.m. the enemy assaulted. Fighting was in progress but the attack had for all practical purposes failed on the Battn front when the CO received a verbal message over the telephone to retire at once. This was passed on to the Coys but at the same time the two Battns on the right flank broke and came back leaving the Coys in the front system in the air. They attempted to come back as ordered but were practically exterminated by machine gun fire.

That night the Battn reassembled at ACHIET-LE-PETIT mustering about 3 officers and 54 other ranks. The casualties suffered in the fighting up to that date amounted to 413."

Charles was killed in action on 24th March and his body was never recovered. His name is therefore recorded on the **Arras Memorial**, Pas de Calais, France, on:

Bay 7

CHARLES RICHARD WHITE
Sergeant
9721
1st Battalion, Hampshire Regiment
who died on
Thursday, 28th March 1918, aged 24.

Charles was born on 2nd April 1894, to George and Eliza White in West Bromwich. His father was working as a boat unloader at the time. He later worked as a general labourer and from where his five daughters and two sons were born, he clearly followed work in Dorset, Sussex and Swanwick, Hampshire. In 1917, they were living in Gosport Street.

Charles enlisted at Winchester into the 10th Battalion the Hampshire Regiment. This "K1" battalion was part of the 10th (Irish) Division, which went to Gallipoli on the 7th August 1915.
Charles went to Gallipoli as a Lance Corporal and later made Sergeant. In 1916 he was posted to the 14th (Kitchener) Battalion, which was serving in the 39th Division. This battalion went to France in 1916 and had two long spells in the Somme. It had fought well in the Ypres battles of 1917 and had a VC action at Pilkem when, on 31st July, Second Lieutenant Hewitt had led a successful attack. After rest in December they briefly returned to the Canal Bank trenches in the Ypres Salient before going south to Saint Quentin at the end of January.

At this stage of the war Lloyd George, who had been politically embarrased by the casualties of Passchendaele, tried to limit the scope for similar future battles by withholding routine reinforcements to France. Normal trench attrition continued, however, and some battalions in France were disbanded to feed other units. The 14th Battalion was one such and when it was disbanded on 23rd February Charles went to the 1st Battalion, which was part of the 11th Brigade in 4th Division in the 4th Army Corps.

Four weeks later this battalion was on the left of the Third Army, and was thus outside the front attacked by the Germans on 21st March 1918. It was, in fact, in brigade reserve north of the Fampoux-Arras Road. That evening it moved up to occupy the trenches east of COLT TRENCH.

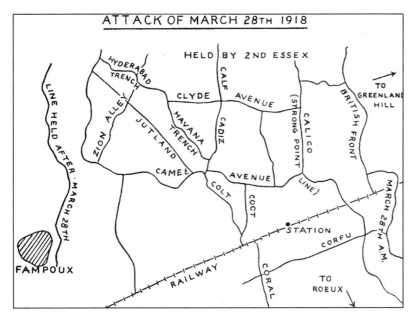

Two days later the troops to the south fell back, leaving the Hampshires right flank on the railway line "in the air." The Hampshires then moved forward to occupy the front line and to extend into CORFU TRENCH.

On 28th March the expected attack arrived with four hours of artillery and mortar bombardment prefacing the enemy assault at 7.15 a.m. By this stage the Hampshires had fallen back to occupy the strong point in CALICO TRENCH from which they offered a very successful defence. By 1'clock, however, the attacking Bavarians had begun to infiltrate the area and gained most of CALF and CADIZ TRENCHES. An hour later the Hampshires had reorganised on HAVANA TRENCH and made a successful counter-attack. German attacks persisted throughout the rest of the day, but with decreasing conviction. This action in repulsing the enemy was the turning point of the German offensive, which soon petered out on this front.

The battalion started the day 604 men strong. This defence cost the Hampshires 43 men killed, 83 others wounded. Charles was one of the 87 additional men missing.

His name therefore appears on the **Arras Memorial** on:

Bay 6

EDWARD MILLER

Driver,
40172
Royal Field Artillery
who died on
14th April 1918, aged 30.

Edward was born in 1888, the second son of Mr and Mrs G Miller of Solent Cottages, Bath Road, Lymington. Before the war he lived in North Kensington, London.

He joined the local Volunteers in 1909 and served with them for five years. In 1914 he enlisted into the RFA and served in  the 87th Brigade taking part – as THE CHRONICLE puts it, in its issue of 9th May 1918:

"in most of the hard fighting on the Western Front."

By 1918 he was a driver in A Battery, which was equipped with 18-Pdr field guns. On 1st April 1918 the battery moved up to the Messines area and for a week fired, mainly at night, on enemy roads and tracks to frustrate the German advance. On 10th April it responded to the German attack on the Armentieres front by retiring in good order and digging in on the forward slope of Kemmel Hill, near Ypres. Edward was killed in action when the Germans overran the battery's position. In the confusion of the time his body was lost as the Germans pressed yet further forward.

Edward's name is recorded on the **Tyne Cote Memorial**, Belgium, on

Panel 4-6 and 162.

JESSE TREGUNNA

Private
25298
1st Battalion, Hampshire Regiment,
Who died on
Monday 22nd April 1918, aged 32.

Jesse was born in Brockenhurst in 1886, one of four sons born to James Tregunna, a railway labourer from St Anthony, Cornwall, and Annie - a London girl. They lived in Lower Buckland. Jesse, a baker, married Ada May Plumbly from Shirley Holms, Sway and continued to live in the same house.

Jesse enlisted in the army at Lymington and served in the 15th, then the 2nd and finally the 1st Battalions of the Hampshire Regiment. It was part of the 11th Brigade in 4th Division in the 4th Army Corps, which had borne the brunt of the German offensive when it attacked Arras in April 1918.

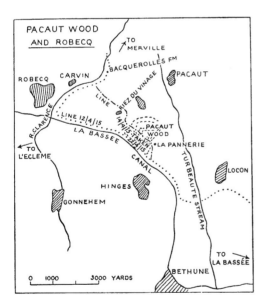

On 22nd April the Hampshires were tasked with the capture of Pacaut Wood, as the opening phase of the British counter-attack. Three companies were used for the attack, which had to cross the canal over footbridges laid for the purpose. The attack went in at 05.15 a.m. and the German counter barrage fell three minutes later. Within 30 minutes the objective was captured. Eighty-five prisoners and thirteen machine guns were taken at a cost of seven officers and 191 men out of the battalion's strength in action of 14 officers and 650 other ranks.

Jesse is buried in **Mont-Bernanchon British Cemetery**, Gonnehem in:

Plot I. C. 4.

THOMAS GEORGE BANKS
Lieutenant
Royal Engineers
who died on
Friday 26th April 1918, aged 28.

George, as he preferred to be called, was born on 7th November 1889. He was the youngest son of David and Sarah Ann Banks (nee Lee), of Belmore Cottage, 2, Belmore Lane, Lymington, where his father worked as a master stonemason employing several men. It was a large family with two daughters, Annie and Muriel and three sons – Frank, an office clerk, Charles, an apprentice surveyor and Thomas.

George attended the Stanwell House School in Lymington and was a member of the Lymington Cadet Corps. His Record of Service shows his enlistment into the Territorial Hampshire (Fortress Company) Royal Engineers in 19th May 1909. At this time he was living in Newport, on the Isle of Wight, where he was working as an electrical engineer for the Electric Light and Power Company. He steadily worked his way up the ranks, becoming a Corporal on 1st July 1909. He specialised as an electrical engineer, and his annual assessment at summer camp showed his progression from **"Skilled"** in 1909, through **"Superior"** a year later, to **"Very Superior"** in 1911.

In 1914 he was a Sergeant in the 1/7th Hants Field Company RE. In September he was nominated for a Temporary Commission in the Royal Flying Corps, but was actually commissioned as a Second Lieutenant on 25th September 1915 into the 2/1st Wessex Divisional Company RE. On 24th January 1917 George was posted to France to the 503rd (Wessex) Territorial Force Field Company. During 1917/18 the Company served as Divisional Engineers to the 58th (London) Division (Territorial) in 4th Army and took part in the Third Battle of Ypres. By 1918 the division was in the Amiens area of the line. In April the company was based 1.5 miles east of Cagny, on the southeast outskirts of Amiens.

It was involved with a variety of tasks from excavating the CAGNY SWITCH TRENCH as well as a headquarters for 2nd Battery RA, to fixing gas blankets in dugouts and consolidating and wiring frontline and support trenches as required.

On the night of 24th April, half the company was engaged in wiring the front line in the Bois de Hangard under the direction of George and Lieutenant G Mentz. It is not known if the wiring party was caught by an enemy patrol, machine gun fire or shelling, but both officers were hit.

George died in the Casualty Clearing Station at Boves. He is buried in **Boves West Communal Cemetery**, Somme, in:

Grave C. 21.

HIS INSCRIPTION ON THE FAMILY GRAVE AT PENNINGTON

WALTER PEARCE
Private
285090
2nd/4th Battalion,
Oxfordshire and Buckinghamshire Light Infantry,
who died on
Wednesday 29th May 1918, aged 38.

Walter was born at Egham, Surrey, the son of John and Elizabeth Pearce. He married Rosina L. M. Pearce and lived at Turnpike Cottage, Buckland, Lymington.

In 1916 he enlisted at Winchester into the Hampshire Regiment, having the regimental number 30626. During the war, however, he was transferred into the Oxfordshire and Buckinghamshire Light Infantry and served with their 2/4th Battalion. This Second Line Territorial battalion had a busy war. It landed in France on the 24th May 1916, as part of the 184th Infantry Brigade in the 61st Division and took over trenches near Neuve Chapelle. Before it had time to find its feet it was pushed into an attack at Aubers Ridge and suffered severe losses. By November it was on the Somme at Mucky Farm and the following year at St Quentin in April, where it conducted a successful trench raid, and made a fine stand in August in front of Ypres during the Passchendaele battle.

It came into its own in 1918. When the Germans advanced on the 21st March, D Company held the Enghien Redoubt for six hours enormously outnumbered and completely surrounded – thus enabling the rest of the battalion to withdraw in good order. The brigade made a stand at Nesle and the battalion counter-attacked the enemy at La Motte, as part of the defence of St Quentin. This effort shattered the battalion.

The battalion was refitted at Avesne, behind Amiens. Walter joined the battalion in a draft of 431 men from England. This draft, coupled with the amalgamation of what was left of the battalion with 300 men from the 25th Entrenching Battalion of the Bucks, brought it back to a strength of over 1000 men.

They left their billet in the chateau at Avesne on the 11th April to go into Army Reserve at Neuve Chapelle. At the station at Hangest they learned from a copy of the Continental DAILY MAIL of the German breakthrough in that area. They detrained behind the Nieppe Forest and marched through it to St Venant, pausing there for a decent breakfast before concentrating behind Les Amusoires and moving up to adopt a defensive posture along the Robecq – Calonne road.

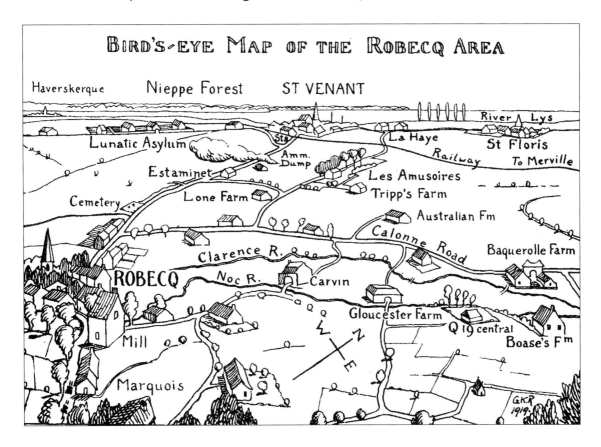

The afternoon saw fighting to secure Baquerolle and Boase's Farms, which the conduct of the new draft helped to secure. The enemy's counter-attack under the cover of the following morning's mist, was frustrated, as was the battalion's attempt the next day to occupy other cottages in the area. The situation was not helped by French civilians, who still occupied some of the farms. One old woman was discovered in a shell-hole sheltering from a machine-gun barrage under a large umbrella.

On the 15th the same cottages were attacked, this time with the planned help from 4th Division to the right of the above birds-eye view. The latter help, however, failed to materialise and German fire from this area caused twenty casualties.

The battalion was relieved by the Gloucesters on the 17th April and went into reserve in the St Venant Asylum, the second largest of its kind in France. This provided well for the needs of the battalion, with its numerous rooms and good laundry and cooking facilities. It was frequently shelled, however, and on the 21st May a shell exploded in a cellar where men of C and D Companies were sheltering, causing many casualties. For the rest of April and May the battalion continued to do tours in the Robecq sector

Walter was wounded in the course of these operations and was evacuated back to the Casualty Clearing station at Aire. Here he died of his wounds on the 29th May 1918.

Walter is buried in **Aire Communal Cemetery**, Pas de Calais, France, in:

Grave II. K. 35.

WILLIAM CHARLES JENVEY

Private
290816
2nd Battalion, Devonshire Regiment,
who died on
Friday 31st May 1918, aged 20.

William was the son of John and Charlotte Eliza Jenvey, of Inkerman Cottage, Middle Road, Lymington. He was raised in Lymington, but enlisted in Winchester into the Devonshire Regiment, with the number 2468 – until he was found to be under-age. He re-enlisted in 1917.

The 2nd Battalion the Devonshire Regiment arrived in France in January 1915 and played a full part in the Neuve Chapelle and Somme battles. William went to France in 1917 and in October was wounded by shrapnel at Passchendaele. He was in hospital in England until March 1918.

By 1918 his battalion had moved south to the Villers-Carbonnel sector of the Somme. The German advance on 23rd March found the Devonshires holding trenches in the St Christ Bridge area. They held the bridge successfully for two days in the face of heavy German attacks and then withdrew to Harbonnieres. After counter-attacking it was then relieved by the French and moved into rest, before taking over the trench line at Villers Brettoneux Plateau with the task of defending Amiens. This it successfully did, despite a determined enemy attack, which included the first appearance of German tanks. This defence of vital ground cost the battalion 346 all ranks killed, wounded or missing.

On 12th May the Corps was then sent to man fifteen miles of French lines near Rheims. The 23rd Brigade was in the centre of this frontage. With the warning of an enemy attack in force the Devonshires were moved from reserve at Roucy, on 26th May, to occupy the underground shelters of the Bois de Buttes.

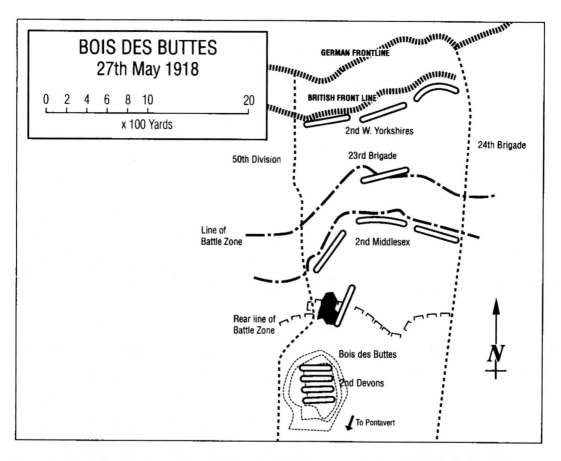

The following day the West Yorks and the Middlesex were overrun in the dawn attack and the Germans, aided by a heavy barrage and a dense mist, achieved a 3,000-yard penetration through the Battle Zone. The Devons left their tunnels to man what was left of their trenches after intense and accurate shelling. They immediately became involved in an infantry battle, which quickly broke down into a series of small, localised and bitterly fought actions. The situation was further confused as the German attack, supported by tanks, aircraft and flamethrowers, was interspersed with retreating Frenchmen and retiring West Yorkshire and Middlesex soldiery.

The Devons held on to their position until midday at a cost of 23 officers and 528 men killed or missing. William was amongst those bewildered and shell-shocked men who somehow escaped from the carnage of the battle. With no rest, the men were put into a thin line of trenches astride the Guyencourt - Ventelay road. Later they were moved to further back to defend Montigny. Then began a series of small but effective delaying actions as the Devons conducted a fighting withdrawal.

Semper Fidelis. The last stand of the 2nd Devons at Bois des Buttes, 27th May 1918. W. B. Wollen (1922).

By 30th May 2 officers and 90 men, all that was left of the battalion, were part of a hastily formed composite Battalion which occupied Bligny Hill. Here they repelled a number of German attacks and brought the German offensive to a halt.

PHOTO CWGC

William was killed defending Bligny Hill. He is buried in **Sissonne British Cemetery**, Aisne, France, in:

Grave 1. 1.

On 5th December 1918 The **Croix de Guerre avec Palme** was presented to the 2nd Battalion in recognition of the successful defence of Bois de Buttes, which bought time or, as General Maistre put it:

> *"Allowed the formation of a dyke against which the hostile flood was in the end to break itself and to be held."*

All ranks of the present-day battalion of the Devon and Dorset Regiment continue to wear this medal ribbon on their arm in memory of this action.

1918 COUNTERATTACK AND VICTORY

By July, it had become clear that the Germans were running out of manpower. The newly unified Allied command structure under Foch, the arrival of the Americans into the Front line, the effectiveness of the British naval blockade and the advent of well-handled tanks and aircraft gave Haig the confidence – almost uniquely amongst the Allied leaders – to believe that the war could be won before the end of the year.

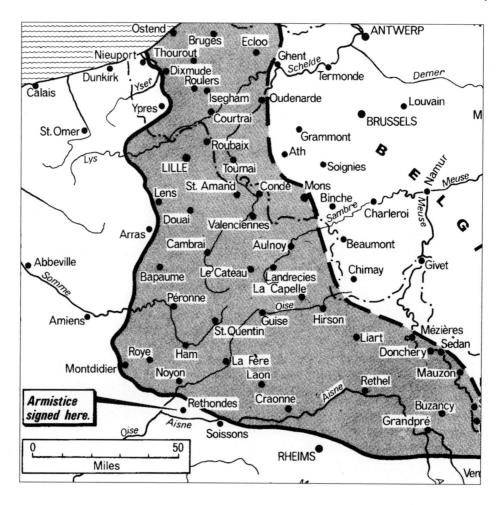

His resultant advance - "The Last Hundred Days" - was to achieve this. For Lymington, however, it was at the expense of the lives of **Henry Harris, James Phillips, Joseph Cleall, Charles Hood, Walter Gannaway, George Lewington, Alfred Scott, Frederick Wellman** and **Oliver Fudge.**

The effect of such heavy losses, all within five months, on the small town of Lymington can be imagined.

HENRY JOSEPH REGINALD HARRIS
Private
35726
12ᵗʰ Battalion, Gloucestershire Regiment,
who died on
Friday 28ᵗʰ June 1918, aged 19.

Henry's father, Henry, a master tobacconist, married Eliza Dewfield Mountjoy and fathered two children – Henry, born on 10ᵗʰ September 1898 and George. The family lived at 32, Commercial Road, Bournemouth. Henry worked as part of the clerical staff at the Capital and Counties Bank at Lymington and in 1917 he enlisted there into the Gloucestershire Regiment.

By this stage the 12ᵗʰ Battalion (Bristol Pals), Gloucestershire Regiment, was in the 95 Brigade of 5ᵗʰ Division. It took part in the Third Battle of Ypres in 1917 but was pulled out as one of the five British divisions to be rushed to Italy to help resolve the crisis caused by the Austro-German success at Caporetto.

When the German offensive began in March 1918 the Gloucesters had ten battalions involved in the fighting. The 12ᵗʰ Battalion returned from Italy and took part in the Battle of Hazebrouck, from 12ᵗʰ – 15ᵗʰ April, which helped to stem the German advance in the Fourth Battle of Ypres. By June we were beginning to push the Germans back and the Gloucesters were warned to attack on the 28ᵗʰ, near Plugstreet.

On the evening of 27ᵗʰ March, Henry's unit moved up through an enemy high explosive and gas barrage to the Assembly position in the Caudescure trenches.

The War Diary map shows the attack:

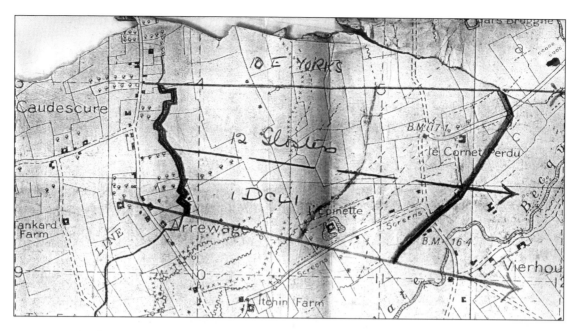

The attack went in at 6.00 a.m. under a creeping barrage and at first met with little opposition, although some casualties occurred when our own men pushed too close under it. All objectives were taken by 7.40 a.m. according to schedule.

About 12.15 pm enemy artillery opened on our new forward positions, and on our artillery retaliating; a general artillery duel ensued until 1 p.m. During the afternoon a few prisoners were rounded up from amongst the corn in rear of our new front line. About 5 pm patrols went out under cover of a barrage but could find no trace of enemy on our side of River PLATE BECQUE

Casualties   2/Lt L C MAY, 2/LT G W FARRINGTON   killed / OR about 150
Capt W BRAY 2/Lt G M WEIR wounded

TNA(PRO)WO95/1580

Henry was killed in this attack and was one of the
"*OR about 150*"
killed or wounded, recorded so casually in the War Diary extract given above. His name is recorded on the **Ploegsteert Memorial**, Belgium, on:

Panel 5

JAMES WILLIAM PHILLIPS

Private
88652
1st Battalion, The King's (Liverpool Regiment),
who died on
Friday 29th July 1918, aged 32.

THE CHRONICLE published on 22nd August 1918 reports:

News has been received by Mr. and Mrs. Phillips, of Bridge-road, Lymington, that their nephew, Pte. W. J. Phillips, of the King's Liverpool Regiment was killed in action on July 25th. The gallant soldier, who was 32 years of age, and who in civil life was in the employ of Mr. John Dimmick coal merchant, has been in the army 2 years, eleven months of which was spent in France. It is a coincidence that he was killed the very day the last letter was received from him.

James was born in Johannesberg, South Africa. In 1913 the Electoral Roll showed him as living at 20 Gosport Street. In July 1916 he enlisted in Brockenhurst into the East Surrey Regiment, but was later transferred to the King's (Liverpool) Regiment.

James arrived in France in August 1917 and by July 1918 was with his battalion in the Ayette sector. They were pulled out of the front line the night of the 25th/26th to prepare for a trench raid on enemy positions between the Courcelles and Moyennesville roads. The War Diary records:

25/7.   Various discussions with support elements for forthcoming raid. Comm Centre Group Artillery called. Comm 6th Trench Mortar Batt. called and fixed up preliminary details

26/7. Staff hard at work on our raid. ...

27/7. CO took Brigade Major round the whole front line early this morning. Col Dunlop CO of 2/Bn MGC called.

28/9.   A Company's patrolling last night was very successful and the location of the enemy posts was now made quite certain.

29/7. A Coys patrols out again last night. Very successful. Saw plenty of Boche. The Regimental Tailors were up today sewing on the white armbands. Buttons were painted with luminous paint. Faces were blacked with burnt cork on (Vaseline) also hands and wrists. Orders issued at 9 am. 2/Lt Ellis was killed, 2 OR's killed, 6 OR's slightly wounded.

The typed report on the raid records that the plan included a Stokes mortar barrage of 16 guns, a standing barrage of 44x18pounders, 14 Vickers machine-guns and a battery of 6-inch Newton Mortars and 22x4.5-inch howitzers.

Assembly in No Man's Land took an hour and a total of 132 all ranks went over top and crawled forward in groups with blackened faces and luminous buttons. At ZERO the barrages fell with a crash. The khaki armbands covering the white armbands were torn off and the raiders rushed the enemy posts. Seven prisoners including a Sgt Major and a Sgt were captured. One gave trouble so was left behind. Our causalities included one officer (Lt Ellis) killed by a bomb and James, believed to have been killed by shell splinters.

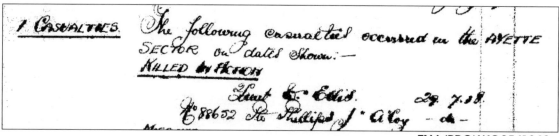

TNA(PRO)WO95/1360

The success of the raid was attributed to a thorough reconnaissance on 4 successive nights, close acquaintance with covering field batteries and the keen personal interest of Capt Harrison MC, 6th Trench Mortar Battery, who in spite of heavy rain managed in 3 days to get 16 Stokes mortars into position and accurately register them. The raiding Section Leaders watched the registration on the enemy posts and were able to move to them with absolute confidence.

James is buried in Bienvillers Military Cemetery, **Pas de Calais, France, in:**

Grave XVIII. D. 9.

148

JOSEPH WILLIAM CLEALL

Sergeant
11609
6th Battalion, Dorsetshire Regiment,
who died on
Friday 23rd August 1918, aged 37.

Joseph was born in East Coker, Somerset, to Mark and Ann Cleall. Before the war he worked as assistant steward at the Conservative Club. He was also connected with Messrs Mew, Langston and Co. He later married Alice Hilda, of Quay Street, Lymington.

He enlisted at Lymington, just after the war began, into the Dorsetshire Regiment. As one of Kitchener's second 100,000 volunteers, he joined the 6th Battalion at its inception in Dorchester on 6th September 1914 and was then attached to the 17th Division. The battalion was originally designated to be pioneers but the men wanted it to be a rifle battalion so the pioneer role was given to the 7th York and Lancasters, who were all miners. The 6th Dorsets were part of 50th Brigade with the 7th East Yorks, the 10th West Yorks and the 7th Yorks.

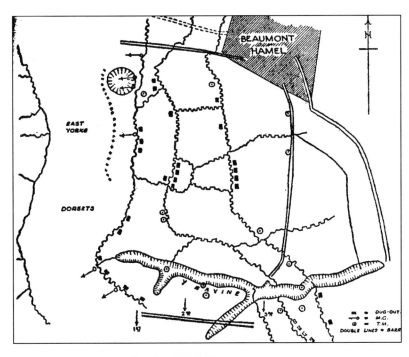

After minimal basic training, the battalion arrived in Boulogne on 14th July 1915, as part of 17 Division.

It had an energetic war, fighting at Ypres in 1915 and 1916, on the Somme in 1916 and at Arras and Passchendaele in 1917.

It was at its busiest, however, in 1918 when it experienced the German Spring offensive - bearing its brunt on the Somme, at St Quentin, at Bapaume and in the stand before Amiens.

On 8th June 1918, the 17th Division went on to the offensive with the East Yorks in trench raid over the old Somme battlefield of 1916, at what is now Newfoundland Park. The Dorsets attacked the "Y" Ravine feature to a depth of 400 yards. The men were well briefed, everyone knew the job they had to do and guns, mortars and machine-guns were used for the box and creeping barrages. The raid began at 10.05 p.m., after a rum ration, and was a brilliant success.

On 1st August the Germans withdrew across the Ancre. Joseph and his battalion moved forward to the southeast of Aveluy wood and the village itself. The ground was full of gas, there were many dead German bodies lying about and booby-trapped dugouts were a hazard. The battalion remained in the area until 5thAugust, restoring the line. It then went back to Herissart for three weeks rest.

The 8th August 1918 was the "Black Day" for the German army. Their collapse led to Joseph's battalion being immediately moved forward to support the opening stages of what was to become a war of movement. Being in reserve they supplied working parties every night and were subjected to shelling and bombing raids from enemy aircraft.

On 21st August 1918 the 17th Division was about to take the first step in the 60-mile advance that ended on 11th November 1918 and the armistice. 5 Corps was tasked with the crossing of the River Ancre and the 50th Brigade was ordered to take over from the 21st Brigade on the night of 22nd August 1918. It was to move to St Pierre Divion and make good a position on the slope of the Thiepval Ridge.

The men set out at midnight heavily laden with kit and tools, leading the Brigade. The night was sultry and the moon slight as they went through the Lustre system of trenches and crossed the flooded marshes of the Ancre. Respirators were worn, as the area was heavy with gas.

There was only one causeway over the Ancre and this was swept with shellfire. Many of the Dorsetshires just waded across and most were wet to the waist. The East Yorks Battalion did not arrive as planned. Nevertheless, the Dorsets occupied the required area of trenches and the next day the sodden and sleepless they pushed the line forward 600 yards. Twenty-seven Germans and eight machine-guns were captured during the day.

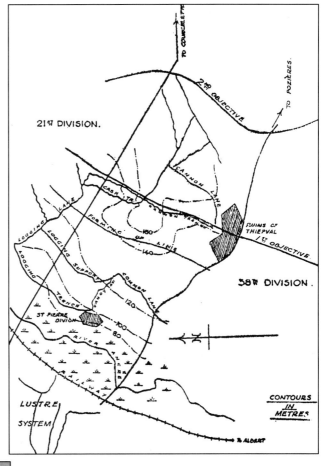

PHOTO AVRIL WILLIAMS

This success cleared the way for the East Yorks to arrive, allowing for the planned joint advance to take place on the 24th.

Sergeant Joseph Cleall was, however, killed in the course of this action.

He is buried in **Poziers British Cemetery**, Ovillers-La Boisselle, Somme, France, in:

Grave I. J. 23.

A joint memorial service for Joseph and Sergeant Walter Gannaway (see page 154) was held at St Thomas Church in September 1918.

151

CHARLES MANSELL HOOD

Lance Corporal
240343
1st/8th Battalion, Middlesex Regiment,
who died on
Saturday 24th August 1918, aged 23.

Charles was born in 1895 in Hackney, Middlesex, the son of Arthur – a bread maker - and Alice Hood – a Lymington girl. By 1901 they had moved to Shirley, Southampton and another son, William, had been born. Charles later married Florence and lived at Clan Cottage, Lower Ashley, New Milton.

He enlisted into the Duke of Cambridge's Own (Middlesex Regiment) before the war and served in the Territorial 1st/8th Battalion as Private (No. 2472). He went with it to France on 9th March 1915 and at Bailleul the battalion was allocated to the 85th Brigade of the 28th Division.

Charles was almost immediately involved in the gas attack in

April 1915 at the Second Battle of Ypres. In the trench fighting later that year, casualties were so high that the 1st/8th was briefly merged with the 7th Battalion, which was in similar state.

Restored, Charles' battalion took part in the actions at Loos in September and was then transferred to the 167th Brigade of the 56th Division, under whom It took part in the ill-fated diversionary attack at Gommecourt and in the subsequent Somme battles.

In 1917, apart from the usual spells of trench duty it fought at the Battles of Arras and Cambrai.

At the end of March 1918 Charles' battalion was relieved from the Arras front by Canadian troops and moved back to rest billets in Villers-au-Bois. For the next four months it was in and out of the trenches in this area, raiding the enemy successfully on 21st May. On 23rd August it had moved to the Somme and was in support trenches near Blaireville. The following day the battalion attacked the enemy in order to secure a "start line" from which the planned attack on the HINDENBURG LINE could be launched.

To do this the battalion was tasked with attacking the right hand part of SUMMIT TRENCH. The attack began at 7.00 a.m. covered by a good barrage. The feature was captured by 10.00 a.m. and the position consolidated with outposts being pushed forward. Orders were received late in the afternoon to continue the attack at 7.30 p.m. – the objective this time being to the CROISILLES RESERVE TRENCH and the HINDENBURG LINE itself. But the latter was a powerful defensive position and the attackers were met with such intense rifle and machine gun fire that the advance soon stalled and the battalion was forced to return to its start line.

PHOTO CWGC

Charles was killed in this attack, which cost the battalion 120 men killed or wounded. His body is buried in **Douchy-les-Ayette British Cemetery**, Pas de Calais, France, in:

Grave 1. A. 2.

WALTER GANNAWAY

Sergeant
D/13983
6th Dragoon Guards (Carabiniers),
who died on
Monday 26th August 1918, aged 42.

Walter was born in Lymington in 1876, being the next to youngest of nine children born to Thomas and Ellen (Bessie) Gannaway. In 1881 the family were living in Cannon Street, Lymington. They were still there in 1917.

ELLEN GANNAWAY AND EIGHT OF HER CHILDREN

Thomas worked as a baker and his eldest son, Frederick, was a baker's assistant. Kate, the eldest daughter was in service and Frank was an errand boy for a local jewellers. In 1881 the other six children were all at school or below school age. Walter grew up in the town and when he left school he worked alongside his father as a baker for Mr F. Shelley at Pilley.

On 2nd January 1905 Walter married Bessie Wearn at Pennington Church. Bessie was born in at Hordle in 1881, the youngest of six children. Walter and Bessie were themselves to have nine children.

Walter was clearly of an adventurous turn as he had volunteered for the Boer War. He served throughout it and was awarded the Queen's South African Medal with 6 clasps as well as the King's Medal for service in 1901-02. The regiment was subsequently posted to India, where this dashing photograph was taken.

He re-enlisted in Lymington on the outbreak of war in 1914 and joined the 6th Dragoon Guards (The Carabineers). By 1918 he was a Troop Sergeant in France. The 2nd Cavalry Division - of which the 4th Cavalry Brigade and the 6th Dragoon Guards were part - were in support of the 18th Division, when it attacked and captured Montauban on the Somme, on 26th August 1918. Cavalry patrols were then used to determine the extent of the German retreat and they reported back that the enemy rearguards were holding Barnafay and Trones Woods in strength. THE CHRONICLE of 19th September reports that he was recommended for bravery in these actions.

Walter was killed in action during these reconnaissance activities. His body was recovered in the subsequent advance and he was later buried in the nearby **Caterpillar Valley Cemetery**, Longueval, Somme, France, in

Grave 1. B. 5.

GEORGE H LEWINGTON
Private
355876
2nd Battalion, Hampshire Regiment,
who died on
Wednesday 4th September 1918, aged 20.

George was born in Waterford, Lymington, in 1898. His father, William, came from Northampton and worked as a general labourer. His mother, Alice, a local girl, sold groceries from her home. George was the youngest of the family, with two elder sisters, Grace and Beatrice, and a brother Albert.

In 1915 George enlisted, at the age of sixteen and a half years, into the 9th Hampshire Regiment (Cyclists). He went to France in 1917 and joined the 14th Battalion. When this battalion was disbanded in February 1918, George was drafted to the 2nd Battalion. As part of 88 Brigade of the 29th Division this battalion had been in the thick of the fighting in 1917, taking part in the major battles of Arras, 3rd Ypres and Cambrai. Cambrai had been a difficult battle for the unit, but after refitting at Sus St Leger, where it was joined by a draft of 274 reinforcements, it moved up in mid January 1918 to the apex of the Ypres Salient. February saw it out of the line, but in early March it was back, this time to the north of Passchendaele where they fought off two enemy attacks. This spell from January to March at Ypres was to cost the battalion nearly 200 casualties.

After being brought back up to strength, the battalion was sent south to Estaires on 10th April, to help counter the second of the great attacks in the German spring offensive.

After stiff fighting, the Hampshires fell back slowly to southeast of Bailleul, where the line finally held until they were relieved by the French on 20th April. The Battle of the Lys had, however, cost the Hampshires over 300 casualties.

On 30th August the Germans evacuated their front line and the 29th Division hastened to follow them. Three days later George and his battalion reached the trenches they had dug and successfully defended on 10th April. Stiffening resistance necessitated a set piece attack, which the Hampshires and Leinsters put in at 8.00 a.m. on 4th September. George at this time was employed as a company stretcher-bearer.

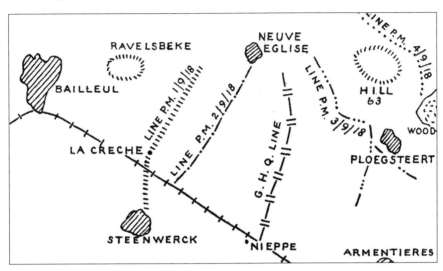

Although Hill 63 was strongly fortified behind swathes of barbed wire, the Hampshires closely followed an accurate barrage, charged up the hill and captured their objective. They spent the rest of the day beating off fierce counter-attacks. The capture of Hill 63 provided 50 prisoners, three large trench mortars and a dozen machine guns. It had cost the battalion 36 men killed and 144 men wounded or missing - George being amongst the latter

PHOTO MARC THOMPSON

His body was later found and duly buried in the **Strand Military Cemetery** at Hainaut, Belgium, in:

Grave VII. F. 10

ALFRED C SCOTT

Corporal
260138
1st/8th Battalion, Sherwood Foresters,
(Notts and Derby Regiment)
who died on
Friday 18th October 1918, aged 26.

Alfred was the youngest son of Vincent and Elizabeth Scott, of Rosetta Place, Lymington. When he left school he was apprenticed as a coach-painter to Mr E Read, of Emsworth Road, Lymington. He later worked in Feltham, Middlesex, where he lived with his wife and child. According to THE CHRONICLE of 24th October 1918:

> *"His widowed mother has had the proud record of seven sons serving their King and Country. Four are now on active service and two – Ex-Sergeant Vincent Scott and Ex-Private James Edward Scott, both of whom were in the retreat from Mons – have been discharged*

Before the war Alfred enlisted at Richmond, Surrey, as a territorial into the East Surrey Regiment and was given the regimental number of 2798. He rejoined the East Surreys in 1916 with the regimental number of 260138 and reached the rank of Corporal. After being hospitalised with a wound or sickness, he was transferred to the Sherwood Foresters and served in their 1st/8th Battalion.

Alfred's battalion was part of the 139th Infantry Brigade in 46 Division. By October 1918 the German line had broken and was in full retreat. On 3rd October, just five weeks before the end of the war, the battalion was involved in a major operation to shift the enemy from Beaurevoir and Montbrehain.

With an Australian division on their left, the battalion advanced at 6.00 a.m. under cover of a creeping barrage. Opposition from Wiancourt, which had not been overrun by the Australians, was dealt with and the village captured.

The battalion then resumed its advance and the machine gun nests at Ramicourt were outflanked and taken. Alfred's battalion suffered heavy casualties from the German guns on the high ground above Montbrehain, which were so close that they were firing over open sights. These guns were mostly put out of action by supporting tanks, which also helped the battalion to gain its objective of Montbrehain. The village had to be evacuated, however, when a neighbouring battalion fell back under a heavy counter attack. Alfred's battalion then consolidated at Ramicourt, before being relieved by the 4th Leicesters.

Nearly a thousand prisoners were taken and many machine-guns. Alfred was shot and badly wounded in this attack, which cost his battalion 257 men casualties. Although he was evacuated back to the Trouville Hospital Area, operated on and the bullet extracted, he died fifteen days later.

Alfred is buried in **Tourgeville Military Cemetery**, Calvados, France, in:

Grave IV. E. 1.

FREDERICK JOHN WELLMAN

Private
241876
1st/5th (T F) Battalion, Gloucestershire Regiment,
who died on
Thursday 24th October 1918, aged 23.

Fred was born in Dorchester. The family moved to Lymington when his father took over "The Fisherman's Rest," in Woodside. Before the war Fred worked as a carter in Totton.

He enlisted at Winchester into the Gloucestershire Regiment in 1915 with the number 5149, and served in France with the 1/5th Battalion, which was part of the 75th Brigade in 25th Division.

In October 1918 the battalion moved to Honnechy to be in reserve to 50th Division for the battle of the Selle. This involved seizing the river crossings and exploiting beyond. The river crossings had been won on the 17th and the following day 50th Division was tasked with capturing the ridge 2000 yards to the east of the Arbre Guernon – Le Cateau road.

The Gloucesters had difficulty in crossing the river, as, despite the early morning mist, enemy shellfire was both accurate and heavy. At 8.45 a.m. Fred's battalion passed through the newly captured ridge and began its attack on the second objective – the securing of Bazuel and the road to Baillon Farm. The Gloucesters successfully took this latter road, but suffered for the rest of the day from heavy sniping and hostile machinegun fire.

160

Rain fell during the night and under cover of the morning mist A Company tried, by "peaceful penetration," to occupy the bank of the river Richemont. This initiative was frustrated by German machine gunners, but a more formal attack on the 20th secured the riverbank.

The battalion was then withdrawn to rest, but success in widening the Selle front north of Le Cateau enabled a major exploitation of the situation to be made to push the Germans back to Valenciennes.

On 23rd October Fred's battalion was tasked with taking the third objective of the day – a line along the northeastern edge of L'Eveque Wood to Bousies. The War Diary of the Gloucesters states briefly:

"Whole objectives gained.
Casualties 7 killed, 14 wounded."

VIS-en-ARTOIS British Cemetery (P.-de-C.)
Showing in the Background, the Memorial to the Missing

Fred was killed before the battalion was relieved, on the night of 24th October - having been at the front for three years.

His body was not recovered and his name is therefore recorded on the **Vis-en-Artois Memorial,** Pas de Calais, France, on:

Panel 6

OLIVER HENRY FUDGE

Gunner
201066
Royal Garrison Artillery
who died on
Friday 25th October 1918, aged 27.

Oliver was the eldest of two sons of Mary Jane and George Fudge of Stanford Road. George was a general labourer who fathered a family of four children. By 1913 Mary was living in Ada Cottage, Brook Road, Lymington.

Olliver enlisted into the Royal Field Artillery at the beginning of the war and went to France on 13th May 1915 with the 9th Scottish Division, taking part in the battle of

Loos. He was seriously wounded on the Somme in July 1916, but was back in action at Passchendaele in 1917. He was later transferred to the Royal Garrison Artillery.

By 1918 Oliver was serving in the 88th Anti-aircraft Section. Whilst the anti-aircraft capability of the army was very limited at the beginning of the war, by 1918 all AA sections were grouped into four gun batteries under Army Headquarters control. They were equipped with the 13-pdr 9-cwt gun capable of shooting to a height of 19,000 feet and were located to defend Army and Corps Headquarters.

Oliver died of influenza in the 13th General Hospital in Boulogne, France and is buried in **Terlincthun British Cemetery**, Wimille, in:

Grave VI. B. 61.

THE FIRST WORLD WAR

THE WAR AT SEA
1914-1918

BRITANNIA RULES

For centuries Britain had practised ruling the seas through the doctrine of the battle fleet. Each ocean had its own British presence and British bases, to ensure the peace of the area, the protection of its trading interests and merchant fleets. The importance of the battleship had been upgraded with the launch of the DREADNOUGHT in 1906, which, at a stroke, rendered the rest of our battleships obsolete and gave other nations – particularly Germany – the chance to develop "Super Dreadnought" building programmes equally with our own.

There were eight naval powers of importance – Britain, France, Germany, America, Austro-Hungary, Italy, Russia and Japan. Of these only the latter two had had recent experience of modern sea warfare. The Battle of Tsushima in 1905 comfortably demonstrated that modern capital ships would defeat not so modern ones, hence the attraction of developing a battleship design incorporating a central battery of heavy guns, steam turbine propulsion and effective armour.

A SMALL PART OF THE SPITHEAD REVIEW JULY 1914

This focus on the battle fleet was a result of an Admiralty manned by senior officers, such as Jacky Fisher, who relied upon their – largely peacetime - experiences to guide them. The absence of a Naval General Staff to think things through, match a building programme to modern need, develop modern tactics and plans, and tailor training to performance meant that in 1914 we were not prepared for modern war at sea.

Submarines were not central to British naval thought, although worldwide, by 1914, there were over 300 in commission. Many of these were modern diesel driven seagoing vessels armed effectively with both gun and torpedo. The sinking of three of our obsolescent heavy cruisers in the North Sea on 22nd September 1914, by U 9, was a mega shock to both the Admiralty and the British public.

As the experiences of the war took hold, so problems were tackled and emergency shipbuilding programmes started.

The danger from mines thus led to the expansion of the minesweeping capability, and the incorporation of trawlers, often with their civilian crews, (here seen using hydrophones) into anti-submarine and minesweeping duties. Wireless communication was developed, which had an effect on Jutland, as did improved means of fire control. Long distance convoy escorts were rapidly built in large numbers. The threat from German U-boats led, not only to an expansion of our own submarines, but also to an effective anti-submarine response. Finally, the effective use of aircraft in support of the sea war was proved by the operations of the Royal Naval Air Service. By the end of the war, three ships had been converted to aircraft carriers and the first purpose-built carrier was under construction.

Much of the Royal Navy's activity in the early phase of the war was inevitably conducted in obsolescent warships. **Arthur Barter** was killed when the pre-Dreadnought battleship BULWARK blew up in Sheerness and **Herbert Torah** was killed when, a month later, its sister-ship the FORMIDABLE, was sunk by a U-boat. **Thomas Mapes** died when another U-boat torpedoed the *S.S. Arcadian*.

ARTHUR SIDNEY JAMES BARTER

Seaman, Royal Navy
239800
HMS BULWARK
who died on
26th November 1914, aged 23.

Arthur was born on 24th August 1891 in Lymington. He lived at 24, Shirley Park Road, Southampton and worked as a barman before joining the Royal Navy, on his eighteenth birthday, as a Boy 2nd Class.

He trained on the old Training Ship IMPREGNABLE before joining EURYALUS. It was on board this ship that he received

his first *"Very Good"* character and his first medal. This cruiser was one of the ships that went to the aid of the victims of the tragic earthquake that hit Messina, Sicily, in December 1908. He therefore received the Messina Medal issued by the King of Italy. He joined the battleship ILLUSTRIOUS as a Boy 1st Class in January 1908, for a fourteen month commission, and then moved to the newly completed battle cruiser INVINCIBLE.
During his two years on this state-of-the-art warship he was promoted to Able Seaman. After a gunnery course he went to the cruiser ROXBURGH for a year, before joining her sister-ship HAMPSHIRE.

On 25th April 1914 Arthur was drafted to the BULWARK. This 15-year-old battleship had been refitted at Chatham in 1912. On the morning of 26th November 1914 the ship was moored at Sheerness and taking on ammunition. At 7.53 a.m., while the men on board were having breakfast, an explosion occurred which rent the ship asunder. When the smoke cleared the ship had gone. The explosion was heard as far away as Whitstable to the south and Southend in Essex, where it shook the pier. There was considerable damage in Sheerness.

H.M.S. BULWARK

Boats from the nearby ships and shore went to rescue those in the water, but only twelve men survived the explosion. An inquest was hastily convened. Sergeant John Albert Budd, RM, who suffered from burns and a broken leg, stated that at 7.30 he was finishing his breakfast on the portside second mess deck, when he saw a sudden flash aft. As he turned, the deck opened up under him and he was thrown into the sea. He remembered coming to the surface of the water but the ship had disappeared. He had not heard the explosion.

The Assistant Coaling Officer at Sheerness, Lt. Benjamin George Carroll, stated that he saw a spurt of flame towards the stern of the after barbette turret which rushed towards the after funnel. The whole interior of the ship blew into the air and everything seemed on fire. Everything pointed towards an internal explosion. BULWARK was almost certainly destroyed while ammunition was being loaded and there may have been some mishandling of the powder charges

Arthur was not one of the survivors and his body was never recovered. His name is therefore recorded on the **Portsmouth Naval Memorial**:

Panel 1

HERBERT CHARLES TORAH

Private, Royal Marine Light Infantry
CH/16728
HMS FORMIDABLE
who died on
Friday 1st January 1915, aged 22.

Bert was born on 21st February 1892, in Middle Road, Pennington, to Henry and Eliza Torah. Henry was a bricklayer, and his own brother Charles – a wheelwright – also lived with the family. Herbert had two brothers, George and Alfred.

Bert was a barman before joining the Royal Marine Light Infantry on 4th August 1910. His record shows him to be 5-feet 4-inches tall, brown eyes and hair, and possessing a large scar on the top of his head. Unusually, he could also swim. He did his basic training at Deal and further training at Chatham before embarking on the pre-DREADNOUGHT battleship KING EDWARD VII. He subsequently served afloat on the battleships TRIUMPH and ALBION, before joining the FORMIDABLE on 27th March 1913.

HMS FORMIDABLE

FORMIDABLE was an obsolescent battleship of 15,250 tons, commissioned in 1901 and refitted in 1908/9. Armed with 4x12-inch and 12x6-inch guns, she was capable of a speed of over 18 knots and carried a complement of 780 men.

At the end of December she went to sea on exercises. At 2.00 a.m. on 1st January 1915 she was 20 miles off Start Point when, in a storm, she was hit by two torpedoes fired by U 24. The first torpedo hit the number 1 boiler port side, whilst a second explosion caused the ship to list heavily to starboard. Huge waves thirty feet high lashed the stricken ship, with strong winds, rain and hail, sinking it in less than two hours. Two of the ship's pinnaces got away from the ship with 140 survivors. One of the pinnaces was seen by the trawler, **Provident**, 15 miles off Berry head, and its occupants saved. Nobody, however, had seen the battleship go down and no ship spotted the other, damaged, pinnace during the day. It was not until nearly twenty hours in continuous gale conditions, after the torpedoing, that this boat was observed from the shore at Lyme Regis and those remaining alive rescued.

FUNERAL AT LYME OF SOME OF THE SAILORS

Bert was not amongst those saved. His name is therefore recorded on the **Chatham Naval Memorial**, Kent, on:

Panel 13

THOMAS MAPES

Quartermaster
SS Arcadian
who died on
Saturday 12th May 1917, aged 42.

Thomas Mapes was the son of John Mapes, a bricklayer, of Burnham, Essex. Thomas married Rose Tomkins at St Thomas's Church on 30th October 1898. Her father, Edward had been born in Cary Street, London, and was a gardener in Lymington. Thomas and Rose lived in The Bethel, Quay Street.

Thomas was a seaman. By 1917 he was serving on the *Arcadian*. This passenger ship started life as the *R.M.S Ortona*, which had been built by Harland and Wolff in 1899. She had a gross registered tonnage of 8939 tons.

She was purchased by the Royal Mail line in 1909 and renamed *Arcadian*. During the First World War she was hired by the government and used as a troop ship. She had been part of the 1st Canadian troop convoy in 1914 carrying 601 soldiers from the cavalry and Royal Engineers, as well as a Field Ambulance.

The Arcadian left Salonica en route to Alexandria, escorted by the light cruiser SENTINAL, at 6.30 p.m. on Saturday 14th of April 1917. She had a crew if 179 officers and men and carried 1,155 passengers, mainly from army units but with a small number of naval men. It was known that a U-boat was in the area so the two ships were zig-zaging at more than 13 knots. Despite these precautions at 5.44 p.m. the following day she was torpedoed by UC 74 on the starboard bow. In a short time her bows were under water and although her boats were lowered smartly, she sank in about six minutes.

THE ARCADIAN SINKING   **PHOTO IWM SP813**

The saving of as many as 944 men by various ships was attributed to Arcadian having completed boat drill only ten minutes before being torpedoed. The Court of Enquiry found that the loss of life was due to some of the boats becoming fouled when the ship capsized, pieces of wreckage shooting up to the surface as the ship foundered and the exhaustion of some of those in the sea.

Thomas was rescued from the sea, landed at Marseilles and hospitalised. The St Thomas Memorial Book records that he died of shock four weeks later.

He is buried in **Mazargues War Cemetery**, Marseilles in:

St Pierre Cemetery Memorial 2.

THE FIRST WORLD WAR

HOME
1915-1919

HOME DEATHS

Before the Great War more servicemen had died in wars from sickness than had died from hostile action. Even in this war more people died from the 1918-20 pandemic Spanish flu than from high explosives.

The medical evacuation system for wounded soldiers ran from the trenches, back through the Casualty Clearing Stations (CCSs), where the degree of severity was determined, through the Base or General Hospitals to the various natures of hospital in the United Kingdom. In practice those who were beyond help died at the forward CCSs, whilst those who required major surgery were treated at the Base Hospitals. If you did get back to a hospital in "Blighty," your chance of recovery was good. Of the 21,000 cases treated in No 1 (New Zealand) General Hospital at Brockenhurst between 1916 and 1921 only 94 are buried in the nearby churchyard.

Those buried in the United Kingdom were mainly servicemen who died from natural causes prevalent in the population at that time. **Jack Urquhart** died from meningitis, **Frank Head** from cancer, **Arthur Shirfield** from diphtheria, **Reginald King** from Raynauds disease, **Thomas Overton**, from tuberculosis and **George Bailey** from nephritis. **Wilfred Clarke** was sent home suffering from shell shock, but succumbed to the Spanish Flu, which also carried away **Robert Parsons, Thomas Hills** and **William Haines.**

Service conditions were harsh and the effects of prolonged exposure to hardships of life at sea experienced by the career sailor in the early years of the Twentieth Century might well have had an influence in bringing on the early deaths of **William Yeatman, Samuel Cooper** and **Henry Barter**.

The war was more directly responsible for the deaths of **George Toms** - whose ship ran aground in bad weather - and **Frank Ball,** who died in a flying-training accident.

JACK URQUHART

Driver
69521
Royal Field Artillery
who died on
Friday 14th May 1915, aged 19.

Jack was born in London, the son of Donald and Elizabeth (nee Wareham, of Poole) who lived in lodgings in Church Street. There were also two daughters in the family. Donald's brother, Hector, lived in Alberta, Spring Road, Waterford. In 1920 Hector and his wife, Edith, ran the "Waltham Arms" in Lymington.

Jack was an iron plater, who responded to Kitchener's call for men to join the New Army.

He was accepted for service at the beginning of the war and trained at the 4th Royal Artillery Depot at Woolwich as a driver in the Royal Field Artillery.

In early March 1915 he was admitted into the Royal Herbert Hospital at Kidbrooke with Cerebro-spinal fever. He died two months later.

Jack is buried in **Greenwich Cemetery**, London, United Kingdom, in:

Grave 3 "C." A. 368.

FRANK ALFRED HEAD

Gunner
3435
Royal Garrison Artillery
who died on
Thursday 18th November 1915, aged 40.

Frank was the husband of Bessie Head, of Brook Road, Waterford, Lymington.

He worked as a grocer's porter, but, before the war, joined the Royal Garrison Artillery. To do this he must have been economical with his age. Having said this, however, whilst the

age on his Death Certificate is given above, the Commonwealth War Graves Commission declares him to be 41 years old. He served in the 67th Company, which was stationed at Portsmouth in the forts guarding the naval base.

In early 1915 he met with an accident on active service, which resulted in his suffering from neck problems. After nine months of great pain and suffering he died in the 5th Southern General Hospital, Fawcett Road, Southsea, of cancer to the larynx and consequent swollen lymph glands in the neck. His wife was with him when he died.

PHOTO NICK SAUNDERS

Frank is buried in **Portsmouth (Eastney or Highland Road) Cemetery** in:

Grave K 14. 8.

ARTHUR SHIRFIELD
Gunner
16952
Royal Field Artillery
who died on
Friday 9th December 1915, aged 19.

The War Memorial records

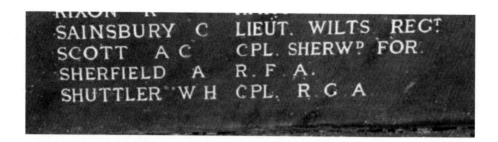

According to official records no She**r**field died in the war. However, one Sh**i**rfield (phonetically identical) is so recorded.

An Arthur Shirfield was born in 1896 to Charles and Lily Shirfield, of The Dean, Alresford, Hampshire. THE CHRONICLE of 31st March 1921 confirms that the Christian name of Gunner Shirfield was, indeed, Arthur. The connection with Lymington, other than the entry in the St Thomas Memorial Book, is unknown.

Arthur joined the Royal Artillery early in the war and reported to the Royal Artillery Depot at Woolwich for training. After basic gunner training he was posted to the 20th Reserve Battery.

He became ill and was admitted to Park Hospital, where he died of diphtheria.

Arthur is buried in **Greenwich Cemetery** in

Grave A. 24

His name is also recorded in the same cemetery on Screen Wall C.

REGINALD KING

Private
2720
1st/8th Battalion, Hampshire Regiment,
who died on
Wednesday 22nd March 1916, aged 21.

Reg was born in 1895 in Spring Road, Lymington, being the youngest son of William and Lilly King. The family later moved to live at 43 Gosport Street. There was an elder brother, William, a house painter, and two sisters - Ethel and Vida. After the war Lilly is recorded as living at The Bungalow, Gosport Street, Lymington.

Before the war Reg enlisted in Lymington into the territorial 1st/8th Battalion of the Hampshire Regiment which had been mobilised on 24th July 1914 at Sandown for coastal duty on the Isle of Wight. It was then sent to Gallipoli, but Reg never got that far.

Reg was diagnosed as suffering from Raynauds disease. The resultant very cold fingers and toes would not have helped his efficiency in a cold and wet trench environment. On his medical downgrading was posted to the 3/8th Hampshires at Gosport. William is recorded as suffering from lead poisoning –

perhaps from preparing the lead-based paints for his brother, who was a decorator. His resultant damaged kidneys could have made it harder to recover from the acute gastritis that he suffered in the last 27 hours of his life. He actually died of a brain haemorrhage in the military hospital in Carrisbrooke Road, Newport, on the Isle of Wight.

Reg was buried on 25th March in **Lymington Cemetery,** in:

Grave 2083

THOMAS OSBERT OVERTON

Lance Corporal
268130
7th (Reserve) Battalion, Sherwood Foresters,
(Notts and Derby Regt.)
who died on
Sunday 19th May 1918, aged 20.

Tom was born on 18th October 1897, in the Castle Inn. His father Henry, a local man, had been a mariner, but also kept the Castle Inn at Hurst. Harry's wife, Esther, had been born in Clapham, London. She gave birth to a very large family. In the photograph below they are, from left to right, – Charlotte, Henry, Thomas, Robert, Ethel and Eliza. There were also three other children – Edward, Minnie and William.

HENRY   THE OVERTON FAMILY ABOUT 1900   ESTHER

Robert John, to the right of Thomas, joined the Royal Naval Reserve and as a Seaman, was awarded the DSM for services in "Q" Ships, in action with enemy submarines.

Tom worked as a lift attendant. He enlisted in Brockenhurst into the Royal Sussex Regiment as a Private, with a regimental number of 7451, but was later transferred to the Notts and Derby Regiment. The second line Territorial battalions of this regiment all served in the 178th Brigade of the 59th Division.

At the time of the German attack in March the Sherwood Foresters were in the line in the Hirondelle Valley. The misty morning of 21st March saw the battalion heavily bombarded at 06.30 a.m. They were initially by-passed by the new infiltration tactics of the lightly armed but very mobile German storm troopers. By 08.30 a.m., however, the division found that it had

"Four if not five enemy divisions facing us."

The battalion's stubborn stand was at the expense of 26 officers and 629 other ranks killed, wounded or missing King George V inspected the survivors on 30th March and a day later the remnants of the 1/7th and 2/7th Territorial battalions merged to form the 7th Battalion.

Before this, however, Tom had been evacuated to a hospital in England to be held, according to his Death Certificate, on the strength of the 5th Battalion.

He died at the Military Hospital in Eastbourne of acute miliary tuberculosis and exhaustion. His funeral was held in St Thomas's Church on 25th May. He is buried in **Lymington Cemetery**, in:

Grave 2503

GEORGE GROVE BAILEY

Sergeant
G/47756
5th Battalion, Royal Fusiliers,
who died on
Wednesday 5th June 1918, aged 45.

The War Memorial shows:

None of the three Baileys who died in the Northumberland Fusiliers had that rank, or the same initials and all had very secure northern roots. It is assumed that "Northumberland" has crept in in error.

George was born in Lymington, a son of the late John Bailey of "Sunnyside," Highfield. Before the war, he worked as a clothier's salesman.

He enlisted in London into the Royal Fusiliers and joined the 17th (Service) Battalion, Royal Fusiliers (Empire). This battalion was raised by a body of gentlemen, led by General Sir Bindon Blood GCB, called "The British Empire Committee." The battalion was raised within ten days and embodied at Warlingham, Surrey, on 12th September 1914 – clothed, hutted and equipped by the Committee.

George sailed with this cosmopolitan, mainly colonial, battalion to France on 17th November 1915. After an introduction to trench warfare in the La Basee canal area the battalion was allocated to 5th Brigade in the 2nd Division. It served throughout the Battle of the Somme from July to November 1916 and then remained in the area.

George's age, however, began to tell against him in the harsh conditions of the trenches. After hospitalisation he was posted to the 5th (Reserve) Battalion in England. Fully equipped for the field its operational task was to man part of the Dover defences. In this location it prepared drafts for the Royal Fusilier battalions overseas and on the Western Front. The battalion was, at times, over 4,000 strong with numerous recruits under training.

By 1918 George had suffered from nephritis for several months and this was later compounded by heart disease. He was admitted into one of the Military Hospitals at Brighton, but at the end of May developed uraemia. He died at 16 Lewes Crescent, Brighton, on 5th June 1918.

His body was brought back to Lymington, where he was buried in the family grave in **St Thomas Churchyard** on 10th June 1918 in:

New Ground

WILFRID DAVID CLARKE

Private
M/14853
Army Service Corps
who died on
Thursday 31st October 1918, aged 40.

Wilf was born in Exeter, the son of John and Emma Clarke, of Launceston, Cornwall. John was a preacher and Emma was involved in the Temperance movement, being associated with the I.O.G.T. The two generations are pictured here.

Wilf worked at a mineral water manufactory in Lymington and rose to be foreman. He married Lily in the early years of the century and lived at 5, Broad Lane, Lymington. By 1914 there were five children to the marriage

FRANCES   WILF   WINIFRED ETHEL   HILDA

Wilf enlisted in Lymington in early 1915 into the Army Service Corps. The following letter has no date, but Grove Park was an ASC Depot and presumably relates to his reception:

Grove Park

Dear Loo

Just a line hoping you and the children are all well. I am all right except my fingers and they are very bad.

I have been unable to go through the test so have no money to draw and have got two-pence halfpenny left. You have to be in uniform before 12 Thursday or you draw nothing. I hope you will be all right. That is all I am thinking about and cant get any address for you to write to me from your end as I have no number and am shifted every day.

I slept in a bell tent about 2 miles from here last night with about six inches of water around your chest. Come and join the army. I have not had my clothes off yet and had one wash and one shave with a shining brick for a glass, no soap, muffler for a towel, 3 wet blankets to keep you warm and no beds. The funny thing is I am as fit as a fiddle. The life agrees with me and I should be as happy as a sandboy if I knew you were all right and I could go in for any test as I feel confident of getting through but it is not a fair test, only bamboozle.

I am saving a penny stamp and as soon as I know any number I will send it on to you. Just had a lot of luck in a empty house for the night on the floor. I have written this letter in little bits to kill time.

Bugle sounding got to answer.

By the end of 1915 he had completed his recruit training and was undergoing Motor Transport (MT) training at Winchester. Wilf is photographed on the far left below.

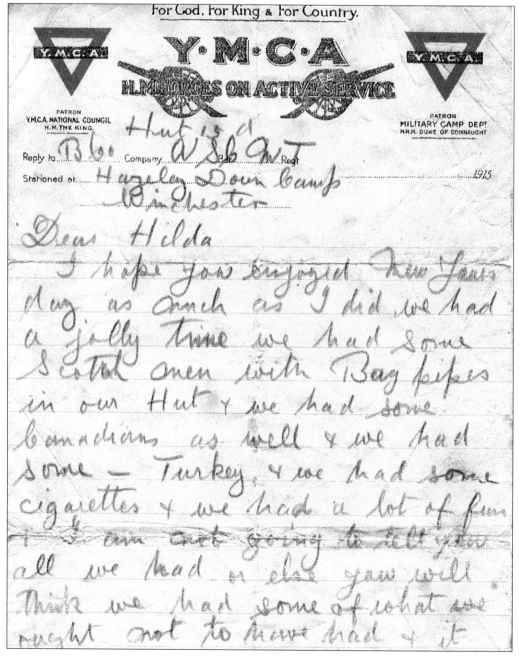

For God, For King & For Country.

Y·M·C·A

H.M. FORCES ON ACTIVE SERVICE

PATRON
Y.M.C.A. NATIONAL COUNCIL
H.M. THE KING.

PATRON
MILITARY CAMP DEPT
H.R.H. DUKE OF CONNAUGHT

Reply to B.60   Company   Hut 13 d   Bat   Regt
Stationed at   Hazeley Down Camp   1915
Winchester

Dear Hilda

I hope you enjoyed New Years
day as much as I did we had
a jolly time we had some
Scotch men with Bag pipes
in our Hut & we had some
Canadians as well & we had
some — Turkey, & we had some
cigarettes & we had a lot of fun
I am not going to tell you
all we had or else you will
think we had some of what we
ought not to have had & it

184

Wilf went to France in early 1916 and at some stage came under shellfire as he was later invalided back to the United Kingdom with shell shock.

By late 1917 he was back in France and wrote the following letter, conforming with the military requirement concerning secrecy of location:

beard reaching to his knees, come along the road in a few years time, call my Grandchildren out to see their Grandfather come home from the great butchers shop.

Wilf's turn for leave came in October 1918.

Wilf, sadly, was not to use this return ticket for the last two weeks of the war. Whilst on leave he contracted influenza. Double pneumonia supervened and he died at home. His wife was by his bedside at the time.

Wilf was buried in **Lymington Cemetery** on 4th November in:

Grave 2417

The following day his mother, Emma, who was staying with Lily for the funeral, was discovered dead in bed, having passed away in her sleep. She was a widow aged 68 and suffered from known heart affliction.

ROBERT PARSONS
Air Mechanic 3rd Class
264865
Royal Air Force
who died on
Thursday 14th November 1918, aged 29.

Robert was born on 6th August 1889 in Jordan Lane, Boldre. His father, James, was a gardener and his mother, Selina, a charwoman. There was an elder brother, Frederick who, in 1901, worked as a groom, and a sister, Ada.

On 2nd August 1913 Robert married Marie Louise Alberton in Bognor. There were two children to the marriage, George, born on 9th May 1915 and Nora, born on 26th July 1918.

George was, for many years, the sacristan at St Thomas's Church.

On enlistment he was medically assessed as *"Grade 1"* and posted to the North East area. He contracted the Spanish Flu and was admitted into the Fulford military Hospital, where he died of Influenza and pneumonia on 14th November 1918.

He was buried in **Lymington Cemetery** on 18th November in:

Grave 2422

THOMAS JAMES HILLS

Staff Sergeant
101645
Royal Engineers
who died on
Tuesday 3rd December 1918.

Thomas James Hills was the son of Elizabeth and William Fordham Hills. According to the 1881 census Elizabeth was born about 1838 in Chatham, Kent. William was born, perhaps a year later, in Malling – a village about twenty miles away – and is shown as working as a fisherman. The family included seven children – Ellenor (1861), Sarah (1864), Mary (1867), Phoebe (1869), Elizabeth (1879), Thomas (1877) and Edward (1880) – all lived in Holborn Lane, Chatham.

Nothing is so far known about Thomas's upbringing, but in December 1898 he married Beatrice Annie Carter at Farnham in Surrey. At this stage he probably lived at Waverley Cottage, Tongham, in Surrey.

The marriage was a fruitful one, with five children. Elsie, who married Oswald Rawlings and had one son, Gerald; Frank, who married Nellie and Florence (Betty) who was twice married - neither children had issue; Ivy, who married John Wiltshire and had a son Trevor; and May Dorothy, who married Robert Charles Hayward and had two sons - John Robert and Michael Charles.

It is John Hayward, of Southampton, who has kindly provided much of the information for this memorial.

At some stage Thomas moved to Lymington, as in 1913 he was residing with his wife, and family at 88 Gosport Street. At this time Thomas was Clerk of Works to Walhampton Manor.

Come the war, with his experience he naturally joined the Royal Engineers, serving in their establishment for Engineer Services. He went to France on 19th December 1915, as a sergeant. He was therefore entitled to the 1915 star, as well as the British War and Victory medals.

PHOTO NICK SAUNDERS

As part of Engineer Services Thomas could have been involved in camp construction, water provision, port or harbour improvement or any other activity involved in creating and maintaining the necessary infrastructure for the BEF in France.

At some stage he was medically evacuated from France to a hospital in Hull but, as the General Registry Office cannot trace his death certificate, it is not known how he died.

He is buried in **Hull Northern Cemetery** in

Grave 65.6

WILLIAM JAMES HAINES

Private
305484

1/7th Battalion, Hampshire Regiment
who died on
Friday 28th February 1919, aged 31.

William was the son of James and Elizabeth Haines of 4, Cannon Street, Lymington. He married Annie Haines (nee Bucknell) and worked as a railway delivery carman out of Lymington station.

William joined the Territorials before war was declared and served in the 7th Battalion as a Private, with the number 1760.

Whilst his personal service records have not survived, the entry on his medal roll shows an entitlement to the Territorial Force War Medal. This indicates that he was embodied before the 30th September 1914, had completed four years service by that date and served outside the United Kingdom after the 1st January 1916.

William joined the 1/7th in India sometime after the beginning of 1916 and moved with it in January 1918 to Aden. Whilst there, his wife died leaving him with two children. He came home on compassionate grounds, before the rest of the battalion, to look after his children.

After hostilities with Turkey were over the battalion lost several men from influenza.

William died at home within four days of catching influenza, which quickly turned into pneumonia. His brother was with him at the time of his death.

THE CHRONICLE of 6th March 1919 reported that:

"The funeral took place on Tuesday afternoon. The coffin was covered with the Union Jack. In addition to the family mourners there were, in the Parish Church, where the first part of the Service was held, Sgt Cooper Quarter Master Sgt Payne, Miss Ouvry and Mr W Haines and other comrades who had served with the deceased in India. The Rev C Bostock (vicar) officiated and there were a number of floral tributes. The funeral arrangements were carried out by Mr FW House, of St Thomas Street."

William was buried on 4th March in **Lymington Cemetery** in

Grave 2403

WILLIAM G YEATMAN

Able Seaman, Royal Navy
182301 P.O.
H.M.S GLORY
who died on
Monday 13th December 1915, aged 37.

William was born on 13th December 1878. He was the son of William and Harriet Yeatman, who lived in Solent, Quay Hill, in Lymington. The family also included a daughter, Beatrice. Father William was a man of many parts as the 1901 Census records his occupation, which he did on his own account working at home, as

"Licensed Victualler Watch Maker Jeweller."

William worked initially as a yacht boy in Lymington, but joined the Royal Navy on 5th December 1894 as a Boy 2nd Class. After training at ST VINCENT, he passed out as a Boy 1st Class and served afloat on BOSCAWEN and ACTIVE before attending a gunnery course at Whale Island, Portsmouth.

On his eighteenth birthday Bill was rated an Ordinary Seaman and sent to IPHIGENIA. It was whilst on this ship that he was promoted to Able Seaman on 1st February 1898. This light cruiser was, incidentally, one of the block ships used in the Zeebrugge raid in April 1918. After more courses he joined the old battleship REVENGE, but almost immediately went to the AUSTRALIA for a years commission. After more courses he was posted to FURIOUS on 3rd December 1903 for thirteen months. Six months then followed on the light cruiser JUNO before going on to the held strength of VICTORY.

On 23rd August 1905 Bill transferred to the Royal Fleet Reserve for five years, to make up his 12-year contract. With a "***Very Good***" character recorded for each of his years of service William had no difficulty, In 1910, re-enlisting for a further five years service with the Reserve

In August 1914 he was taken on the strength of GLORY.

HMS GLORY

GLORY was a Canopus Class pre-DREDNAUGHT battleship completed in 1900. Armed with 4x12-inch guns she carried a complement of 682 and was capable of a maximum speed of nearly 18 knots. She served throughout the First World War and saw action on 7th March 1919 in the naval operations against Murmansk and Archangel.

He served on her until 2nd October 1915, when he was admitted into hospital in Malta for a week with enteritis. He was then quickly sent back to England, taking passage on the cruiser EUROPA. The infection spread systemically to the whole body and became Enteritis Pachymeningitis. It resulted in meningitis, coma and death.

Bill died on his birthday, 13th December, in St George's Hospital, London.

He was buried in **Lymington Cemetery** on 17th December, in

Grave 2705

SAMUEL THOMAS COOPER

Chief Stoker, Royal Navy
167174
HMS MINOTAUR
Who died on
8th April 1916, aged 42.

According to his Service Record, **Samuel** was born in Lymington on 11th May 1873 and worked as a labourer before joining the Royal Navy on 26th May 1892, when he was nineteen. After training he joined the newly commissioned cruiser ROYAL ARTHUR as a Stoker 2nd Class on 2nd March 1893. He gained his 1st Class rating a month later and left the ship on 25th September 1896 for six months shore training.

Sam reported to the torpedo gunboat SHARPSHOOTER on 24th November 1896, but quickly moved on to TERRIBLE, a cruiser, where he served alongside Henry Barter. This commission ended on 24th October 1902, when the ship returned from the Boer War.

On 22nd January 1903 he joined ST VINCENT, serving on her until May 1905. During this time he was disrated to Stoker 2nd Class, but recovered to 1st Class and became a Three-Badge man before he left the ship to join the light cruiser EGMONT. For the next seven years he served on ten different ships from a battleship, through a cruiser to a succession of torpedo gunboats. During this time his character was consistently graded as **"Very Good"** and in 1911, on CORMORANT he achieved Chief Stoker rank.

On 5th May 1912, having completed more than twenty years service Samuel moved to the Royal Fleet Reserve, being held on the books of VICTORY.

On 1st June 1914 he was called up for summer training with the Reserve Fleet. Churchill as First Lord of the Admiralty refused to release the reservists at the end of the month. The Royal Navy – and Samuel – were ready for war.

HMS MINOTAUR   PHOTO IWM Q 39623

PHOTO VIA NICK SAUNDERS

Samuel had joined the heavy cruiser MINOTAUR, which had been laid down in June 1906 at Devonport. Built by Harland and Wolff she was completed in March 1908. As a cruiser of 14,600 tons displacement capable of 23 knots she was heavily armed with 4x 9.2inch and 10x 7.5inch guns and carried a compliment of 755 men.

He served until stricken by heart disease. He was taken aboard the Naval Hospital Ship SOUDAN, but died at 10.45 a.m. on 8th April. The St Thomas Memorial book notes that he died from the effects of the war.

Samuel is buried in **Lyness Royal Navy Cemetery,** in:

Grave B. 22.

HENRY ROBERT BARTER

Able Seaman, Royal Navy
197764
HMS INVINCIBLE
Who died on
22nd December 1916, aged 34.

Henry was born in Lymington on 9th September 1882, another of the sons of Frank, a ships fireman, and Bessie Barter of Quay Hill. His brother Walter (see page 36) was killed at Gallipoli. Before the war Henry married Caroline Sully.

When Henry joined the Royal Navy at Portsmouth on 14th January 1898 he was nearly 5 feet 5 inches tall, possessed grey eyes and brown hair, and had a large scar on his chest. He passed out from his training at ST VINCENT a year later as a Boy !st Class and gained sea time aboard the cruisers MINOTAUR and AGINCOURT. He then attended a gunnery course at Portsmouth. When he left the course at eighteen years old he had grown 3 inches and his eyes were now described as *"Brown."*

Over the following nine years Henry served on ten different ships ranging from battleships to destroyers and including the Admiralty Yacht ENCHANTRESS. Henry also attended six more courses and had become a Two-Badged Able Seaman. On 9th March 1909 he joined – what was to be - his last ship, the brand new battle-cruiser INVINCIBLE.

The INVINCIBLE was laid down 2nd April 1906 and commissioned on 20th March 1909. The concept was that such battle-cruisers, with their superior firepower and speed, would be able to operate either alone or in a scouting role or as part of a battle fleet in an anti-cruiser role. INVINCIBLE, capable of 28 knots as its armour was only 7 inches thick, could avoid action with battleships whilst its own 12inch guns could be devastating. She displaced 17,250 tons and Henry was one of its war complement of 837 officers and men.

HMS INVINCIBLE

Henry left the ship as a Three-Badged Able Seaman when INVINCIBLE started a major refit at the end of 1913 and

rejoined her on the completion of the refit at the outbreak of war. After North Sea duty she was sent to the South Atlantic where, on 8th December she took part in the successful Second battle of the Falklands and took part in the search for the DRESDEN. In April 1915 she had a refit to replace some of her 12-inch guns, which had been worn out in the Falklands battle. Another refit, a year later, left her in prime condition for the battle of Jutland.

PHOTO NICK SAUNDERS

Five weeks before her destruction at Jutland – from which only 5 of the crew survived - Henry was invalided out of INVINCIBLE with neurasthenia.

He is buried at **Portsmouth Cemetery** in

Grave 12. 10 1/2

GEORGE TOMS

Able Seaman, Royal Navy
J/39110
H.M.S. NARBOROUGH
who died on
Saturday 12th January 1918, aged 19.

George was born on 14th September 1898 in Upway, Dorset. His father, James, was a general labourer. His mother, Beatrice, also raised another son, James, and two daughters, Rose and Margaret. They later moved to Lymington, living in Waterford Lane.

George joined the Royal Navy at Portsmouth on his eighteenth birthday, having previously worked as a garden boy. His Record of Service describes him as being nearly 5 foot 1 inch tall, with brown hair and eyes and being of a fresh complexion. After training on IMPREGNABLE he joined the old heavy cruiser KING ALFRED for two years, during which time he gained an Able Seaman rating. After a course ashore he joined NARBROUGH on 31st October 1917.

HMS NARBOROUGH

NARBOROUGH was a three-funnelled destroyer of about 1000 tons displacement, armed with three 4xinch guns and four 21" torpedo tubes in two pairs of two. The class was a popular one with the continuous building of 85 of them between 1914 and 1917. On 12th January 1918 OPAL and NARBOROUGH were part of the Escort Force "P" taking a convoy from Peterhead to Lerwick. A gale sprang got up and the Convoy Commodore ordered the two destroyers to take shelter.

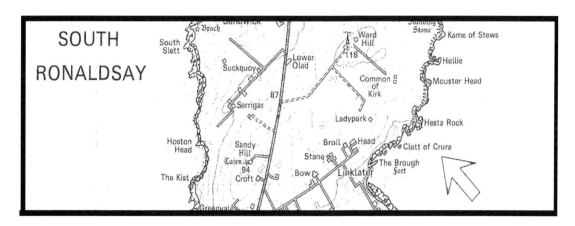

Both ships ran aground in Windwick Bay on the East Coast of South Ronaldsay while making for Scapa Flow.

The Admiralty Enquiry (AD137/3726) into the loss of NARBOROUGH found that the ships had missed the entrance channel and in the blinding snowstorm had struck the rocks at the Clett of Crura. NARBOROUGH capsized and immediately broke in two. There was only one survivor from the two ships.

PHOTO K AYMER ORKNEY PHOTOGRAPHIC

The people of Ronaldsay have erected a memorial to those lost. It reads:

"In memory of the 188 men who perished here when HMS NARBOROUGH and HMS OPAL were lost on the rocks of Hesta during the snowstorm of 12th Jan. 1918."

The above photograph shows the memorial with the Clett of Crura cliffs in the background. George Toms' body was recovered. He is buried in **Lyness Royal Naval Cemetery**, Orkney, in:

PHOTO NICK SAUNDERS

Grave O. 21.

FRANK EPHRAIM BALL
Lieutenant
Royal Air Force
Who died on
Monday, 8th April 1918, aged 29.

Frank was born 1st February 1889, the son of Frank, an estate manager, and Helen Ball, of Smethwick, Birmingham, and grew up in the developing world of automobile engineering. He was always interested in flying and in the early days of aviation designed and started to build an aeroplane, but was unable to complete it. On moving to Lymington he became chauffeur to Mr Jebb-Scott of Linden house and accompanied him to South Africa. On returning in 1913 Frank started business in St Thomas Street as a motor engineer. He was a member of both the Conservative Club and the Literary Institute.

On 1st February 1915 Frank married Ida de Jersey Browning at St Thomas's Church. The Brownings lived in Weston Road and Ida's father, Frederick, worked as a house decorator. The newly married couple lived at Hurstlea, Waterford.

Frank joined the Royal Flying Corps on 8th August 1917. As a trained mechanical engineer he declared knowledge of gauge making and twelve years engine repair experience. On the back of such engineering knowledge he soon flew, as an engineer, in large aircraft such as the DH 6 and DH8.

On 17th November Frank was commissioned as a temporary Second Lieutenant (on probation) into the General List. This rank was confirmed on 16th February 1918, when he was selected for pilot training. Successfully negotiating initial flying training on the Avro 504 he 1918 progressed, on 2nd April, to being a pupil pilot at No. 1 School of Aerial Fighting, which was operating from the Race Course at Ayr in Scotland. This unit operated advanced training on, mainly, Sopwith Camels.

This single-seat fighter had only entered front-line service in 1917 and, although it proved a difficult aircraft to fly, it was very manoeuvrable. Once mastered, however, it out-flew the enemy aircraft to became the most successful of all British fighters.

Frank was killed six days later when he was involved in a mid-air collision with another pupil, Lt. Robert Elesmere Brooks, also aged 29. They were both flying Sopwith Camels and the collision occurred at 3,000feet over the parish of Kilwinning.

Frank's Service Record sheet notes that his service was deemed sufficient for the grant of service medals.

His wife, Ida, later married again and as Ida de Jersey Gosling, lived at 6, St Helen's Place, St Thomas Street, Lymington.

PHOTO RICHARD WILLIAMS

Both pilots are buried in **Ayr Cemetery**, Ayrshire, Scotland, Frank being buried in:

Grave K. 3937

THE MEMORIAL

1919-1921
1991

CELEBRATION AND COMMEMORATION

A General Committee was established to consider details of how to celebrate and commemorate the Armistice. Twelve weeks after the Armistice was signed, the Mayor caused the following notice to be issued:

BOROUGH OF LYMINGTON.

MAYOR'S FUND.
Roll of Honour and Memorial.

NOTICE.

A Public Meeting

of Subscribers to the above Fund, and all interested, will be held at The Town Hall, Lymington, on

MONDAY, FEBRUARY 10th, 1919,

at 8.0 p.m., for the purpose of discussing the most appropriate method to be adopted for perpetuating the memory of those of our residents who have lost their lives in the Great War.

In view of the importance of the subject to be discussed I trust that the Meeting will be well attended.

EDWARD A. C. STONE,
Mayor.

Town Hall, Lymington,
5th February, 1919.

This meeting was well attended, The Mayor started a Fund with a £10 donation, and the meeting resolved:

> *"That no sums of money be accepted towards this Fund if raised at Whist Drives, Dances, Balls or any Public Entertainment."*

At its next meeting on **18th February** it was reported that the Fund had reached £327.10.6 and that offerings had practically ceased. It also considered the acquisition of the cricket field as a permanent Memorial, but considered the price was too high. Another site considered for such a purpose was the Sea Baths. Two other matters were considered. A list of those killed was inspected and matters put in hand to update it. Regrettably this list has not survived in what are otherwise remarkably complete records. It was also agreed that all proceedings of the Committee would be conducted in camera and that no account be accordingly furnished to the Press.

Progress was made at the next meeting on **27th February**. It was resolved to invite comprehensive designs for the proposed Obelisk, cost not to exceed £250, and to provide names for about 70 of the fallen, with brief naval or regimental description.

The meeting held on **2nd April** considered estimates for the Obelisk from sixteen suppliers. As the £250 cap on expenditure was resulting in *"Obelisks of a diminutive character,"* It was agreed to defer the matter to a Mr Whitaker of Folkestone, who was asked to make observations on the designs submitted by Mr Newbury A Trent of Chelsea, Messrs Stoute and Murray of London and Mr Banks of Lymington. Of the two possible land purchases, Commander Shrub declined to reduce his price for the cricket field and the sea baths were considered too run down and expensive. A new suggestion to purchase 4-6 acres of land adjoining the Cottage Hospital was referred back to the owner, Mr Aman, to see if he would reduce his asking price from £150 down to £100 per acre.

The Meeting held on **29th April** was notable for being the first time that the possible location of the Obelisk *"Near the Parish Church"* had been mentioned – the alternative site being in front of "Home Mead." Whilst the estimated cost was assumed to be £750, Mr Richards thought a suitable memorial could be supplied for £500. It was then agreed that Mr Richards, Mr Newbury and Mr Trent would each produce the best sketch of a memorial they could offer for £500, in the form of an obelisk or Celtic Cross.

The three sketches were considered at the meeting on **27ᵗʰ May**. The sketch by Mr Richards was selected for recommendation to a public meeting.

At the committee meeting on **19th June** doubts were expressed about the production costings provided by Mr Richards for his Cross. Details were requested! The sub-committee recommended that the cricket ground be purchased for £1600, with an additional sum of £400 to be spent on necessary expenses. The ground would be vested in the Mayor, Aldermen and Burgesses of the Borough of Lymington.

Mr Richards was pleased to learn of the acceptance of his design and promised to check his sub-contractors costings. He suggested that work on the foundations should be carried out by a local firm. This was agreed and the site was confirmed as being opposite Church House in the High Street.

The Meeting on **15ᵗʰ July** focused on the possible purchase of the cricket pitch. The Mayor was requested to issue an Appeal at once for £2000. The timing of this appeal neatly meshed with the Victory Celebrations that were due to take place four days later.

Edward. A.S. Stone.

Chairman.

VICTORY CELEBRATIONS

The Council planned its victory celebration for 19th July 1919. Whilst most soldiers had returned by then, it was indeed a celebration for the town. Those Lymingtonians not in uniform had all been affected by the war and had played their part, collecting eggs and rolling bandages for the local hospitals, raising money for the war, knitting troops' comforts, etc. Women filled jobs previously done by men – and in general supporting the war effort in whatever ways necessary.

It was a four-day spectacular.

19th July:

6 a.m.	Reveille by Buglers
	Decoration of Town
7.00	Church Bells rung
8.30	Town Band plays
10.00	Church Bells rung
10.30	Procession
12.30	Dinner for
	65+ year olds
1.30.	Church Bells rung
2.30	Adult Sports
4.30	Children's Tea
6 .00	Church Bells rung
7.00	Evening Concert
9.00	Illumination of Town

21st July:

    2.30 p.m. Children's Entertainment at the Lyric
    8.00p.m. Free Entertainment for Service and
                    Ex-Servicemen

22nd July:

    2.30 p.m. Children's Entertainment at the Lyric
    8.0 p.m. Public Entertainment at the Lyric

23rd July:

    9 p.m.   Peace Ball. Tickets five shillings each.

The Procession formed up at the Railway Station, headed by the Town Band. It was led by the Royal Navy, followed by C Company of the 4th Hampshires, Ex-Servicemen, Youth contingents, VADs and nurses, Councillors et al. It paraded up Queen Street, down Avenue Road and back to the Town Hall.

PHOTO ST BARBE MUSEUM LYMINGTON

The Mayor, Councillor Stone, pictured here, delivered an address and presented Lymington medals specially struck for the occasion.

SELECTION OF NAMES

Residence is the usual criteria for the selection of names for commemoration on any War Memorial. In some locations, e.g. Brockenhurst, post-war residence of the widow has, however, been deemed sufficient qualification. In Lymington, at the committee meeting held on **18th February**

"A list of those killed was inspected and matters put in hand to update it."

This list was submitted by Mr Osborne of Quay Hill and the Hon Sec was deputed to take all necessary steps to bring it up to date. A sub-committee was later formed to fulfil this task. No records of this committee have survived, but we can try to determine how they thought by the cases that were noted in the Minutes of the main committee.

On **2nd April 1919** Mrs E Taylor of 23 Morelow Street Westminster, SW1 requested that her husband's name be included on the Roll of Honour. Lance Corporal **Edward Taylor** served in the Scots Guards and died of wounds on the 5th March 1917. Although Edward was born in Lymington, as he had re-enlisted in Sunbury-on-Thames it was held that his name was not eligible for the Lymington list.

A letter from Mrs C Gates of 6, MAPLE terrace, Western Road requesting that her late son's name might appear on the Roll of Honour was discussed at **29th April** meeting. Private **Charles Gates** was both born and enlisted in Lymington. He died whilst serving in India on 14th October 1917. This request was agreed.

A request from Mrs L Parsons of 9 Nelson Place that her husband's name be included on the Roll of Honour was approved at the meeting held on **4th July**. Air Mech (3rd Class) **Robert Parsons** RAF died on 14th November 1918 and is buried locally.

At the meeting on **13th October** it was resolved that Mr D Banks, Mr F Trevor-Garrick, and the Hon Sec be deputed to go through and bring up to date a list of the names entitled to be inscribed on the Memorial. The definition of "entitled" regrettably, however, is not given.

They duly reported on **23rd October**, producing a list of names recommended for inclusion, a list of those not so recommended and a list of men who were doubtful but who were recommended for inclusion. Unfortunately these lists have, also, not survived. It was resolved to publish the "final" list as a last chance for corrections and omissions.

On **6th January 1920** the minutes recorded:

List of names to be inscribed on Memorial. A full list was now submitted. Resolved: "That the names of Douglas Bodman and Arthur Tom Munden be omitted". Also "That the name of Frederick John Wellman" be added. And "That the name of Jesse Tregunna be included although his name already appears on the Brockenhurst list".

Claims. Claims were submitted on behalf of the following and dealt with as set forth:-
Clifford Howard Warder.
Frederick Seaman.   } Rejected.
C.E.A. Harding. Brevet Major.

Arthur James Baxter.
Sydney George Ellis Jones.   } Admitted.
Francis Willoughby Loxton.
Ronald Ford.   D°

It has not been possible to trace **Douglas Bodman**. **Arthur Munden** served in the Hampshire Regiment. He was born in Fordingbridge and lived in Bordon. **Frederick Wellman** of the Gloucestershire Regiment lived in Lymington.

Jesse Tregunna of the Hampshire Regiment was born in Brockenhurst but lived in Lower Buckland. He was killed in action on the 22nd April 1918.

Clifford Warder, of the Royal Fusiliers, was killed in action on 4th February 1916. He was born in Boldre and lived in Walhampton.

Frederick Seaman of the Hampshire Regiment was killed in action in the Balkans on 18th September 1918. He was born in Chelmsford and lived in Brentwood, Essex.

Charles Harding of the Royal Fusiliers was born in Newcastle. Eton records show his father as Major GH Harding 5th Fusiliers of Lynden House Lymington. Charles lived in Lynden House, Lymington with his wife and son. He died in France on 10th December 1917. He has a personal memorial in St Thomas Church.

Arthur Barter lived in Southampton, but came from a Lymington family. **Sydney Jones** of the London Regiment, who was killed in action on the 1st March 1917 was born – and lived – in Hammersmith. Corporal **Francis Loxton** of the Somerset Light Infantry was born in Lymington, but lived in Harringay, Middlesex. **Ronald Ford** of the Hampshires was born in Lymington but lived in Goring-on Sea.

Whatever the merits of their case, requests for the names of **Henry Cresswell Delamain** (KIA 17/4/15) and **David Patrick Laing** (KIA 20/10/14) to be included had to be refused, at the meeting of **17th April,** on the grounds that there was not enough space on the Memorial.

Clearly, whilst residence was an important factor in selection, in some cases other local criteria came into play. At this distance from the event we can only respect the judgement of the Committee.

THE MEMORIAL

The Peace Celebrations were very successful. The implementation of the Appeal was discussed on **5th August** and subscriptions were invited from residents and local businesses. Mr Richards now stated that his own sub-contractor, Messrs Martyn & Co, could do all the work, including foundations and steps, for less than £500 and that if the lowest quote was to be accepted he:

"Would have to decline to have
anything more to do with the matter."

He also proposed to charge 25 Guineas for his services. The committee resolved unanimously

"That the subject of the Cross do
remain in abeyance for the present."

At the same meeting Flushards Field of 7 acres and the Baths were offered to the committee for £2,300.

The Appeal wasn't appealing enough, according to the meeting of **14th August**. Lady Crawford of Cox Hill was proposing to provide an entertainment at the Lyric Theatre, Mrs Heppenstall was asked to arrange a confetti battle on the cricket field and the Freemasons were to be approached – all activities being to raise money for the fund.

By the **22nd** Lady Crawford had agreed to arrange a concert as agreed in October and the confetti battle was imminent. It was also resolved to appeal to outside parishes. Given the problems of raising money for the cricket field the Buckland Road project - at £150 an acre – was reinstated. This was just as well, as at the next meeting on **6th September** Commander Shrub withdrew his offer to sell the cricket ground. It was agreed to return all subscriptions. Mr Aman stalled on the sale of the Buckland Road site. Mr Richards was requested to provide full specifications and quotations for the memorial.

The meeting on **13th October**:

> 'Resolved
> (a) That the surnames of the fallen men, initials of Christian names, rank and unit be inscribed on the Cross.
> (b) That Mr Richards be asked whether there was to be carving on both sides of the Cross, or in other words, whether the Cross was to have a double front, and
>
> c) That the dedicatory inscription be as follows:-
> "To the Glory of God, and in grateful memory of the men of this Borough who fell in the Great War - 1914-1919."
>
> It was further resolved:-
> That Mr D. Banks, Mr F. S. Trevor Garrick, and the Hon: Sec: be deputed to go through and bring up a list of the names entitled to be inscribed upon the Memorial"

The Town Council opened negotiations with the committee relative to the diversion of the gas mains and electric cables, which would apparently be necessary under the proposed site, also as to the cost of making up the pavement near the site. This was later done at public expense.

On **23rd October** Mr Richards proposed that all the names should be together on the front of the base. This, unfortunately, would require a bigger panel than previously anticipated.

The restrained language of the minutes of the meeting on **6th January 1920** clearly reflects a difficult situation caused by a letter from Mr Richards stating that Cornish granite was too expensive and proposing two designs in Portland stone for £600 or £485. Neither plans, however, matched his original proposals. The committee was not impressed with Portland stone. Mr Richards was told to go back to his drawing board.

The meeting held on **18ᵗʰ February 1920** was a triumph. An estimate from Mr Richards was received for the

Proposed Celtic Cross	£475
Excess number of names to be inscribed	£ 22
Extra for back and sides to be carved	£ 80
	£577
Mr Richards' fee	£ 25
Total	£602

It was resolved

"That the estimate be accepted, and that the list of names to be inscribed be in accordance with the one prepared by Mr Trevor-Garrick now produced."

Martyn & Co was asked to complete the Memorial within six months. Unfortunately, as the sum so far raised was insufficient, another appeal was made through the LYMINGTON CHRONICLE. Certain subscribers were approached again and the cricket field appeal monies were, by agreement of the subscribers, devoted to the Celtic Cross scheme. Progress on the setting-out of the names on the base of the Cross was such that at the Meeting on **17ᵗʰ April** two late requests for names could not be accommodated.

The next meeting held on **7ᵗʰ October,** was not so happy. The architect, Mr Richards, explained that Cornish granite had proved more difficult to obtain and the sub-contractor –Sweet & Sons of Liskeard – had many similar orders in hand, but would proceed as soon as they could. The Committee bit the bullet and resolved that the hope be expressed to the contracting firm that the memorial be completed at the earliest possible date. A sample of the type of lettering and another of the Delabole slate, to be used for the panels, was presented and approved at the Meeting on **5ᵗʰ November**.

The next meeting on **8ᵗʰ February 1921** was difficult. The Cross was in a packing case at Lymington station but, after inspection, was not considered to be in accord with the original drawing. The committee was

"greatly disappointed."

The committee then moved on to arrangements for the unveiling of the memorial. A Sunday afternoon was proposed. Major General Seeley was to be invited to do the honours. An ecumenical dedication was agreed.

The approximate Balance Sheet to date showed a £44.1.6 deficit.

The following meeting on **2nd March** determined to install a set of railings around the memorial for safety reasons. The photo below shows the Monument in pre-rail use. The date for the dedication was set for Easter Sunday, 27th March and the Mayor was to officiate in the regretted absence of the Lord Lieutenant. A bid by the Ex-Services Club to be represented on the Unveiling Committee was politely refused, as their interests had already been taken into account. Funds now stood at between £580-£590. Two further meetings were to be held on **25th April** and on **10th December**. Martyn and & Co was paid £589.10.0 but payment of £31.19.8 to Mr Richards was deferred as the fund was under-subscribed by £31.18.4.

The Town Council agreed to take over the Memorial and to maintain it hereafter on behalf of the inhabitants.

PHOTO MIKE REED

THE DEDICATION

215

PRAYERS to be offered by the REV. A. W. BONSEY.—

O ALMIGHTY Lord, the God of the spirits of all flesh; Fulfil, we beseech Thee, the purpose of Thy love in those who are at rest, that the good work which Thou has begun in them may be perfected unto the day of Jesus Christ, who liveth and reigneth with Thee and the Holy Ghost, one God, world without end. *Amen.*

GRANT, we beseech Thee, merciful Lord, to Thy faithful people pardon and peace, that they may be cleansed from all their sins, and serve Thee with a quiet mind; through Jesus Christ our Lord. *Amen.*

ALMIGHTY God, with Whom do live the spirits of them that depart hence in the Lord, and with Whom the souls of the faithful, after they are delivered from the burden of the flesh, are in joy and felicity; We give Thee hearty thanks, for that it hath pleased Thee to take our brothers into Thy merciful keeping; beseeching Thee that we, with all those that are departed in the true faith of Thy holy name, may have our perfect consummation and bliss both in body and soul in Thy eternal and everlasting glory; through Jesus Christ our Lord. *Amen.*

O HEAVENLY Father, Whose Son our Saviour Jesus Christ did weep at the grave of Lazarus His friend; Have compassion upon those who are in sorrow; comfort them with the sense of Thy love; give them sure confidence and trust in Thy care, and make them to know that all things work together for good to them that love God; through the same Jesus Christ our Lord. *Amen.*

HYMN.

CHRIST the LORD is risen again;
CHRIST hath broken every chain;
Hark! Angelic voices cry,
Singing evermore on high,
Alleluia!

He, Who gave for us His life,
Who for us endured the strife,
Is our Paschal LAMB to-day;
We too sing for joy and say
Alleluia!

He, Who bore all pain and loss
Comfortless upon the Cross,
Lives in glory now on high,
Pleads for us, and hears our cry,
Alleluia!

He, Who slumber'd in the grave,
Is exalted now to save;
Now through Christendom it rings
That the LAMB is King of kings.
Alleluia!

Now He bids us tell abroad
How the lost may be restored,
How the penitent forgiven,
How we too may enter Heav'n.
Alleluia!

Thou, our Paschal LAMB indeed,
CHRIST, Thy ransom'd people feed:
Take our sins and guilt away,
Let us sing by night and day
Alleluia! *Amen.*

The Cross will then be Unveiled by
The Mayor (MR. ALDERMAN E. A. G. STONE).

The Cross will then be Dedicated by THE REV. C. BOSTOCK.

O ALMIGHTY FATHER, Lord of heaven and earth; Vouchsafe, we beseech Thee, to accept this Offering at our hands, and to consecrate this our gift to Thy glory and ourselves to Thy service: for Jesus Christ's sake. *Amen.*

IN the Faith of Jesus Christ we dedicate this Cross to the glory of God and in memory of His servants, in the Name of the Father, and of the Son, and of the Holy Ghost. *Amen.*

ALMIGHTY and merciful God, of whose only gift it cometh that Thy faithful people do unto Thee true and laudable service; Grant, we beseech Thee, that we may so faithfully serve Thee in this life, that we fail not finally to attain Thy heavenly promises; through the merits of Jesus Christ our Lord. *Amen.*

OUT of the deep have I called únto | thee, O | Lord : Lórd | hear | my | voice.

2 O let thine éars con- | -sider | well : thé | voice of | my com- | -plaint.

3 If thou, Lord, will be extreme to márk what is | done a- | -miss O Lórd | who | may a- | -bide it ?

4 Fór there is | mercy . with | thee : thérefore | shalt | thou be | feared.

5 I look for the Lord ; my sóul doth | wait for | him : ín his | word | is my | trust.

6 My soul fléeth | unto . the | Lord : before the morning watch, I sáy, be- | -fore the | morning | watch.

7 O Israel, trust in the Lord * for with the Lórd | there is | mercy : ánd with | him is | plenteous . re- | -demption.

8 And hé shall re- | -deem | Israel : fróm | all | his | sins.

Glory be to the Fáther, | ánd . to the | Son : ánd | to the | Holy | Ghost ;

As it was in the beginning * is nów, and | éver | shall-be : wórld without | end. | A- | -men.

THE LESSON. To be read by the Rev. W. H. Cory.

(Wisdom iii. 1-6).

BUT the souls of the righteous are in the hand of God, and there shall no torment touch them. In the sight of the unwise they seemed to die : and their departure is taken for misery, and their going from us to be utter destruction : but they are in peace. For though they be punished in the sight of men, yet is their hope full of immortality. And having been a little chastised, they shall be greatly rewarded : for God proved them, and found them worthy for Himself. As gold in the furnace hath He tried them, and received them as a burnt offering.

Then shall the Minister, The Rev. H. A. Tree, *say—*

DEAR Brethren in Christ : Whereas the Cross, now to be unveiled and dedicated, is set for a Memorial to those who died for their Country on active service during the late war, let us commend their souls to the mercy of God, first recalling their names :—

Frederick Backhurst, George Grove Bailey, Frank Ephraim Ball, Thomas George Banks, Arthur James Barter, Robert Henry Barter, Walter James Barter, Ben Broomfield, Cecil Edmund Carpenter, Alan Clark, Arthur Clarke, Wilfrid Davis Clarke, Joseph William Cleal, Samuel Thomas Cooper, Herbert Henry Croucher, Edgar Robert Darlington, Edwin Charles Elliott, Edward Frampton, Joseph Frampton, Ronald Ford, Henry Oliver Fudge, Walter Gannaway, Charles Henry Gates, James Gates, Walter E. Gilmore, Herbert Sydney Haines, William James Haines, Henry Joseph Reginald Harris, Ernest Hart, Harry Hayter, Frank Alfred Head, W. J. Heaste, Thomas James Hills, Frank Harry Holloway, Charles Mansell Hood, Samuel Maurice Hurford, William Charles Jenvey, Sydney George Ellis Jones, Douglas Cumming Paget Kindersley, Harry King, Reginald King, Walter Nike King, Bertie Kingswell, Evelyn Anthony Klitz, Henry Jack Leonard, George Henry Lewington, George Edward Lewis, William Charles Lock, Francis Willoughby Loxton, Jack Stanley Lydford, Thomas Charles Stuart Mac Gregor, Frederick Mansfield, Thomas Mapes, William Charles Marshman, Edward Miller, George William Mutter, Cyril Harvey John Osborne, Thomas Osbert Overton, Robert Parsons, Arthur George Payne, Walter Pearce, Thomas William Pelfrey, Oswald

Perry, James William Phillips, Edward George Rickman, R. Rixon, Charles Sainsbury, Alfred Cecil Scott, Arthur Sherfield, Walter Henry Shuttler, George Albert Smith, Sidney St. John, Edward Stokes, William Tilley, George Toms, Herbert Charles Torah, Jesse Tregunna, John Urquhart, Charles Everard Warder, Alfred George Wearn, Frederick John Wellman, Charles Richard White, William Edward Wild, William Yeatman.

HYMN.

FOR all the Saints who from their labours rest,
  Who Thee by faith before the world confess'd
Thy Name, O JESU, be for ever blest.
                        Alleluia !

Thou wast their Rock, their Fortress, and their Might ;
Thou, LORD, their Captain in the well-fought fight ;
Thou in the darkness drear their one true Light.
                        Alleluia !

O may Thy soldiers, faithful, true and bold,
Fight as the Saints who nobly fought of old,
And win, with them, the victor's crown of gold.
                        Alleluia !

O blest communion ! fellowship Divine !
We feebly struggle, they in glory shine ;
Yet all are one in Thee, for all are Thine.
                        Alleluia !

And when the strife is fierce, the warfare long,
Steals on the ear the distant triumph-song,
And hearts are brave again, and arms are strong.
                        Alleluia !

The golden evening brightens in the west ;
Soon, soon to faithful warriors comes their rest ;
Sweet is the calm of Paradise the blest.
                        Alleluia !

But lo ! there breaks a yet more glorious day ;
The Saints triumphant rise in bright array :
The King of glory passes on His way.
                        Alleluia !

From earth's wide bounds, from ocean's farthest coast ;
Through gates of pearl streams in the countless host,
Singing to FATHER, SON, and HOLY GHOST.
                        Alleluia ! *Amen.*

The Benediction.

THE LAST POST.   THE REVEILLÉE
THE NATIONAL ANTHEM.

218

SECOND WORLD WAR NAMES

THE LYMINGTON TIMES of 25th August 1990 carried the following article:

52 ADDITIONS FOR WAR MEMORIAL

A GREAT deal of time has been spent trying to rectify a serious omission by the old Lymington Borough Council who, for some unknown reason, failed to honour those men from Lymington and Pennington by not adding their names on the war memorial in the High Street. Thanks to the diligence of Keith McDonnell, of Tranmere Close, a list of 52 men killed on active service has now been drawn up, which it is hoped will be recorded on a plaque on the memorial in time for this year's Remembrance Sunday. Any last-minute additions must be received by him by the end of this month, on Lymington 673891.

Following an interim list published in the "A. & T." last month, more names have been received, including a letter from Saltash in Cornwall which told of Lymington postman Frank Whittingstall who had been killed as a soldier.

Mr. McDonnell, an Army captain during the war, expresses his thanks to divisional librarian Norman Gannaway for making available the library facilities, also the "A. & T." for their investigative research. Now the Royal British Legion branch is meeting with the Town Council with a view to erecting a plaque. "We will be as helpful as possible," says town clerk Allon Clark.

The up-to-date list of known names now reads: S. J. Bran, L. Brown, R. H. Bygott, F. S. Cassey, J. E. M. Chamberlain, G. H Charles, W Clarke, A. G. Cole, R. K Collins, E C. Cowdery, A. E. L. Crosthwait, L R. Croucher, R. J. Dashwood, C. R. Day, R. Dimmick, H. O. Foster, C. Freeman, A. G. T Frogley, J Gregory, J. Gunnell, H. L. C. Hall, W. G. Hawkins, G Hayter, E Hayward, F. A. Hayward, V. R. Hobby, G. P. Huddart, W. C. Hurst, H. R. Ireland, P. H. Isted, R. C Isted, J D.F. Jeans, V. H. Jones, J Lawrence, W C. Lewington, H. Lewis, R. H. Maxted, R. C. McLeod, A. G. Payne, D. A. Pirie, G. Plumridge, T. Race, K. Renyard, G Thomas, P. C. Todd, F. J. R Walsh, J R. Welsh, P. White, F. Whittingstall, R. Wilson, J. H. C. Wort, F. A. Young.

This effort, by a number of individuals and agencies, was happily successful. Trying to research all the names on the list, however, has been difficult – and in three cases impossible. Christian names are not given in the article above, the records of those concerned in 1991 have not survived and official records are not yet available for research. This has made the contributions by relatives and friends of those who died even more valuable and appreciated.

The unveiling and dedication of the memorial plaque was appropriately conducted.

Lymington & Pennington Town Council

**Unveiling and Dedication
of the
Memorial Plaque**

**In memory of
Those who died in the 2nd World War
1939 - 1945**

**Sunday, June 30th, 1991
at 3.00 p.m.**

This service is an almost exact replica of the Borough of Lymington Service of Unveiling and Dedication of this Memorial Cross, in memory of those who died in the war 1914 - 1919, which was held on Easter Sunday, March 27th, 1921 at 3.00 p.m.

The war was not kind to Lymington as the seventy-three men killed is a disproportionately large number of men for a small town.

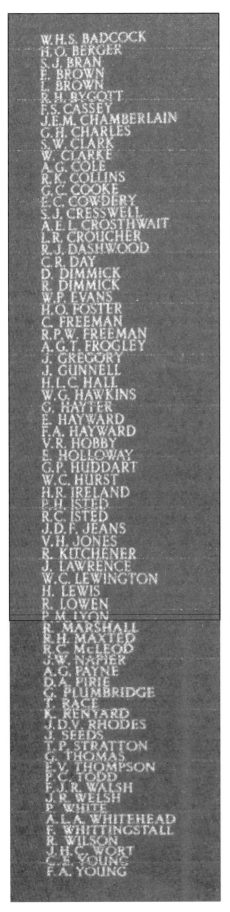

W.H.S. BADCOCK
H.O. BERGER
S.J. BRAN
E. BROWN
L. BROWN
R.H. BYGOTT
F.S. CASSEY
J.E.M. CHAMBERLAIN
G.H. CHARLES
S.W. CLARK
W. CLARKE
A.G. COLE
R.K. COLLINS
G.C. COOKE
E.C. COWDERY
S.J. CRESSWELL
A.E.L. CROSTHWAIT
L.R. CROUCHER
R.J. DASHWOOD
C.R. DAY
D. DIMMICK
R. DIMMICK
W.F. EVANS
H.O. FOSTER
C. FREEMAN
R.P.W. FREEMAN
A.G.T. FROGLEY
J. GREGORY
J. GUNNELL
H.L.C. HALL
W.G. HAWKINS
G. HAYTER
E. HAYWARD
F.A. HAYWARD
V.R. HOBBY
E. HOLLOWAY
G.P. HUDDART
W.C. HURST
H.R. IRELAND
P.H. ISTED
R.C. ISTED
J.D.F. JEANS
V.H. JONES
R. KITCHENER
J. LAWRENCE
W.C. LEWINGTON
H. LEWIS
R. LOWEN
P.M. LYON
R. MARSHALL
R.H. MAXTED
R.C. McLEOD
J.W. NAPIER
A.G. PAYNE
D.A. PIRIE
G. PLUMBRIDGE
T. RACE
K. RENYARD
J.D.V. RHODES
J. SEEDS
T.P. STRATTON
G. THOMAS
E.V. THOMPSON
P.C. TODD
F.J.R. WALSH
J.R. WELSH
P. WHITE
A.L.A. WHITEHEAD
F. WHITTINGSTALL
R. WILSON
J.H.G. WORT
C.E. YOUNG
F.A. YOUNG

The **Royal Navy** sustained heavy losses at the beginning and early part of the war. Eighteen Lymington men were to die in the war at sea whilst serving with the Royal Navy, with a further four being killed whilst serving with the **Merchant Navy**. Merchant seamen suffered the highest casualty rate, with one in four seamen not surviving the war.

Seventeen men died whilst serving with the **Royal Air Force**, mainly in the middle part of the war when the bombing of German-occupied Europe was achieved only at the cost of a high casualty rate.

The thirty-one **Army** casualties tended to occur later in the war as the North African, Italian and Burma Campaigns developed and the Invasion of Europe occurred. Seven of these men died whilst serving with the Hampshire Regiment.

Sadly, three men remain unidentified

Finally, there has been the tragic death of the Lymington man who died in Bosnia in 1997, whilst on UN peacekeeping duties.

Many people in Lymington today have personal memories of these men who died in the wars and military actions of the last century. It is to be hoped that justice has now been done to their memory.

THE SECOND WORLD WAR

1939-1941

1939-40: THE OPENING PHASE

The Second World War began, for Britain, on 3rd September 1939.

In the air, the country – and particularly London – was braced for immediate bombing attacks. These did not occur, although school children were evacuated to "places of safety." RAF Fighter Command sent some squadrons to support the British Expeditionary Force (BEF) in France and Bomber Command limited itself to leaflet raids over Germany and some small-scale attacks, mainly against shipping and naval targets. The RAF had used the extra year, bought by the Munich Agreement, to hasten its process of re-arming with modern performance aircraft, and so had modern fighters like the Hurricane and Spitfire, although in small numbers. Aircraft production was stepped up, but in 1939 the short and medium range bombers were no match for the German airforce.

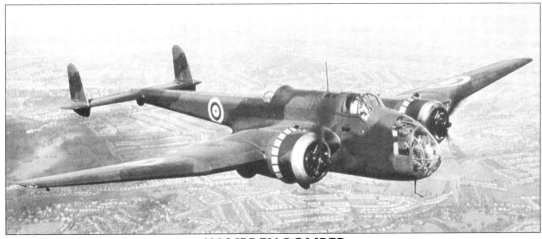

HAMPDEN BOMBER

Although Lymington had a surprisingly significant number of men serving in the RAF, it suffered no casualties in this phase.

For the army, mobilisation went to plan and the BEF made its way to France in the same way their fathers had done in 1914. In the absence of any aggressive moves by German Forces the BEF built defensive positions along the Franco/Belgian border to extend the French Maginot Line defences. It then settled down to tactical and fitness training. A Norwegian expedition was also mounted, but was not a military success.

BEF IN FRANCE IN WINTER 1939-40

Arthur Payne – whose father was the second casualty in 1914 (see page 8) – became the first one in this war, when he was accidentally shot and killed in France in February 1940.

The Royal Navy experienced no such "Phoney War." Within four minutes of war being declared Donald Pirie's submarine SPEARFISH had been (unsuccessfully) attacked by a U-boat's torpedo. The navy began its war at a canter with aggressive and comprehensive worldwide patrolling. It re-introduced convoys, took a very positive part in the Norwegian campaign and had success at the battle of the River Plate. On the other hand the battleship, ROYAL OAK, was sunk in Scapa Flow and the navy began to lose ships and experienced crews that, at this stage of the war, were not easy to replace. **Herbert Ireland** was lost in January 1940 when his destroyer hit a mine in the North Sea and **Geoffrey Charles** was killed the following month in the same area, when his destroyer was sunk by a U-boat.

Apart from this naval activity the country resigned itself to being at war – for the second time in twenty-five years – against the same enemy. The mood of the country appears, with hindsight, to be one of confident resignation. Business continued to be

"as usual."

ARTHUR GEORGE PAYNE

Lance Bombardier
815477
Royal Artillery
Who died on
Thursday 8ᵗʰ February 1940, aged 26.

Arthur was the youngest son of Arthur and Alice Payne and born in China. His father, a sergeant in the South Wales Borderers, was killed at Tsingtau in 1914 (see page 8).

On leaving school Arthur worked at Wellworthys until he was 18, whereupon he enlisted as a gunner in the Army. Before the war he married a local girl, Maud. They lived - with his mother - in Carlton Gardens, Lymington.

When war broke out 19ᵗʰ Field Regiment, Royal Artillery, was sent to France as part of the British Expeditionary Force. Arthur's older brother, Reginald was already serving in the Royal Marines and his married sister, Mrs David, was also living in Lymington. Arthur came home on Christmas leave and was photographed with Maud and their 2-year-old daughter Barbara Ann. His wife later commented that

"He had always seemed so very happy."

Arthur died in France on 8ᵗʰ February, being accidentally killed by a gunshot. The day after Maud was notified by telegram of his death she received a letter from Arthur, which he had posted on the 6ᵗʰ of the month. She also received a letter from his Battery Commander who wrote that

"The loss had caused a gap it would not be easy to fill."

Arthur was buried with full military honours in **Douai Communal Cemetery**, France, in

Row L. Grave 6.

HERBERT RICHARD HENRY IRELAND

Leading Stoker, Royal Navy
P/KX 81258
H.M.S. GRENVILLE
Who died on
Friday 19th January 1940, aged 26.

The Irelands were an old Lymington family. Herbert's father, also named Herbert, was a painter and decorator. They all lived in Station Street until the father's death in July 1934. Just before the war, his mother, Fanny Ireland, moved with her daughter to Parkstone, Dorset. Herbert's aunt, however, remained in Lymington, living at Elgar's Cottage, in the High Street.

Herbert was a scholar at Lymington Council School and a member of the 1st Lymington Scout Troop. He later joined the Sea Scouts, before enlisting in the Royal Navy just before his father's death.

HMS GRENVILLE   PHOTO NMM N8706

GRENVILLE was the Flotilla Leader for the "G" Class destroyers of 1335 tonnage that entered service in 1935. Capable of 36.5 knots, she was the only one of the class to be armed with 5 x 4.7-inch guns as her main armament.

She was one of the 184 flotilla leaders and destroyers with which the Royal Navy began the war. GRENVILLE was only the fourth destroyer to be sunk in the war when, under the command of Captain G E Creasey MVO, she struck a mine and sank 23 miles east of the Kentish Knock lightship on 20th January 1940.

Leading Stoker Ireland was amongst the 81 of her complement of 175 officers and men who were lost.

PHOTO NICK SAUNDERS

Herbert's name therefore appears on the **Portsmouth Naval Memorial**, on:

Panel 41, Column 3

GEOFFREY HOWARD CHARLES

Ordinary Seaman; Royal Navy Volunteer Reserve
P/JX 165586
H.M.S. DARING
Who died on
Sunday 18th February 1940, aged 24.

Geoffrey was the only son of Walter and Emily Charles of Avenue Road, Lymington. Shortly after his birth in Buckinghamshire the family moved to Fordingbridge, and Geoffrey attended a private school in Salisbury.

In 1935 they moved to Lymington, where Geoffrey worked in partnership with his father in the builders merchants business in Gosport Street. Geoffrey was a parishioner of St Mark's Church, Pennington, where he had signed the Electoral Roll and regularly worshiped. He was able to indulge his keenness for sailing, owning his own yacht. He was reported as being very popular amongst a large circle of friends with his

"Ever-smiling countenance."

He joined the Royal Navy in October 1939 with two friends – Bill Johnson - the well-known amateur actor and Gordon Priddle - who both worked for Lloyds Bank in Lymington. They went together to a depot on the North East coast for their basic training. Geoffrey went on alone to do a gunnery course, and then had home leave before joining DARING.

HMS DARING   PHOTO NMM N12174

DARING had been completed in 1932 by John L Thornycroft and Co., of Southampton and was a modern oil-burning destroyer, displacing 1,375 tons, capable of a speed of 36 knots. She had the standard destroyer main armament of 4 x 4.7 inch guns and carried eight torpedo tubes. Before the war she served on the China station and in June 1939 was one of the two warships blockaded by the Japanese Navy at Foochow.

Geoffrey had only been on the ship for a short time when, on 18th February 1940, she was torpedoed by U-23 in the North Sea off Duncansby Head. This U-boat was commanded by Kretschmer, who sank forty-seven ships before he was captured in 1941.

The Southern Daily Echo, for Monday 19th February 1940, reported:

> *"The Admiralty regrets to announce that HMS destroyer DARING, Commander S A Cooper, has been torpedoed and sunk. One officer and 4 ratings have been picked up. Nine officers and 148 ratings are missing and it is feared have been lost. The loss of the DARING strikes home with added intensity so far as Southampton is concerned, for she was built at Woolston, where a sister craft, HMS DECOY, was also constructed."*

There were actually 15 survivors and 157 men were lost.

PHOTO NICK SAUNDERS

Geoffrey's body was not recovered. His name is therefore recorded on the **Portsmouth Naval Memorial** on:

Panel 39, Column 3

1940 DUNKIRK

The German attack on 10th May 1940 came as no surprise, although the speed of the advance, the brutality of the blitzkrieg tactics on the civilian population and the collapse of our allies, France and Belgium, came as a nasty shock to Britain at large. It followed the collapse of the ill-fated Norwegian campaign, which coincidentally led on the same day to the fall of the Chamberlain government and its replacement by a Churchill-led coalition pledged to vigorously prosecute the war.

In France the advance of the British Expeditionary Force up to the River Dyle in Belgium was swiftly followed by an immediate about turn and the retreat to Dunkirk.

A BOAT LOADED WITH TROOPS

The "miracle" of Dunkirk was that the Royal Navy was able to organise, in very short notice, the evacuation of 338,226 troops from the beaches, including 123,000 French soldiers. Whilst most of the latter were repatriated to France, the saving of three-quarter's of the BEF provided the cadre of trained manpower upon which UK military expansion could take place. **Patrick Lyon** was killed in the retreat.

Success did not come cheaply as the RAF lost 106 aircraft over the beaches, whilst the Navy lost 9 destroyers and countless small craft. Other evacuations took place further down the coast. **Eric Cowdery** was killed heading for such a port.

Britain was alone against Germany and operations now switched to the Mediterranean and the Atlantic.

PATRICK MAXWELL LYON

Lieutenant
73167
2nd Battalion, The Middlesex Regiment,
Who died on
Tuesday 28th May 1940, aged 24.

Patrick was the second son of Admiral Sir George Hamilton Lyon KCB and Lady Lyon (nee Helenora Pierson). They were married in 1912, lived in London and before the war had a country property, Greenfields, Sway Road, Lymington. They later moved to Ramley Cottage, Pennington.

Admiral Lyon entered the Royal Navy in 1899 from the King's School, Bruton. He was an early specialist in gunnery and was known in the Navy as "Torpedo" Lyon. He was also a well-known sportsman and played rugby for England as well as cricket for Hampshire. His ability to play good rugby, however, did get him into trouble. A Labour MP, in the 1920s, raised a question in Parliament demanding to know why this serving naval lieutenant had been sent by destroyer to Scotland to play for England in a match against Scotland. The Navy, however, rose to this occasion by simply stating that Lieutenant Lyon had been on duty carrying important despatches to Edinburgh and as such had been sent by destroyer to Rosyth. He merely took part in the game after they had been delivered and whilst the destroyer was coaling for its return journey! In March 1939 Admiral Lyon became Commander-in-Chief of the Africa station. He died in 1947.

Patrick was born on 8th November 1916. He entered Cheltenham College in September 1930 and left in July 1935 for the Royal Military Academy Sandhurst. He was commissioned into the Middlesex Regiment in 1937 and was promoted to Lieutenant in 1939.

The 2nd Battalion mobilised on 1st September 1939 and joined the 3rd Division, under the command of Major General BL Montgomery DSO as its machine-gun battalion.

The battalion arrived in France at the end of the month and its companies allocated to its constituent brigades. D Company, in which Patrick was serving, was at this time attached to the 7th Guards Brigade as it was holding the line of the River Marcq. Defensive positions were dug and the "phoney" war endured. 1940 began with a long cold spell occupied by training and the digging of many alternative defensive positions.

Five days before the German attack the battalion held a sports day near Lille. They forgot to retrieve their sports flag, which was found by some Frenchmen, who cherished it as an emblem for the local Resistance movement and returned it after the war.

On 10th May the division moved forward to the River Dyle. By the 15th the Belgians had fallen back and 3 Division was holding the line. With the French collapse at Charleroi the retreat began and the battalion held positions on the River Dendre and then on the Escaut. On the 22nd they fell back to Wattrelos – this at a time when the Belgians were giving way to the north and French resistance to the south was ceasing.

On the 27th the battalion moved to the defence of thirteen miles of the Yser canal near Dunkirk. They were relieved on the 28th, but the disengagement of D Company was held up

by snipers, mortar fire and constant air attacks.

Captain Parsler, the OC, was killed and Patrick, who took over command, almost immediately suffered the same fate.

Patrick is buried in **Coxyde Military Cemetery**, Belgium, in:

Grave V. E. 4.

ERIC CLEMENT COWDERY

Leading Aircraftman
547793
Royal Air Force
who died on
Friday 7th June 1940, aged 25.

Eric was the eldest son of Clement and Eva Cowdery of 3, Nelson Place, Lymington.

Eric, or "Jim," as he was affectionately known to his friends and family, joined the RAF and underwent training at RAF CRANWELL as a wireless technician. He was afterwards transferred to an *"RAF station in Hampshire."*

He went to France as one of the ground staff of the Air Component of the BEF. He was reported missing in France in June 1940. In the LYMINGTON TIMES of 16th January 1943 his family were reported as being still optimistic of his safe return. In the same article it reported on his two brothers. Dorian, the youngest at nineteen years of age, had been successful in passing out as an RAF photographer after four months of intensive training; and Gerald, who had just completed four years' service, including his time as a member of the 5th Battalion of the Hampshire Regiment in the Territorial Army, was a radio telephonist at the Bournemouth Garrison.

It was finally confirmed that Eric had, indeed, been killed by bombing on the way back home in the final evacuation from France, after Dunkirk. He is buried in **Vernon Communal Cemetery**, France, in:

> ### ROLL OF HONOUR
> Cowdery.—Dearest memories of L.A.C. Eric C. Cowdery, R.A.F., reported missing in France, June 1940, dearly beloved eldest son of Mrs. and the late Mr. C. Cowdery and brother of Gerald and Dorian.
> "Per ardua, ad astra" "Never in the Field of human conflict was so much owed, by so many, to so few."

Plot 1. Grave 12.

1940/41 THE NEXT STEP

At sea the surface and sub-surface threat to our Atlantic lifeline of convoys from commerce raiders and U-boats, which had so nearly defeated us in 1917, had to be countered. *James Seeds* was lost when his Sunderland was shot down whilst on an anti-submarine patrol in the North Sea. *Donald Pirie* was lost when SPEARFISH was finally sunk whilst on patrol off the Norwegian coast.

After Dunkirk the threat of invasion across the channel was very real. *Arthur Whitehead* was shot down whilst observing invasion preparations in Dutch ports. Pre-invasion targets for the German air force included our coastal trade.

A COASTAL CONVOY

Cyril Day and *Edgar Brown* were both killed in such attacks, whilst *Robert Dashwood* was lost when his destroyer was sunk responding to a false invasion report. As winter approached so this threat receded and Britain – supported only by its Empire troops – got on with the war.

When Italy entered the war, attention turned to the Mediterranean. Allied Troops were sent to North Africa to defend Egypt and to neutralise the Italian colonies of Libya and Eritrea. The success of the Wavell campaigns brought Germany in to bolster its ally. The Italian invasion of Greece similarly needed support and in April 1941 Germany was compelled to reinforce this venture. Se found the troops for this campaign by delaying her invasion of Russia by a vital four weeks. If she had attacked Russia in May, as planned, she

234

would have had a longer period of good weather in which to advance and may well have captured Moscow before winter – thus changing the course of the war.

An allied Expeditionary Force was rushed from North Africa just as the campaign there was in the process of being successfully concluded. In the face of overwhelming German forces the Greek Expeditionary Force soon found itself having to organise an impromptu evacuation to, and then out of Crete. **David Dimmick** was lost in the latter evacuation.

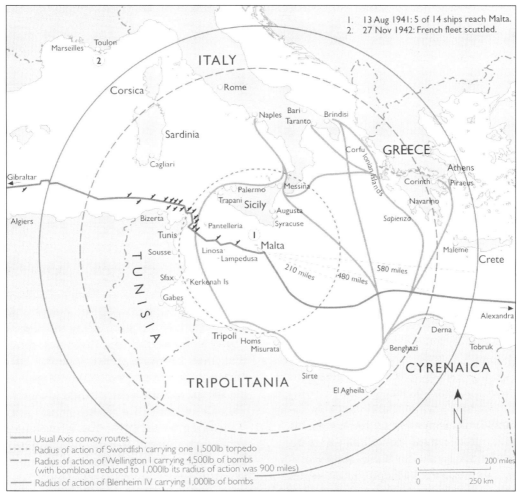

MAP ARTWORK BY THE MAP STUDIO, TAKEN FROM ESS 48 THE SECOND WORLD WAR (4) THE MEDITERRANIAN 1940-45 WRITTEN BY PAUL COLLIER COPYRIGHT OSPREY PUBLISHING LTD

Malta became the lynchpin of our Mediterranean strategy and was reinforced. **James Lawrence** died on the island, whilst **Robert Bygott** left there in his submarine to sink Italian convoys to Libya and was not heard of again. **Geoffrey Cooke** died when his battleship BARHAM was torpedoed late in 1941 whilst patrolling south of Crete

John Welsh and **William Scott-Badcock** both died in Egypt in 1941 from accident or illness.

JAMES SEEDS

Pilot Officer
Royal Air Force
who died on
Tuesday 9th July 1940, aged 20.

James was the youngest of three sons of Sir William Seeds KCMG, who was our Ambassador to Russia at the beginning of the war. The other brothers were Robert, who was in the Field Police and Hugh, who was a career officer in the Royal Navy. James was born in Greystones, West Dublin and educated at Rugby school, from which he went directly to RAF Cranwell on the Prize Scholarship as an Officer Cadet. There was also an older sister Sheila, who has kindly provided the picture below, taken in the garden of Fairfield, their Lymington home.

FAIRFIELD   PHOTO JOHN KELEAY

After graduating from Cranwell James successfully passed a number of courses until, in 1940, he was posted as a pilot with No. 201 squadron flying the long-range Short Sunderland flying boat. At the start of the war, this squadron was stationed at RAF SULLOM VOE in the Shetland Isles operating long-range maritime patrols looking for German surface-raiders and submarines. The Sunderland was the only allied aircraft capable of flying out to 500 miles from the British coast on patrols lasting 14 hours, but their numbers were limited and 201 squadron had only fully converted to the type in April 1940, when they were involved in the Norwegian campaign.

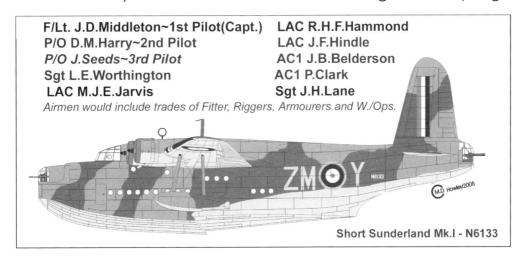

F/Lt. J.D.Middleton~1st Pilot(Capt.)   LAC R.H.F.Hammond
P/O D.M.Harry~2nd Pilot   LAC J.F.Hindle
P/O J.Seeds~3rd Pilot   AC1 J.B.Belderson
Sgt L.E.Worthington   AC1 P.Clark
LAC M.J.E.Jarvis   Sgt J.H.Lane
Airmen would include trades of Fitter, Riggers, Armourers and W./Ops.

Short Sunderland Mk.I - N6133

The Operational Record Book (ORB) for 201 squadron records the departure of James's aircraft, 'Y' N6133, from RAF SULLOM VOE at 1300 hours on an anti-submarine patrol. Its fate is recorded as "***FTR***" (Failed to Return). It is now known that it was shot down at 14.47 hours, at a position 90 miles West of Sumburgh, by Oblt Gollob, flying a Messerschmitt Bf 110 of 3/ZG76 operating from Norway. There were no survivors.

The names of the 10 men are all recorded on the **Runnymede Memorial**, Surrey, with James's name appearing on

Panel 10.

James is also remembered in St Thomas's Church.

DONALD ANTHONY PIRIE DSC

Lieutenant, Royal Navy
H. M. Submarine SPEARFISH
who died on
Friday 2nd August 1940, aged 26.

Donald was born in March 1914, the first of four sons and two daughters to Commander Wilfrid Pirie DSO RN and Leonora Pirie of Westhorpe, Kings Saltern Road, Lymington. Wilfred was awarded the DSO for service in submarines in the Dardenelles. After the war the family moved to Hurlingham, London. All four brothers followed the father's example and joined the Royal Navy. Three of them were awarded the Distinguished Service Cross. The family was comparatively lucky with Roger surviving the sinking of ROYAL OAK in Scapa Flow and Lindsay, who has kindly provided this information, reaching Australia after the sinking of JUPITER in the Battle of the Java Sea.

Donald joined the Royal Navy as a Dartmouth cadet in 1927. He served from April 1931 as Cadet and Midshipman in the battleships VALIANT and WARSPITE - and in the cruiser HAWKINS when it was flagship in the East Indies. On promotion to Sub-Lieutenant he specialised in submarines. Amongst the submarines on which he served were OSWALD, in China, and UNDINE, a new quick-diving submarine of the "U" class.

HM SUBMARINE SPEARFISH   PHOTO COURTESY RNSM

In April 1939 Donald was posted to be second-in-command of SPEARFISH, one of nine Swordfish Class submarines of 640 tons, built between 1932 and 1933.

SPEARFISH was early into action when, four minutes after war was declared a German U-boat fired a torpedo at her, but missed. Donald spent the early part of the war patrolling the North Sea, the Skagerrak and the Norwegian coast. On the 22nd September SPEARFISH was badly damaged by a depth charge attack in the central North Sea and had had to be escorted home by Home Fleet ships. Donald was Mentioned in Despatches for his part in this successful recovery. On 11th April 1940, off Norway, she put three torpedoes into the German pocket battleship, LUTZOW. For this successful action Donald was awarded the Distinguished Service Cross.

DONALD PIRIE (FOURTH FROM RIGHT FRONT ROW)   PHOTO COURTESY RNSM
AND WATCH ON SPEARFISH

On 31st July 1940 SPEARFISH put to sea from Rosyth for a patrol off the Norwegian coast. Two days later she was seen by U-34, who was returning from a successful patrol in the Atlantic, having sunk the destroyer WHIRLWIND and 11 merchantmen.

In fairly rough seas Captain Rollmann of the U-34 fired his last torpedo and heard an explosion. Rollmann surfaced to find AB William Pester, who had just joined SPEARFISH, swimming in a sea of diesel. There were no other survivors. Pester was made a POW. Repatriated at the end of the war, he was sadly killed, six weeks later, in a motorcycle accident.

In a personal tribute published in the Times of 2nd September 1940, G. M. S. writes:

"Donald Pirie will always be associated in my memory with the open air; sunshine, rain, wind, and the sea. Driving an open car, a tramp on the moors, rough shooting, or sailing a boat: these were his delights. Indoors was the place where one ate or slept, but to be avoided as much as possible. He considered it more profitable to sleep than to waste time playing cards.

Brought up in the traditions of the Service to which he belonged, he followed his father in specialising in submarines. He and his brothers were taught sea-craft before reaching their "teens." He possessed a natural sense of command, which he exercised in a quiet, modest manner, and the courage and determination, which are required in those on whom in early youth such great responsibility falls.

He accepted with cheerfulness and without complaint the discomforts associated with life on a submarine, which were inwardly distasteful to him, as he specially appreciated good living and comfort. His short life was a happy one. He had the capacity to enjoy it to the full. He was a shrewd observer of human nature. His terse, humorous comments will remain long in the memory of his many friends."

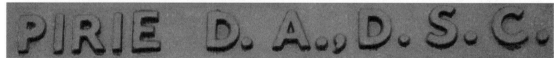

PHOTO NICK SAUNDERS

Donald's name is recorded on the **Portsmouth Naval Memorial** on:

Panel 37 Column 1.

ARTHUR WILFRED ALEXANDER WHITEHEAD

Flying Officer
Royal Air Force
who died on
Thursday 11th July 1940, aged 29.

Arthur was born in 1911, one of the five sons and a daughter born to Sir James Beethom Whitehead KCMG, MA, JP and the Hon Marian Ceclia Whitehead (nee Brodrick), of Efford Park, Lymington. The second son, Edgar, later became Prime Minister of Southern Rhodesia from 1958 – 1962. Arthur was a keen aviator and flew his own aircraft from the "splendid landing ground hidden by trees" at Efford Park.

Arthur first appears in the records of No. 500 (County of Kent) Squadron, Royal Auxiliary Air Force in April 1940, when he is listed as the pilot of a reconnaissance patrol in the English Channel. No. 500 squadron was part of Coastal Command and was equipped with the twin-engine Avro Anson Mark I, which they operated from RAF DETLING in Kent. Their duties were principally maritime reconnaissance, which included anti U-boat and E-boat (fast motor gun-boats) patrols and convoy escort. Indeed, one of the specific tasks, at this time, was to escort the leave ships that ran regularly between Dover and the French ports.

AVRO ANSON MK I   PHOTO JARROD COTTER/FLYPAST MAGAZINE

The Avro Anson was a 1930's design for a small civil transport, and was adapted to a military role by the addition of a single Vickers machine gun turret; another Vickers fixed in the nose and a small bomb load. A restored Anson in 500 Squadron markings, part of the IWM Duxford Collection, is shown above.

No 500 Squadron rapidly came to find that this armament was inadequate when opposed by the Messerschmit Bf109s and Bf110s of the Luftwaffe, so they arranged privately for the fitting of two additional Vickers machine guns firing through the side windows. The net result was that 500 squadron ended 1940 with a score of 4 enemy aircraft shot down, of which 2 were Bf. 109 fighters.

This period through May and June 1940 was one of intense activity. The Dunkirk evacuation saw Arthur taking part in patrols, either singly or in flights of three aircraft, looking for German fast surface, vessels which could have caused havoc amongst the ships trying to rescue the British Expeditionary Force. From the 27th to 30th May he flew each day for four hours and on the 31st made two flights - airborne at 05:23 landing at 09:40, then up again at 17:20 and returning at 22.34 p.m.

Once the evacuation was over, Arthur was again involved in escorting convoys. His report of 10th June describes an attempt to bomb German E-boats, although without success. His navigator suggested that they should use more and smaller bombs. The E-boats were well armed and other squadron aircraft had been lost in similar attacks. He reported a large fire in Dunkirk on 21st June and fired at a floating mine on the 25th. In all, Arthur flew 15 operational sorties in June.

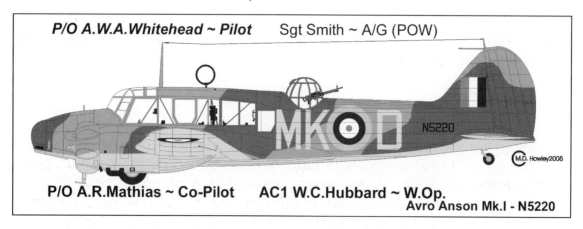

P/O A.W.A.Whitehead ~ Pilot   Sgt Smith ~ A/G (POW)

MK D   N5220

P/O A.R.Mathias ~ Co-Pilot   AC1 W.C.Hubbard ~ W.Op.
Avro Anson Mk.I - N5220

Other tasks included reconnaissance of the occupied Channel ports. Following two convoy escorts on the 7th and 9th July, Arthur was detailed on the 11th for a HOOKOS - a patrol of the Hook of Holland and Ostend areas. They took off at 21:15 and failed to return.

The fate of Whitehead's Anson and crew was discovered by Dutch friends with an interest in their local history. They found

a reference in a contemporary diary, kept by a German Officer who was posted to the Hook of Holland during the war. The diary notes the time of the crash as 11:30 p.m. Dutch time and goes on to state:

"Thursday 11TH July 1940, an Avro Anson from No. 500 Squadron, on patrol between Ostend and Hook of Holland, crashed South-West of Hook of Holland. 3 pilots, Whitehead, Hubbard Mathias, were killed."

PHOTO EDDY VAN DRIEL

Sergeant Smith, the air gunner, survived the crash and was taken prisoner by the Germans.

Arthur Whitehead is commemorated on his parents' grave in Milford. Arthur, Pilot Officer A.P. Mathias and Aircraftsman W.C. Hubbard are buried together in **Rotterdam (Crooswijk) General Cemetery**.

Quote from CWGC about the Rotterdam cemetery:

"In May 1941, the local civil authorities set aside for Allied war casualties a plot in the immediate vicinity of the Dutch war graves. A number of British airmen were moved to this plot from other parts of the cemetery and from scattered graves in the surrounding countryside; and subsequent Allied casualties were buried there. These graves were constantly tended and provided with flowers by the people of Rotterdam, in contrast to the German graves, which were ignored. The enraged Germans therefore caused them to be removed, in May 1943, to the remotest corner of the cemetery. They were fenced off by wooden hurdles, and even for a short time guarded by an armed sentry to keep away visitors."

CYRIL RALPH DAY

Leading Seaman, Royal Navy
P/JX 133111
H.M.S. DELIGHT
who died on
Monday 29th July 1940, aged 27.

Cyril was the second son of Mr and Mrs Cyril George Day of "Sunnypatch," All Saints Road, Lymington. The family was a large one with a younger brother Sidney, who served in the Merchant Navy, two other brothers and two sisters. Cyril's father was a retired Royal Naval Petty Officer who, at the time of Cyril's death, was working as a Customs Officer at Lymington.

Through his father's service Cyril went to the Greenwich Naval School when he was 13 years old. He then joined the Royal Navy and by 1939 he was serving with the Far East Fleet in China. He returned home early in 1940 to join DELIGHT – a sister ship to DARING (see page 228). Six of the eight destroyers of this class were lost in the war.

HMS DELIGHT   PHOTO 1935 WRIGHT & LOGAN

Cyril was on home leave in the beginning of July. Shortly after rejoining his ship she was subjected to an aircraft attack off Portland on 29th July 1940. The ship was badly damaged, set on fire and later sank in Portland harbour.

Out of a complement of 145 men, six ratings - including Cyril - died of wounds and three officers (including Commander Fogg-Elliott, the ship's captain) and fifty-seven ratings were wounded.

Cyril was accorded a Naval funeral on Friday 9th August.

He is buried in **Portland Naval Cemetery**, Dorset, in:

Grave 690.

PHOTO NICK SAUNDERS

245

EDGAR BROWN

Quartermaster
73167
HMS WILNA
who died on
Thursday 8th August 1940, aged 22.

Edgar Brown was the youngest of the three sons of Mr and Mrs R. Brown of "Ringwood", Southampton Road, Lymington. As a boy he went to the local Church of England School and was a member of the 9th Lymington Sea Scouts. One of his brothers, Albert, was called up as a Sergeant in the 5th Hampshire Regiment when war was declared, whilst his other brother worked at a local factory.

In 1940 Edgar was called up for the Naval Auxiliary Personnel (Merchant Navy) and served with the Yacht Patrol. This unit comprised private yachts requisitioned by the Admiralty on the outbreak of war. They were then given light armament and used for coastal convoy duties.

He was drafted as quartermaster to WILNA, a modern vessel of 461 tons, built in 1939. In May of that year she was hired by the Admiralty, as part of its preparation for war. The ship was then armed with a 4-inch gun and given two machine-guns for anti-aircraft protection. From the outbreak of war she was used for escorting coastal convoys up and down the English Channel.

On Thursday 15th August WILNA was yet again escorting a Channel convoy when she was attacked by enemy aircraft. This first large-scale enemy attack on a convoy left Edgar dead and another Lymington man, William Woodford - who lived with his parents at 66 Flushards Estate badly wounded. William actually lost his left arm below the elbow. Lymington Rovers, for whom he had played, raised a benefit fund for him.

*"He deserves everything that can be done
to give him a good start in life."*

Edgar was buried a week later. The coffin was draped with the Union Jack and there were many flowers. The Reverend M R Bethune conducted the funeral, which was attended by friends and relatives and Edgar's fiancée, Miss Hogan.

WILNA was finally sunk by enemy aircraft off Portsmouth on 24th March 1941, whilst on escort duties with another convoy.

Edgar is buried in **Lymington Cemetery**, in:

**Consolidated Plot
Grave 863**

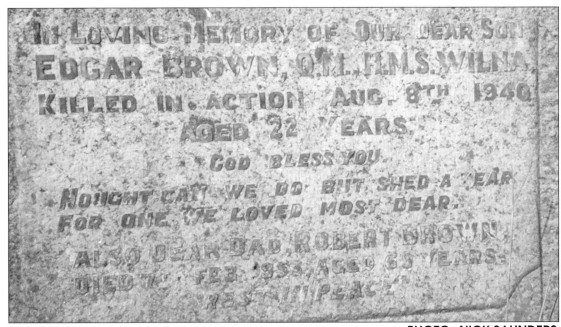

ROBERT JOHN DASHWOOD

Ordinary Seaman, Royal Navy
P/JX 192481
H.M.S. ESK
who died on
Sunday 1st September 1940, aged 20.

Bob was one of the sons of Charles and Annie Dashwood of 20, Hazel Road, Pennington. In April 1945 a younger brother,

Richard, was captured in Germany whilst serving with the Royal Scots Fusiliers. Another brother, Charles, served in the REME in North Africa and Italy; whilst another brother, Peter, also joined the Royal Navy.

According to his sister Catherine - herself in the WRNS - Bob's chief interest as a boy was singing, particularly in St Mark's Church where he was Head Choirboy from a very early age. He was also a member of the church's Social Club, swam in the Lymington Swimming Club water polo team and was a keen and popular member of Lymington Rovers Football Club. In September 1940 the Rovers reported that the club had 50 members serving in His Majesty's Forces and 30 serving in Home Defence.

Bob's love of the sea, inherited no doubt from his grandfather – a Chief Boatswain in the Coastguard Service and a Royal Navy pensioner – and his seafaring father, took him into the 9th Lymington Sea Scouts. From there he became a founder member of the Oxey (Pennington) Sea Scouts. He served his grocery apprenticeship with Mr Rowland Hill in Lymington.

Bob joined the Navy at the outbreak of war and, after signals training at COLLINGWOOD – where this picture was taken - was sent to join the ship's company of ESK. She was an "E" Class destroyer built in 1934 and was one of the two ships of this class to be equipped as minelayers.

HMS ESK   **PHOTO NMM N3046**

On 31st August 1940 ESK, EXPRESS and INTREPID– reinforced by ICARUS and IVANHOE of the same 20th Destroyer Flotilla - sailed from Immingham on a mine-laying mission off the Dutch coast. They were escorted by KELVIN, JUPITER and VORTIGERN from the 5th Destroyer Flotilla. Aerial reconnaissance detected a German force and – believing, wrongly, that these ships were part of a German invasion force - the destroyers were ordered to intercept. In the action EXPRESS struck a mine and was badly damaged. ESK went to her assistance and hit another mine and sank immediately. IVANHOE also went to her assistance, hit a third mine and was so badly damaged that she had to be sunk by KELVIN. EXPRESS was towed back to Hull and took 13 months to repair.

PHOTO NICK SAUNDERS

ESK sank in less than two minutes at 11.25 p.m. with the loss of 9 officers and 151 ratings. Robert was one of the many crewmen whose bodies were not recovered. His name is therefore inscribed on the **Portsmouth Naval Memorial** on:

Panel 39, Column 3

DAVID ROWLANDS DIMMICK

Sergeant
T/187639
Royal Army Service Corps
Who died on
Saturday 26th April 1941, aged 28.

David was the second son of the Reverend F T Dimmick and his wife, Florence, of Kingsfield, Woking. The Reverend Fred was a well-known Lymingtonian and a former Minister of Milford Baptist Church.

David attended the Brockenhurst County High School from 1923-1928 and left to be an accountant in the office of Messrs Jackman and Masters in Lymington. David's brother Paul also worked with this firm before taking up an appointment with Woking Council. At the time of David's death Paul had been temporarily released from the army for urgent valuation work for the Government. Paul was a keen musician and was the organist at Milford Baptist Church whilst his father was the Minister. An elder brother, Corporal F T I Dimmick, was also serving in the Royal Army Service Corps.

In 1941 Hitler and Mussolini turned their attention towards Greece. On 1st March they occupied Bulgaria and by 24th March Yugoslavia had joined the Axis Powers - although this was reversed three days later when a military takeover occurred. A German invasion had, however, been foreseen and a month earlier an Expeditionary Force of 57,000 British, ANZAC and Polish had begun to land to support the Greek army.

On 6th April Hitler invaded both Yugoslavia and Greece. Over-stretched Allied forces swiftly crumbled in the face of a blitzkrieg attack and a withdrawal and evacuation were rapidly organised. Despite the absence of friendly air cover 43,000 Imperial soldiers were evacuated over the nights of 26th-27th and 27th-28th April.

250

Unfortunately, David was not amongst those saved. He was initially reported as missing. Six months later the distress of his wife, Nora, was increased when 40 letters that she had written to him between December 1940 and May 1941 were returned to her.

There was still no news of him in November 1941 and it was finally ascertained that he had been lost at the time of the evacuation.

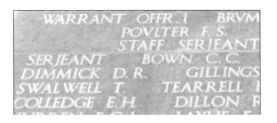

As his body was never found, David's name is recorded on the **Athens Memorial, Greece**:

PHOTOGRAPHS DON CORDING

Face 8.

JAMES LAWRENCE

Private
5498441
1st Battalion, The Hampshire Regiment,
Who died on
Sunday 9th-10th November 1941, aged 25.

James was the son of Charles and Frances Lawrence of Stony Marsh, Hampshire. By 1940 Charles had moved to *Rosemary*, at Everton.

James was called up in 1939 and joined the Hampshires. When war was declared the 1st Battalion of the Hampshire Regiment was stationed in Egypt. In December 1939 they moved to Palestine to help keep the peace between the Jews and the Arabs. However, on 2nd June 1940 they moved back to the Canal Zone and when Italy declared war on the allies the battalion moved into defensive positions at Mersa Matruh. The expected invasion did not materialise.

On 21st February 1941 the battalion left Egypt for Malta, sailing on the fast cruisers ORION and AJAX. In Malta the Hampshires joined the 2nd Devons and the 1st Dorsets to form 231 Brigade, whose role was to defend Safi airstrip and part of Luqa airfield

against airborne attack.

Towards the end of 1941 the German Luftwaffe moved to Sicily and gained mastery of the air in the Mediterranean to such an extent that no convoys were run to Malta between November 1941 and March 1942.

John Mizzi, of The Royal British Legion in Malta, has reported that the period over which James was killed were "ordinary" days for Malta at that time. The bombing was sporadic and not at one specific spot and the Situation Report for that day and night does not specify any one location.

Although James experienced all this as his battalion guarded the two airfields, the War Diary records, for 9th November:

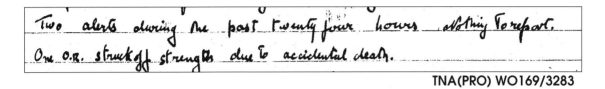

TNA(PRO) WO169/3283

He is buried in **Pembroke Military Cemetery**, Malta, in:

Collective Grave 1. 4. 8.

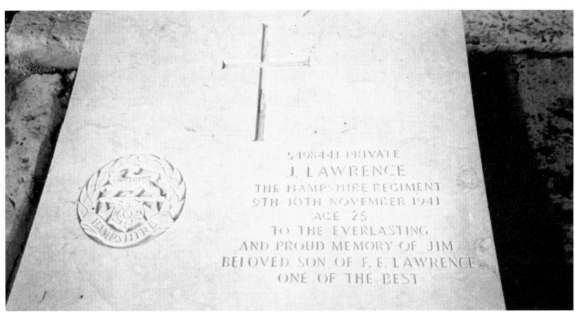

PHOTOGRAPHS BY COURTESY TRBL MALTA

ROBERT HUGH BYGOTT

Lieutenant, Royal Navy
H.M. Submarine P 33
who died on
Wednesday, 20ᵗʰ August 1941, aged 21

Bobby Bygott was the elder son of Hugh Cecil Bygott and grandson of the Reverend John Parkinson Bygott, who was vicar of Longdon, near Litchfield, for some forty years. Roger, the younger son, has written this memorial. Hugh had been a subaltern in the Irish Guards and after the war was training to be an electrical engineer. He died of meningitis in 1925. Bobby's mother, Joyce Mary Hadfield (nee Wire), had connections with Lymington as her father, who died in 1911, was an architect. He had designed some houses along Beaulieu River and also restored part of the abbey. The Wire family lived at Blakes, in Walhampton. Joyce's great grandfather, a lawyer, was Lord Mayor of London in about 1852 and her maternal uncle, Sir Robert Hadfield, was a very famous metallurgist in Sheffield.

In 1928 Joyce married again another parson's son – Flight Lieutenant John Horton Woodin RAF – whose father was Rector of Yarmouth, Isle of Wight. John, or Jack, as he was known, flew flying boats out of RAF CALSHOT. Joyce and Jack bought Gordleton Mill at Sway and had a daughter, Anne. Jack Woodin was an excellent stepfather to Bobby and Roger.

Bobby attended a prep school at Highfield, Liphook and left at age thirteen to become a cadet at RNC Dartmouth. This photo was taken about 1936. His passion was sailing and he was able to keep Jack's boat, a Montague Sharpie, there part of the time

Bobby joined the modern cruiser, SHEFFIELD, as a midshipman on 1st January 1938 and early in the war was involved on convoy work to Russia. In February 1940 he was commissioned Sub-Lieutenant RN and posted to the battleship NELSON. He was at Dunkirk in May/June 1940 in charge of a rescue launch and was wounded by a shell, which damaged his wrist and destroyed his wristwatch.

His interest in submarines was stimulated by the fact that Jack Woodin had two family connections with well-known submariners – Admiral Max Horton RN and Commander Holbrook VC RN. Bobby joined the submarine training course at DOLPHIN, Gosport, on 30th September 1940 and completed six weeks later. On 12th December he was posted to the submarine USK, working out of Portsmouth. In a letter he wrote to his cousin, Leo, he commented :

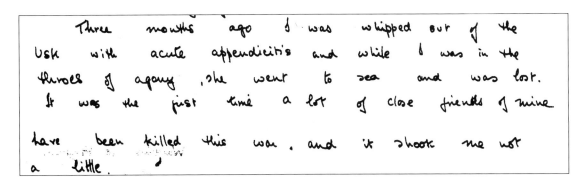

Three months ago I was whipped out of the USK with acute appendicitis and while I was in the throes of agony, she went to sea and was lost. It was the first time a lot of close friends of mine have been killed this war, and it shook me not a little.

Bobby was promoted to Lieutenant in July 1941 and posted to UPHOLDER in Malta. In May he had his twenty first birthday and received a number of cheques. He wrote to his cousin Leo:

"I and another chap out here decided in view of my suddenly acquired wealth to buy a little dinghy we had wanted for a long time and so we bought it this morning."

The photograph shows Bobby sailing in Malta.

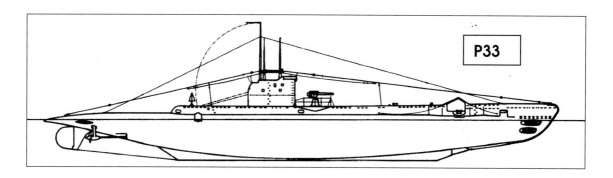

He was posted to P33 in August 1941. P 33 was a modern "U" class Group II, which had been laid down at Vickers Armstrong in Barrow-in-Furness in June 1940. Launched in January 1941 and completed on 30th May it was a smallish submarine displacing 658 tons at full load. Armed with four 21-inch bow torpedoes it was crewed by 4 officers and 29 ratings. Its operational range was 5,500 nautical miles at 10 knots.

On 6th August she sailed from Malta to attack one of the Italian convoys re-supplying Libya. Nothing further was heard from the submarine and there were no survivors. Naval records state that she was probably mined off Tripoli.

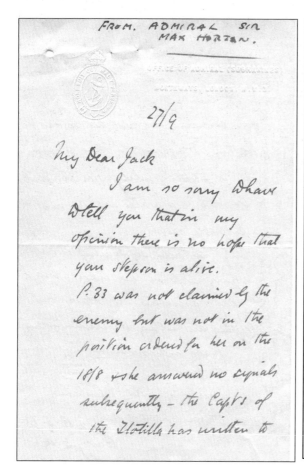

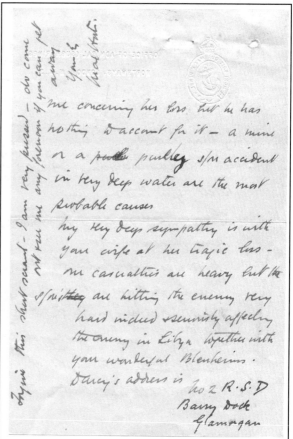

In October 2000 Brian Cox, a neighbour of Anne, wrote to the Submarine Museum requesting information, on her behalf, about her late brother. Part of the letter read:

> *My neighbour was a child of only ten years old, and an evacuee from London, living in a hostel or similar in Cornwall. On the day in question, she was happily playing with other children, gradually becoming dextrous with the intricacies of a Yo - Yo. Her mind was totally concentrated on her efforts, her skill, or her lack of it, when the toy went somewhat high. At that moment, she suddenly became aware of her brother Bobby's face in the overcast sky above her, and she was immediately struck by his look of distress. As she says, "I instantly felt that I wanted to reach up and hug him." Apparently she told no-one, but she vividly remembers, that, in bed that night, she desperately cried herself to sleep. She was a lonely evacuee, and there was no-one with whom she felt she could share her distress.*
>
> *Several days later, a school teacher called her aside and was about to gently take her into a quiet room, when she was totally astonished to learn that her pupil already knew that her brother was dead, and all she could utter, was, "Why, why, have I been asked to tell you this terribly sad news again, when someone has already told you," In fact nobody ever gave her any positive news, either earlier, then, or later.*

PHOTO NICK SAUNDERS

P33 was overdue on 20th August 1941 and officially posted as missing three days later. Robert's name is therefore recorded on the **Portsmouth Naval Memorial:**

Column 1 of Panel 45

GEOFFREY CLEMENT COOKE

Captain, Royal Navy
H.M.S. BARHAM
who died on
Tuesday 25th November 1941, aged 51

Born on 20th March 1890, **Geoffrey** was the youngest son of the late Mr Henry Cooke of Whittlebury, Hampstead. Between the wars Geoffrey and his wife, Constance May, lived at Farnley, Belmore Lane.

Geoffrey was a career naval officer who had joined Dartmouth as a cadet in 1905, in one of the last terms under the BRITANNIA scheme. In January 1907 he passed out as Midshipman to the battleship CORNWALLIS. He was promoted Sub-Lieutenant in April 1910 and Lieutenant in July 1912. As a watch-keeper in the light cruiser FEARLESS he was present at the Heligoland Bight action on 28th August 1914. In December 1915 he was appointed to the destroyer ATTENTIVE in the Dover Patrol, moved to a sister-ship, ACTIVE, in 1917, but in April of that year returned to ATTENTIVE as its gunnery officer. A year later he returned to FEARLESS, which at that stage was senior officer's ship of the 1st Submarine Flotilla.

Between the wars Geoffrey served in the cruisers CHESTER, INCONSTANT and YARMOUTH and the battleship EMPEROR OF INDIA, both in home waters and the Mediterranean. Early in 1925 he became the senior Lieutenant Commander in the training ship IMPREGNABLE at Plymouth and was promoted to Commander on 30th June 1926. During the next two years he commanded PETERSFIELD in China, before serving on the staff of HMS ST VINCENT, a training establishment at Gosport, Portsmouth. When promoted to Captain on 30th June 1933 he became the Commander of the battleship RODNEY, later commanding CALCUTTA and the net-layer GUARDIAN.

In February 1938, he was appointed Deputy Director of Naval Intelligence at the Admiralty, where he served until 1940, when he was appointed Captain of BARHAM - a Queen Elizabeth Class battleship of 27,500 tons completed in December 1914. A heavily armoured Dreadnought she had director-controlled 15-inch and 6-inch guns and was capable of nearly 25 knots.

BARHAM's war had been mainly spent in the Mediterranean. At 4.30 p.m. on 25th November 1941, whilst patrolling with the battle fleet south of Crete, she was hit by three torpedoes fired by U-331. This U-boat had come undetected right through the destroyer screen and fired her torpedoes 200 yards ahead of the battleship. She then broke surface and passed so close down the side of the following battleship, VALIANT, that the latter could not depress her guns sufficiently to hit the submarine.

BARHAM SINKING

BARHAM soon listed to port and men began to collect on her upper side. After a couple of minutes, however, a main magazine detonated and the ship disappeared within five minutes of being attacked. Vice-Admiral Pridham-Wippell and nearly 450 survivors were rescued, but Geoffrey Cooke, 55 other officers and 806 men were killed.

Their names are all recorded on the **Portsmouth Naval Memorial** on

Panel 45, Column 1

JOHN RICHARD WELSH AFM

Squadron Leader
Royal Air Force
who died on
Friday 27th September 1940, aged 41.

John was a son of Thomas Welsh MBE and Kate Welsh. He later married Edith and in 1939 the family was living at Littlecot, Milford Road, Pennington.

The first indication of Squadron Leader Welsh's career is the entry in the Air Force list for 1929 on the occasion of his promotion to Warrant Officer on 1st August that year. Further achievements are recorded with the award of the Air Force Medal in August 1930. It has not been possible to discover the exact reasons for the award but eligibility is quoted for:

"exceptional valour, courage or devotion to duty whilst flying, though not in active operations against the enemy".

Obviously John was involved in some form of development work as he was posted to the Marine Aircraft Experimental Establishment at Felixstowe in April 1932. His seniority date of 20th July 1934 resulted in a posting to RAF WORTHY DOWN in Hampshire where No. 7 Squadron, commanded by Bert Harris (later Marshall of the Royal Air Force Sir Arthur Harris KCB CB OBE, Commander of Bomber Command), operated Vickers Virginia bombers. In 1935 the squadron re-equipped with another biplane bomber - the Handley Page Heyford. In December 1936 John moved to RAF DRIFFIELD in Yorkshire where Bomber Squadrons 75 and 215 were in residence - both equipped with Handley Page Harrows.

This posting lasted for just a year before John was sent overseas to the British Forces in Iraq, which consisted of stations at Basra, Diwaniyah, Shalbak and the headquarters at Habbiniya. He took up this post in February 1938 and on 14th April 1939 received his commission as a Flight Lieutenant. He is listed as part of the decorated team of Signals staff consisting of Squadron Leader JG Weston MBE as the Chief Signals officer, F.O. FWG Aggett MBE and himself with the AFM.

By 1940 John is listed under the Active List as a Commissioned Signals officer – Technical Branch. To have risen through the ranks in such a manner indicates he probably entered the Royal Air Force under the Aircraft Apprentice Scheme that was started in 1920 at RAF HALTON.

The 1930s was a period of expansion in the field of air to ground communication and radio navigation. The Middle East was an important destination and staging post for the expanding civil passenger airlines on their journeys into Africa, as well as the military's need to be able to communicate and navigate over this difficult terrain. John Welsh would no doubt have been involved in the technical aspects of this specialisation.

PHOTO CWGC

His Death Certificate indicates that he died on 28th September 1940 in the 15th Scottish General Hospital in Cairo from injuries sustained from an accidental fall. He is buried in **Cairo War Cemetery** in:

Grave P. 258.

WILLIAM HENRY SCOTT BADCOCK

Squadron Leader
75559
Royal Air Force
Who died on
Monday 16ᵗʰ March 1941, aged 59.

THE LYMINGTON TIMES of Saturday 26ᵗʰ April 1941 reported:

"The death has occurred on Active Service in the Middle East of Squadron Leader William Henry Scott Badcock, RAF, who was a retired Captain in the R.A.M.C.

The deceased officer, who was a native or Lymington, had had a long and distinguished career in the Army and R.A.F; extending over a period or 40 years with a break of two years after his retirement in 1937.

The only son of the late Mr. Henry Badcock, chemist, and Mrs. Badcock - one of the oldest families in Lymington – the deceased officer- joined the, R.A.M.C. in 1900 as a private, but quickly rose to the rank of Sergeant. He saw service in the South African War and Cape Colony, receiving the South African medal with three bars and later did foreign service in Mauritius.

He served in France through out the 1914-18 war as a Sergeant Major and was several times mentioned in' dispatches.

He was the proud possessor of the 1914 Star and of the Meritorious Service Medal for long-service and good conduct, while he was also awarded the Jubilee medal.

Shortly after the Armistice he was sent to Singapore for 3 years and received his commission in 1924. He went East again in 1930, when he served in Shanghai for three years and was promoted Captain. On returning home in 1934, be was stationed at the Military Hospital. Colchester, and he retired in 1937 with the rank of Captain in the R.AM.C.

In May 1939 he joined the R.A.F. receiving his equivalent rank of Flight Lieutenant, and was stationed at an aerodrome in Scotland. In June 1940, due to his efficiency, he was promoted Squadron Leader and was sent overseas to the Middle East in November last. On 2nd March 1941 he became a casualty and passed away on the 16th, being laid to rest on the 18th March.

He leaves a widow and three sons, two of whom are serving In the R.A.F., - while the youngest. is employed in a key occupation. He also leaves a sister, Miss Amy Badcock, who is living in St. Albans."

William was an officer in the 103rd Maintenance Unit of the Desert Air Force. According to his Death Certificate he died in the 8th General Hospital at Alexandria, Egypt, of **"Pleural effusion left,"** most likely caused by lung cancer.

He is buried in **Alexandria (Chatby) Military and War Memorial Cemetery** in:

Grave N. 135.

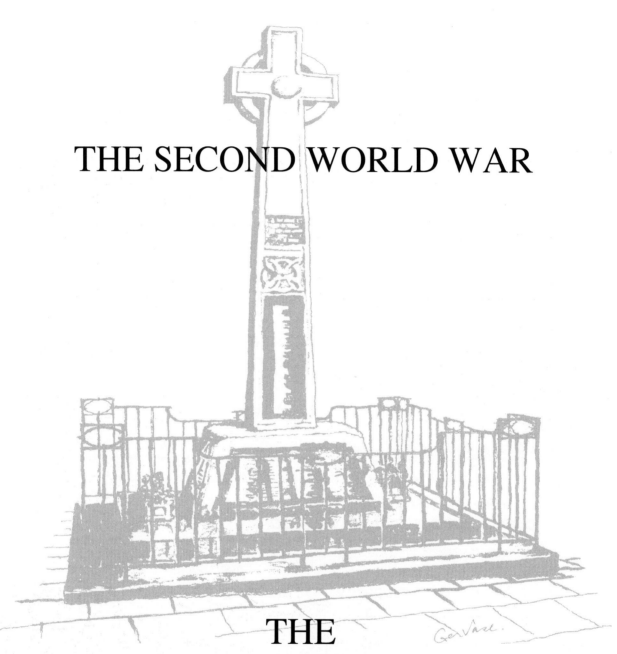

THE SECOND WORLD WAR

THE
NORTH AFRICAN
AND
ITALIAN CAMPAIGNS

THE NORTH AFRICAN AND ITALIAN CAMPAIGNS

The fighting in North Africa was initially against Italian forces and resulted in a number of early victories. The campaign was weakened at vital moments by the need to send in theatre forces to Greece and then the Far East, which destabilised allied plans in North Africa. When Germany inserted its own units to bolster its Italian ally the action became more difficult and fortune swung backwards and forwards, depending on Rommel's supply situation and who was commanding British Forces.

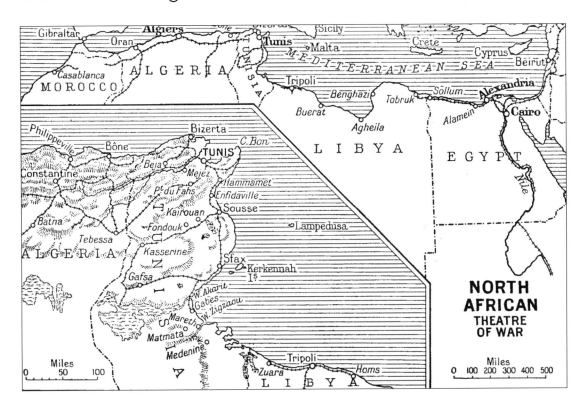

The appointment of Montgommery to command the 8th Army and his conduct of the battle of El Alamain was one of the early turning points of the war. The invasion of Algiers by Anglo/American forces, code-named TORCH, under Eisenhower and the appointment of General Alexander in overall command of the 1st and the 8th British Armies made ultimate victory possible. Sadly **John Napier** and **James Wort** were to be killed before it was achieved.

Victory in North Africa took pressure off Malta, which had been a lynchpin for our operations in the Mediterranean.

Once Axis forces had been defeated **Sicily** could then be invaded as the springboard to the invasion of Italy. *Peter White* was not to recover from the injuries he received when his fighter crashed in Sicily whilst he was working-up to support the invasion of the Salerno beaches

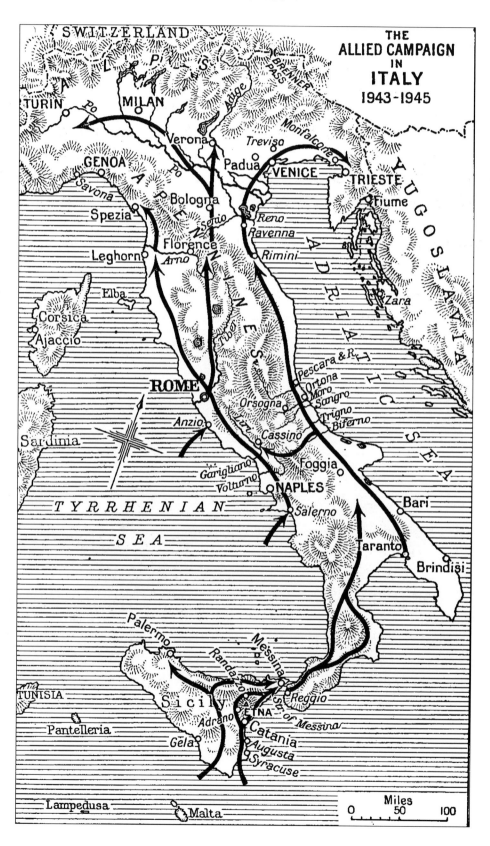

THE
ALLIED CAMPAIGN
IN
ITALY
1943-1945

The Italian campaign, which lasted for the remainder of the war, was to cost Lymington dearly.

Roderick McLeod, Charles Wittingstall and *Cecil Freeman* all died in attempting to break out of the Salerno bridgehead.

As the allies fought their way up the increasingly mountainous spine of Italy, with its plethora of easily defensible rivers, so the German defence hardened. Conditions were frequently cold and wet and fighting took on the trench characteristics of the First World War. *Sidney Bran,* and *Frederick Haywood* were lost in the long fight for Cassino. *Roy Wilson, Robert Williams-Freeman, Thomas Race, Leonard Brown, Joseph Chamberlain* and *Edgar Holloway* were all killed or died of wounds in Italy.

Stanley Clark, of the RAF, was killed in a road accident.

Walter Hawkins was killed in his LC(G), as was *Robert Collins* in his cruiser, both off Anzio.

AFRICA STAR   **ITALY STAR**

JOHN MORILLYON NAPIER MC

Captain
108067
Royal Armoured Corps
Who died on
21st November 1941, aged 26.

John was the second son of the Reverend Arthur Wilson Napier M.A. and Isobel of Boldre Hill, Lymington. Arthur himself had been born in 1871 in Devonport and had held benefices in Hampshire and Dorset, but retired to Boldre hill where, during the war, he commanded the local Home Guard. The eldest son, Captain Lennox Napier DSO DSC RN, had a distinguished naval career - as had his grandfather, Admiral Gerard Napier.

John was commissioned into the 7th (Queen's Own) Hussars and joined the regiment in North Africa as a Second Lieutenant on 26th January 1941. He became an acting Lieutenant in March and was awarded the Military Cross whilst regimental navigator. He clearly impressed, as he was made Adjutant, with its associated captain's rank, on 20th July.

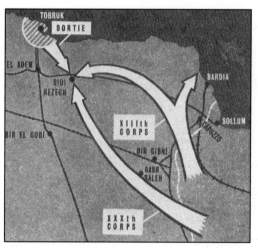

On 16th November orders for the advance, to sweep the enemy right out of Cyrenaica, were given. The aim was for the XXXth Corps to trail its coat for the enemy armour, which would respond and be smashed. Tobruk would then be relieved and Rommel forced to retreat. Two days later the regiment, with its mix of A10 and A15 tanks, advanced with B Squadron in the lead. Towards dusk two enemy vehicles were destroyed. The next morning an enemy camp was identified, but the arrival of a strong force of enemy armour dictated caution. The regiment was then directed to take the airfield at Sidi Rezegh to the north. This was done and prisoners and aircraft captured.

At dawn on 20th November the enemy attempted to recapture the airfield, but were beaten off. In the afternoon the regiment was dive-bombed by Stukas, but without any damage being done.   The next day the regiment were guarding the flank of the assault group, who were tasked with capturing the ridge beyond the airfield, when it was attacked by about fifty enemy tanks. C Squadron was sent to help A and B Squadrons, but the enemy penetrated between A Squadron and RHQ. John's tank was hit and his spare tank also knocked out. This meant that both links to brigade were now out of action and the regiment was on its own.

John died the next day of his wounds. He is buried in the:

Knightsbridge War Cemetery

Acroma, Libya, in:

Grave 4. D. 19.

PHOTO CWGC

The remainder of the action is worth telling.

B Squadron was reduced to two tanks left in action and the regiment started to withdraw, engaging the enemy closely. At this stage of the battle the Colonel was killed and the enemy got between the regiment and brigade. The regiment now comprised twelve tanks, some of which had mobility and main armament problems.   It was also totally surrounded. As the War Diary noted:

"It was going to be a difficult problem to rejoin our brigade."

The remaining tanks slipped through two enemy columns and made contact with 22nd Armoured Brigade. Unfortunately John's unit was identified as the enemy, so no help was received. The situation was so desperate that the remnants were patched up and kept in battle until the 25th November, when it consisted of two serviceable tanks and a Dingo armoured car.

Despite the initial setback Torbruk was relieved on the 27th November.

JAMES HENRY CHARLES WORT

Private
5500656
5th Battalion, The Hampshire Regiment
Who died on
Friday 26th February 1943, aged 23.

James was the son of Mr & Mrs J Wort, who lived at 10 Bath Road, in Lymington.

After leaving school James worked in a local factory, and with a number of other local lads joined the 5th/7th Hampshire Regiment (Territorial Army) before the outbreak of war. In 1939 the 1/4th, 2/4th and 5th Hampshire Territorial battalions formed the 128th Brigade of the 43rd (Wessex) Division. In 1940 this brigade became part of GHQ Mobile Reserve before moving to East Kent for coastal defence duties.

In 1941 he married Irene Lilian of Raynes Park, Surrey, and a son was born in March 1942.

In August 1942 128 Brigade became part of 46th Division and on 6th January 1943 James embarked with his unit on the LEOPOLDVILLE at Gourock for North Africa.

The brigade arrived at Bone on 17th January and by the end of the month occupied a defensive position astride Hunts Gap. 5 HAMPS were posted, with 155 Battery RA, 12 miles ahead at Sidi Nsir to blunt the expected attack on the main position. The German Commander, General Von Arnim attacked Sidi Nsir on 26th February using three battalions of parachute troops and heavy tanks. By evening, the battalion and the 9 survivors of its supporting 25 Pounder battery withdrew, having stopped an enemy who were desperately determined to break through to Hunts Gap.

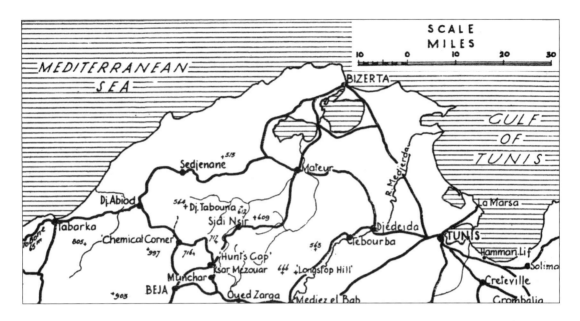

The 200 survivors of the battalion then occupied a portion of the defences at Hunts Gap and awaited their next battle. By 2nd March the German attack at Hunts Gap was finally defeated, although the brigade remained in contact with the enemy there until early April.

James was one of those killed in the ferocious German attack on Sidi Nsir.

PHOTO CWGC

He is buried in **Beja War Cemetery**, Tunisia, in

Grave 1. E. 8.

271

PETER LEONARD WHITE

Sergeant Pilot
Royal Air Force Volunteer Reserve
who died on
Tuesday 19th October 1943, aged 23.

Peter was the only son of Mrs Brown of Eastern Road, Lymington, by her first marriage.

He joined the RAF when he was seventeen years old and later qualified as a fighter pilot. By 1943 he was in Malta as the allied forces were built up for the liberation of Sicily and Italy.

He was initially assigned to 683 photo-reconnaissance squadron. This unit was led by the famous Wing Commander Warburton DSO* DFC** and operated various marks of PR Spitfire, although Peter does not appear to have made any operational flights with them.

On August 13th 1943, Peter joined No. 1437 Strategical Reconnaissance Flight, which was operating from Francesco landing ground in the recently occupied Sicily. They were operating Mustang aircraft, which they flew as pairs, for low level observation of military and transport targets. They would also attack these targets and the resultant anti-aircraft fire was particularly hazardous.

Probably as a result of their losses, two Spitfire Vbs were issued to the Flight on 16th August. However, the performance of the Spitfire was felt to be inferior to the Mustang and not suitable for operations. It was therefore used to provide flying practice for pilots waiting to go on operations.

It was while undertaking such practice that Peter crashed on landing at Lentini in the South east of Sicily. Despite being bravely rescued from the burning aircraft by two 81 Squadron airmen, he suffered severe injuries.

Sgt P.L.White

Supermarine Spitfire Vb Trop.   ER 532

He was hospitalised in Sicily and his mother immediately sent him cablegrams and airmail letters to the Field Hospital to which he was reported to have been admitted.

She was therefore surprised and grieved to hear later, from a padre, that during the eight weeks that he lived after his accident, her son did not receive any of her messages. This was apparently due to the fact that he was moved to a hospital in North Africa and that either her messages were not forwarded to him, or were lost in transit.

Peter is buried in the **Medjez-el-Bab** War Cemetery, Tunisia, in:

Grave 13.A.2

RODERICK CAMPBELL McLEOD

Lieutenant
186926
2nd Battalion, The Scots Guards,
who died on
Saturday 11th September 1943, aged 21.

Roderick was born on 4th October 1921, the eldest son and heir of Sir Murdoch Campbell McLeod, 2nd Baronet, and Lady McLeod (nee Whitehead) of Pennington. His father was an East India merchant who served with the Seaforth Highlanders in the First World War. His mother was the daughter of Henry Hammond Whitehead JP, of Pelham Crescent, London. Sir Murdoch died in 1950 and was succeeded by Roderick's only brother Charles. His mother - Lady McLeod - died in 1964.

Roderick joined the army from Winchester School at the beginning of the war and was commissioned into the Scots Guards. The 2nd Battalion had fought in the North African campaign since April 1941as part of the 201st Guards Brigade. Towards the end of the campaign, on 6th March 1943, the battalion took part in the battle of Medenine. Ten days later the brigade attacked the Horseshoe feature five miles to the northwest, which screened the Germans final position of the Mareth Line. The attack, with over 400 men killed, wounded or missing, was described by the regimental historian as

"One of the most terrible nights in the history of the Guards."

Roderick's battalion returned to this position on 26th March. Two days later he was wounded, two of his men killed and four others wounded whilst crossing a minefield. That night the Germans evacuated the Mareth Line. They surrendered on the 12th May and the North African campaign was over.

Roderick rejoined his battalion and was posted as a platoon commander to F Company. On the 5th September the brigade sailed for the beaches of Salerno and the invasion of Italy.

The battalion landed at midday on 9th September. The beachhead had been secured and by last light it had married up with its vehicles in the assembly area. A limited night march brought it to a mile and a half short of the Tobacco Factory on an important crossroads. The War Diary states

"The situation in front is fluid, to say the least; and dawn is awaited with mixed feelings."

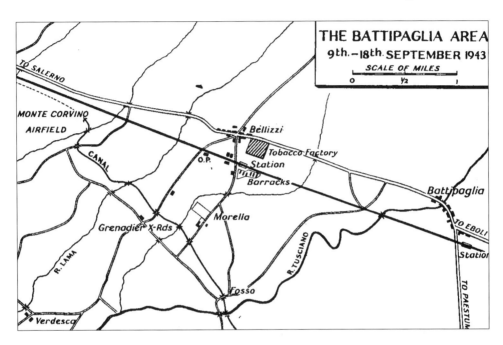

On the 10th it moved up to attack the Tobacco Factory. It was initially captured, but the War Diary goes on to say:

Summary of Events and Information.

Owing to the very heavy fire from the cross-roads and village, 'G' Coy. and L.F. had to withdraw *slightly* , the former retaining an O.P. on the railway line which was to become the most valuable place in the Battalion's position, and the latter evacuating the station and barracks. Lt. Fyfe-Jamieson got his platoon out of the station very well but got caught by his trousers on some wire. Sgt. Lumsden cut Lt. Fyfe-Jamieson's trousers off under heavy fire and both returned safely. R.F. also became involved in the fighting in the Barracks and Lt. Bowen-Colthurst was wounded in the hand.

The day was marred by the death in the morning of Capt. Sir H. Astley-Corbett when an 88 mm shell landed in Battalion Headquarters. Major Crichton-Stuart was badly, and Capt. Romer slightly, wounded. Two A/Tank gunners killed and three wounded. The Commanding Officer and Brigadier had miraculous escapes. As a result Lt. Phillipson took over command of 'F' Coy. The Padre was wounded by a bullet in the ribs.

The following other ranks were killed in action:-
2699435 L/Cpl. PEDDIE C., 2699109 Gdsn. JARVIE W.,2700447 Gdsn.
WILSON J.

TNA(PRO)WO171/1394

Roderick's company had so far been in reserve. On the night of the 11th three companies again attacked the objective, with F Company tasked to capture the crossroads. The Right Flank (RF), whose task it was to secure the Battipaglia-Salerno road, lost a number of men captured. G Company took the factory, but was forced once again to withdraw suffering casualties. F Company came under very heavy spandau fire from the crossroads.

PHOTO THELMA STOLLAR

Roderick and another subaltern were killed and two other company officers were reported missing. Apart from those captured the battalion suffered 3 officers and 11 other ranks killed in this attack.

The War Diary entry for the day after this attack laconically reports:

"Battalion slept and sorted itself out."

Roderick is buried in **Salerno War Cemetery**, Italy, in:

Grave II. A. 36.

CHARLES ARTHUR WHITTINGSTALL

Private
13048645
2nd/5Th Battalion, Queens Royal Regiment (West Surrey)
who died on
Friday 17th September 1943, aged 27.

Charlie was a son of George and Leonora Whittingstall who, in 1938, lived together in Pitmore Lane, Pennington. When he left school Charlie worked in the Post Office in Lymington, employed initially in 1932 as a Telegram Boy, but, according to a contemporary, Chris Saunders, in January 1937 he was promoted to postman.

WALTER DIBBS   HARRY LEWIS   LEN PLUMLEY
CHARLIE WITTINGSTALL

This picture has been kindly provided by Isabel Satherley. It was taken in the Post Office yard about 1935. Her father, Harry Lewis, has his hands on Charlie's shoulders.

Charlie joined the Queens Regiment when war was declared.

277

By 1943 he was part of the 2/5th Battalion, which was serving with its two sister battalions – the 2/6th and 2/7th battalions – in the 131st Brigade of 7th Armoured Division. This division was part of the follow up force, which landed three days after the initial beech assault at Salerno. It found itself in a small, increasingly overcrowded, beachhead where the enemy were resisting fiercely and the outcome was assessed as being very much in the balance. The crisis was over by the 15th, however, and on 18th September Charlie's battalion entered Battipaglia without resistance.

Charlie, however, was not with his mates as he had become a casualty in the first few days after his battalion landed.

PHOTO CWGC

Charlie is buried in **Naples War Cemetery** in:

Grave III H 4

CECIL FREEMAN

Corporal
5496466
1/4ᵗʰ Battalion, The Hampshire Regiment
who died on
Tuesday 28ᵗʰ September 1943, aged 28.

Cecil, or "Tic" as the family called him, was the son of George and Florence, who lived at 14, Flushards Estate, Lymington. He went to the local Council School until he was 14 years old and then worked in W H Smith's as a paperboy. His father was known in Lymington as "Punch," as he enjoyed entertaining the children, although his real work was as a labourer and with his donkey cart he would turn his hand to any local odd jobs.

Tic's eldest brother, Leslie, was born in 1904. He exaggerated his age and went for a soldier, serving in Ireland in the "Black and Tan" period. He gained his 2ⁿᵈ Class Certificate of Education in 1923 and became a Warrant Officer at an early age. Leslie married Maud Harvey, whose father was a local shepherd, in All Saints' Church, Woodside, in 1927. I am indebted to their daughter, Jean Smith, for this family information. Tic's other brother, Harold also joined the army.

Tic followed Leslie into the army and was posted to the 1ˢᵗ Battalion the Hampshire Regiment, which had gone to India in 1925. Tic joined them in 1937 in time to take part in the Frontier operations in the Khaisora valley against the followers of the Faqir of Ipi. Tic was wounded and returned to England in a hospital ship in 1937.

He was posted to the local 1/4th Territorial Battalion, as a Lance Corporal and was well known as a boxer and footballer. The Hampshire Brigade, comprising the 1/4th, 2/4th and the 5th Territorial Battalions, was sent to North Africa in early 1943 and played a full part in the campaign. It was recognised as a good fighting brigade and as such had been selected to be one of the three assault brigades of X Corps at Salerno.

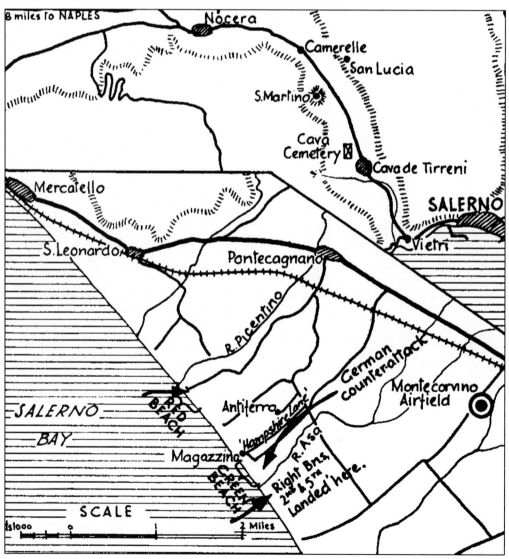

At 3.0 a.m. on 9th September 1943 the landing craft carrying Tic, now a Corporal, moved towards Red Beach and by nightfall had pressed forward to secure the northern flank of the bridgehead. His battalion then moved forward into the foothills above Salerno, occupying The Crag and White Cross Hill. On the 14th the Germans recaptured these positions and despite several determined Hampshire counterattacks remained in possession until their general withdrawal northwards six days later. Tic's battalion was then pulled out for a short rest, which included swimming in the sea.

By the 25th, however, they were back, joining the advance to Cava. They advanced on the village of San Lucia, suffering casualties from snipers and then took part in the capture of the terraced hill of San Martino.

Tic was amongst the 159 casualties incurred by the battalion since the landing. THE NEW MILTON ADVERTISER reported that he died of his wounds on the 28th September 1943.

FAMILY PHOTOS JEAN SMITH   PHOTO THELMA STOLLAR

He is buried in **Salerno War Cemetery**, Italy, in

Grave III. A. 13.

SIDNEY JOHN BRAN

Private
5509977
2nd Battalion, The Hampshire Regiment
Who died on
Sunday 30th January 1944, aged 31.

Sid was born in 1913 at Rose cottage, Pennington, to Jack and Eva May Bran. An older sister, Freda, was later to marry Cyril Hurst (see page 328). A younger sister, Ivy, died aged 10, of heatstroke and is buried in St Mark's churchyard. Jack was to die in 1940 at the age of 61.

Sid's wife, Joan, lived in Millbrook, Southampton. There were no children of the marriage and after the war she married an army vet and emigrated with him to Australia in 1954.

Sid joined the Hampshires in 1939 and served with the 2nd Battalion in France. After the battalion escaped from Dunkirk it was part of the coastal defensive scheme in Lincolnshire before sailing for North Africa on 11th November 1942.

The Hampshires played a full part in the defeat of Rommel in North Africa and fought particularly well at Tebourba, for which the battalion was subsequently awarded a Battle Honour. It then went on with the 128 (Hampshire) Brigade to invade Italy at Salerno and fight its way up country. By autumn the Brigade had crossed the Volturno River (see map page 266).

After a three-week rest in November the battalion went back to the front line and sent fighting patrols out towards the next German defensive line on the River Garigliano. Christmas was spent at a camp behind Monte Camino, but in mid January 1944 the battalion assembled for the assault crossing of the River Garigliano. The Hampshires were on the right of this disastrous attempt on 19th January. The Germans opened the sluice gates and the river was soon in flood.

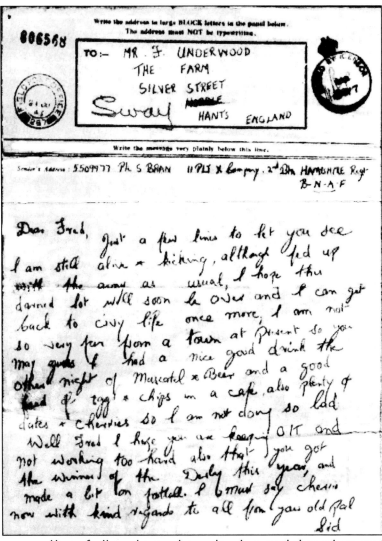

The battalion was withdrawn from the line and whilst "at rest" Sid sent this upbeat letter to an old friend in Sway.

Two days after the letter had been sent the battalion crossed the river further north, to support the attack on Monte Damino by the 1/4th Hampshires. The attack went in at 2.30 p.m. in bright sunlight on 29th January. Sid's battalion took over the following day, but could not capture the bare razor-backed feature. Sid was initially thought to be missing, with the hope that he might be a prisoner of war, but some time later his mother received a letter from Sid's platoon commander confirming his death. His name is recorded on the **Cassino Memorial**, Italy, on

PHOTO THELMA STOLLAR

Panel 7.

283

FREDERICK ARTHUR HAYWARD

Fusilier
5504827
2nd Battalion, Royal Fusiliers (City of London Regiment)
who died on
Friday 19th May 1944, aged 24.

Fred was one of the four sons of Frederick and Nellie Hayward of Lymington, the other brothers being Bill, Jack and Stan.

It is not known when Fred joined the army, but by 1944 his battalion was in Italy with 12 Brigade. On the 5th May 1944 the unit was relieved from the line at Cassino by the Guards Brigade. Two days later they found themselves camped next to the 1st Battalion and they held an impromptu "Fusilier Day" with sports, entertainments and a general party.

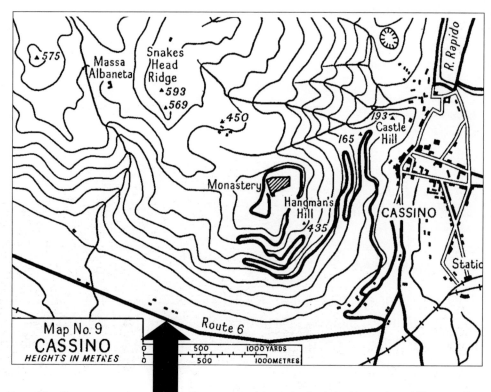

The battalion was soon thrown back into the battle. On the 17th, Cassino and the Monastery were virtually surrounded by 12 Brigade. As resistance crumbled the battalion was ordered to cut Route 6 to the south, in order to prevent the escape of the Cassino Garrison.

That night 57 deserters from the garrison gave themselves up. On the 18th May Major Thomas, of W Company, took a patrol up the mountain and claimed to be the first British troops to enter the Monastery. He brought back 28 Germans and the white tablecloth under cover of which they surrendered.

The next day the battalion moved further along Route 6. At 12.40 p.m. the enemy mortared the carriers of the Mortar and Pioneer platoons, which were stuck down a narrow lane. Two Fusiliers were killed outright and Fred was one of the 10 soldiers wounded in this attack.

Fred died from his wounds and is buried in **Cassino War Cemetery**, Italy, in

PHOTO THELMA STOLLAR

Grave VIII. E. 20.

Two days later the battalion suffered further casualties including its Commanding Officer, who was killed.

On 28th May, the battalion held a Remembrance Service in honour of the officers and men who had given their lives in the recent fighting.

PHOTO THELMA STOLLAR

ROY WILSON

Trooper
5573604
Royal Armoured Corps
Who died on
Tuesday 1st February 1944, aged 23.

Roy was born on 5th March 1920 to Albert and Ethel Wilson of Boldre. His father was a groomsman at the East Close Farm. Their marriage produced three sons – Bert, who served in the Pioneer Corps, Jack a Coldstream guardsman and Roy. There were also four daughters – Freda, Nora, Joan and Vera. The family later lived at Gorse Cottage, Sandy Down, Boldre.

Roy, who was keen on boxing, worked as a gardener until he joined the army early in the war. By 1942 he was serving with the 3rd Reconnaissance Regiment of the Royal Armoured Corps, in North Africa. On the 5th November Roy was reported ***"Missing"*** From a patrol. A Casualty Card was raised on him and his mother informed. A month later he was found by 571 Field Squadron RE. He sent this greeting card in 1942 or 1943.

PHOTOS CLIFF STRIDE

Roy then went on to serve with the 44th Reconnaissance Regiment in 56 Division, which took a very active part in the North African campaign fighting in Tunisia, before taking part in the invasion of Italy at Salerno on 9th September 1943.

Roy and his unit fought their way up Italy until, In January 1944 Roy's regiment, was pulled back for rest to Montanaro to reform after the disorganisation caused by its most recent battle.

At midnight on the 1st February Roy's regiment took over the line from the 8th Royal Fusiliers at Lorenzo. It suffered considerable shelling, during which Roy was killed. Mrs Wilson wrote to the War office requesting details of his death. Lieutenant Brodigan replied:

"Your son was in my troop and I was very proud of him. He was a very good soldier and always a cheerful comrade. I was terribly upset that morning he was killed. We were defending a small village and my troop were in a house next to a road leading to the German positions. At 7.30 in the morning the Germans landed a shell in the road next to the house, your son was just going out to take up his position at the time. He received a piece of shrapnel in the head and died instantaneously. I was just behind him when he fell and I can assure you that he suffered no pain at all.

Please accept my sincerest condolences in your tragic loss. Your son died a hero's death doing his duty for his country, and was missed by us all."

He is buried in **Minturno War Cemetery**, Italy, in

Grave I. H. 4.

287

ROBERT HENRY PEERE WILLIAMS-FREEMAN

Major
52624
Duke of Cornwall's Light Infantry
Who died on
Thursday 3rd February 1944, aged 32.

Robert was the only son of Lieutenant Colonel Arthur Peere Williams-Freeman DSO OBE and Mrs Williams-Freeman. Colonel Arthur was born on 21st February 1877, the son of the Reverend HP Williams-Freeman, the Rector of Affpuddle, Dorset. In 1908 he married Hilda Saunders and fathered one son – Robert – and two daughters. He was educated at Wellington and Sandhurst, joining the 1st Battalion the Duke of Cornwall's Light Infantry (1 DCLI) in 1897. He served in the Tirah Campaign (1897/8), the European War (1915/8) and retired in 1926. The family lived originally in Lyndhurst, but moved to Lymington in 1937, living at Bridge End Cottage. His interests were shooting and fishing.

PHOTO DCLI MUSEUM

Robert, who was born on 8th July 1911, was very much his father's son. Educated at his father's old school, he followed the tradition by passing out of Sandhurst and joining the DCLI - receiving his commission on 27th August 1931.

Robert joined the 1st Battalion in India. Promoted Lieutenant three years later, he commanded a platoon in D (Support) Company and later served in Battalion Headquarters. In 1935, whilst on leave in England he attended the Annual Regimental Dinner at Claridges, with his father.

Robert was an all-round sportsman and in India played for the battalion in the Dinapore Divisional Cup Hockey Tournament. Unfortunately they lost to the European Institute, a strong railway side, by 2-0. He was also a particularly fine golfer, with a handicap of 2. He was a popular member of the Brockenhurst Golf Club and in 1938, again on long leave from India, he won the championship of the Light Infantry Regiments at Camberley Heath Golf Club.

In 1938 the battalion moved from Bihar to the Punjab. On the outbreak of war, it took part in the rounding up of enemy nationals. Robert left them in early 1940 to take up the appointment of Adjutant to the Bristol University Signals Unit. On 29th June 1940 he married Cynthia Joan Young, in the Parish Church at Burnham-on-Sea, Somerset. Their son, Derek was born at Burnham on 12th September 1941.

On 28th April 1941 Robert was promoted Temporary Major and returned to his battalion six months later – which, by this time, was stationed in Iraq. In May 1942, however, it began the long road journey to North Africa, covering the 2000 miles in three weeks.

Robert went to the Army Staff College in 1942 and then became GSO2 of the 55th Division in England. Towards the end of 1943 he took up an appointment on the staff in North Africa and moved with an 8th Army formation to Italy.

On 17th January 1944 the River Garigliano was crossed and the bridgehead was stabilised a week later. Robert arrived there on the 25th/26th January 1944 and was almost immediately wounded.

He died of his wounds only a week after his arrival in Italy. Along with the many other casualties incurred in crossing the Garigliano in January, he is buried in **Minturno War Cemetery**, Italy, in:

Grave 1, A, 5

THOMAS RACE

Warrant Officer Class II
5498237
5th Battalion The Hampshire Regiment
Who died on
Thursday 14th September 1944, aged 30.

Tommy Race was a native of Coundon, near Bishop Auckland. He came to Lymington in 1931 and worked for Tarrants in New Milton. He later became a gardener at Great Ballard Preparatory School and in 1936 was employed as a machinist at *"a well-known Lymington factory."* He played football for Hordle and an entry on 1st July 1939 in Hordle Parish Register records the marriage of Thomas Race to Elsie Edith Sheppard. A daughter, Cynthia, was born in 1940.

In 1935 Tommy enlisted into The 5th Battalion of the Hampshire Regiment. D Company was based at Lymington. By 1939 he

was a corporal and drilled recruits on the New Milton "Rec." The battalion was part of the 128th Hampshire Brigade of 46th Wessex Division Brigade, which arrived in North Africa to reinforce the 1st Army in mid January 1943. It did not have an easy time as it was involved in the battle for Hunts Gap where it had taken the full brunt of the German attack (see James Wort, page 270), as well as the Battle of Beja – where so many local men were captured and made prisoners of war.

On 7th September 1943, 128 Brigade sailed from Bizerta for Salerno, where they landed as part of the initial wave of the assault. In the following six months 5th Hampshires fought their way continuously northwards, leading the assault crossing of the Volturno and on the 19th January repeated the process for the crossing of the Garigliano. By February Tommys battalion was fighting very successfully in atrocious conditions at 2,000 feet in the mountains around Ornito.

On 16th March 1944, 128 Brigade was withdrawn to Palestine for three months rest and retraining. It returned to Italy in July.

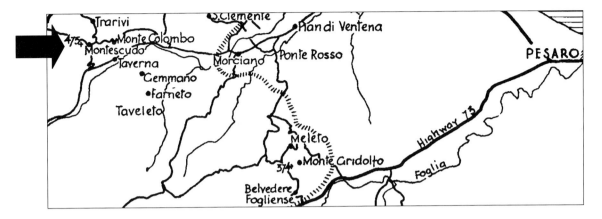

In August the battalion captured Monte Gridolfo. On 14th September Tommy's battalion attacked Montescudo to clear the way for the assault on Hill 475. The battalion occupied the cemetery outside the village, but were up against the 100th Mountain Regiment of picked Austrian troops. The fighting for Montescudo was bitter house clearance under constant shelling. Tommy, as Company Sergeant Major of Support Company, was bringing up ammunition in a bren-gun carrier to the forward company when it was hit by a shell and blown to pieces. Tommy's colonel wrote to Mrs Race:

"I am most dreadfully sorry. I had known him well since 1939, when I took over Adjutant of the 5th/7th – he was a very fine man, always cheerful and a fine example to all. He was universally popular and respected by all ranks."

THE LYMINGTON TIMES gave pipes to servicemen at that time and Corporal Carr received one. On the 12th August, just before Tommy's death, Corporal Carr asked that one might be sent to Sergeant Major Race

"who is one of the few old soldiers left, and I am proud to be in his company, as we have soldiered together in this regiment now for over seven years."

CSM Thomas Race is buried in **Gradara War Cemetery**, Italy, in:

Grave II. E. 9.

He is also remembered on the Hordle War Memorial.

LEONARD BROWN

Lance Bombardier
919086
Royal Artillery
who died on
Thursday 5th October 1944, aged 33.

Len was the son of Edwin North Brown and Elizabeth Brown. He later married Gladys Mary of Lymington.

He joined the Royal Artillery at the beginning of the war and by 1944 was a Lance Bombardier with 306 Battery, 77 Field Regiment (Highland), in Italy. This regiment was equipped with twenty-four 25 Pdr gun/howitzers and was part of 4 (British Infantry) Division. It was commanded at this time by Lieutenant Colonel H Wainwright DSO RA.

25 PDR GUN TEAM FIRING IN ITALY

The regiment had spent the winter helping its division to slowly fight its way up the Liri Vally. In May 1944 it was one of the twenty-one artillery regiments that supported the crossing of the Rapido river. It then moved forward to help in the capture of Monte Cassino and Rome. The division later advanced to the northeast to take Reiti, but had a stiff fight on the way at Palombara.

In the Summer the division moved to the east coast, where it supported the capture of Pesaro and then Rimini.

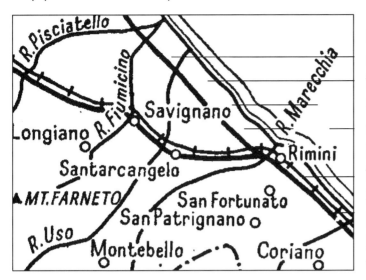

On 1st October Len's regiment came under the command of 5 Corps, which was advancing north from Rimini. On 3rd October the regiment was at Santarcangelo when Len's battery was heavily shelled and he was wounded.

PHOTO THELMA STOLLAR

Len died in hospital two days later. He is buried **in Salerno War Cemetery**, Italy, in

Grave V1.F. 17.

JOSEPH ERNEST CHAMBERLAIN

Lance Sergeant
5512761
5th Battalion, The Hampshire Regiment,
who died on
Monday 4th December 1944, aged 22.

Joe was born in Devonshire to Alfred Thomas and Gladys Marjory Louise Chamberlain. This couple later took over the management of the "Sportsmans Arms" in Pennington, but when Alfred died his widow moved to Lorne Road.

Joe worked for Messrs. Rashley & Co. as a plumber, but joined the local TA battalion on the outbreak of war. He went through the actions in North Africa and Italy, sharing the same experiences as CSM Tommy Race (see pages 290/91).

Montescudo and Hill 475 were both occupied by the 5th Battalion on 17th September after bitter and costly fighting which, once again, had fought itself to a standstill. After resting, the brigade was back in the line and on 28th September tasked, once again, with leading the assault on a river crossing. Poor weather delayed the action on the River Fiumicino until 7th October. Joe's battalion crossed at midnight and occupied San Lorenzo. The bridgehead was held by the brigade, against fierce counter-attacks, for 36 hours - cut off to their rear by the swollen river. The crossing of the Fiumicino is described in the Regimental History as

" A magnificent achievement."

The end of October saw the whole division come out of the line for rest. The next mission for Joe's battalion was to assist in the capture of Forli. The brigade plan was to attack, on 7th November, through San Martino-in-Strada. After a slow start the attack went to plan with infantry/tank cooperation supported by RAF ground-attack aircraft and Littlejohn anti-tank guns successfully defeating the enemy armour.

The next river, the Montone, was then crossed – although with some difficulty – and Forli occupied.

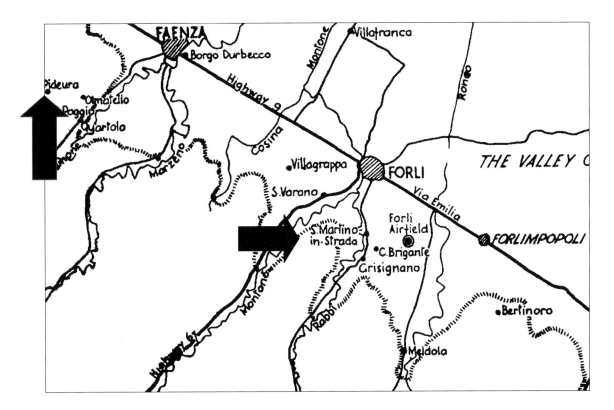

The 128th Brigade came back into the line on 24th November to take the lead in the advance towards Faenza. They forced a crossing over the Marzeno and expanded the bridgehead despite heavy rain and the rising river. The next obstacle, the River Lamone, was reached on the 26th.

The advance had, however, outstripped supplies and a week was taken to improve recently captured roads and crossing places. The night of 3rd December saw the other two battalions in the brigade cross the Lamone. Joe's battalion passed through the 2nd Battalion's positions on top of a steep ridge at Olmatello and advanced towards Pideura in the growing light of dawn until it was held up by a strong German position on another ridge. Attempts throughout the day to expand the bridgehead were unsuccessful in the face of heavy machine-gun fire.

Joe was killed in the course of the day. He is buried in **Faenza War Cemetery**, Italy, in:

Grave III. A. 9.

EDGAR LEWIS HOLLOWAY

Trooper
5507991
Royal Armoured Corps
who died on
Saturday 27th January 1945, aged 31.

Eddie Holloway was a son of Mrs Holloway, who lived at Rose Cottage, Woodside in Lymington.

After leaving school he worked for nine years for Mr J Orman, the farmer, and then did six years with Lymington Borough Council. During this time he married, lived in Hordle, and successfully raised a family of a son and a daughter, Doreen.

Eddie was called up for the army and joined the 7th (Queens Own) Hussars of the Royal Armoured Corps.

When Eddie joined the army in 1943, his wife and family moved to 77, Tennyson Road, Portswood, Southampton. The Hussars was part of 9 Armoured Brigade Group and was serving with the 5th (Canadian) Armoured Division. It had taken part in the Anzio landings in January 1944 and fought its way up Italy with the 1st Canadian Corps

By January 1945, given the nature of this phase of the Italian campaign, Eddie's regiment was operating away from its tanks, in an infantry role.

It was involved in the battle for San Alberto, during which A Squadron, in which Eddie was serving, made a successful fighting patrol, which killed many enemy and took several prisoners - at no cost to the squadron. Eddie's unit was congratulated by the Army Commander for this action.

The regiment then moved to a new and much more difficult sector of the line. On 25th January Eddie's squadron sent out another patrol, this time to recce the enemy positions. The patrol lay up in a German dugout for two hours watching a German sentry on a plank bridge 15 yards from their position. The sentry changed every hour, but the patrol were seen when they tried to capture him and although he was killed the patrol also lost a man. The next day A Squadron was mortared during the evening. Eddie was hit and evacuated back to hospital.

In February 1945 his wife was officially notified that Eddie had died of wounds on 27th January, whilst serving in the 8th Army with the Central Mediterranean Force.

PHOTO CWGC

Eddie is buried in **Argenta War cemetery,** Italy in

Grave III, F, 17.

STANLEY WILFRED CLARK BEM

**Leading Aircraftman
Royal Air Force Volunteer Reserve**
who died on
Sunday 16th July 1944, aged 30.

Stan was born on 16th July 1914, the second son of Henry and Maud Clark of Rosetta Cottage, Lymington. He grew up with his brothers Fred and Ron and went to the Church of England School, playing football for the school team. He was also a choirboy at the Parish Church and a member of the 1st Lymington Scouts. He later joined the Town Band, playing the cornet or the trumpet with the little local dance band. On leaving school he became an apprentice carpenter with Rashley and Co and did some work on the Parish Church in helping to build the new vestry on the north side. Stanley later

worked as a driver for SCATS as well as being a driver with the Hants and Dorset Bus Company. He also became engaged to Betty Perrin, of Bournemouth.

At the start of the war he and his brothers all joined the RAF. Stan became a driver and as his younger brother, Ron, has expressed it

"Began his experiences in earnest in North Africa."

In time Stan moved on, via Sicily, into Italy. His brother understands that at some stage he had, unarmed, rounded up some of the enemy – but whether this was in North Africa or Italy is not known.

This picture shows Stan (second from the left) with some of his unit. It was taken in Sicily on 15th September 1943.

Stan was fatally injured in a road accident on his thirtieth birthday. He had driven many thousands of miles on duty all over Italy and the accident happened on a rare day off. He was not, on this occasion, driving, but was a passenger in a vehicle, which overturned – whether by enemy action or driver error is not known. Stan was not killed immediately, but died later from a broken neck in an RAF General Hospital.

His parents were officially notified, after his death, that he had been awarded the British Empire Medal.

Stan is buried in **Naples War Cemetery**, Italy, in:

Grave I. B.8.

299

WALTER GEORGE HAWKINS

Lieutenant, Royal Naval Volunteer Reserve
who died on
Wednesday 8th September 1943, aged 33.

Walter, always known as **George**, was the eldest son of Mr Sidney Hawkins. The photograph, taken with Joan Stephens (nee Tizard), was taken in the mid 1920's sitting in a sand boat they had built on the beach at Milford. George was educated at the County Grammar school in Brockenhurst, after which he worked for his father, for whom he later managed Priestlands Dairy.

PHOTO JOAN STEPHENS

George had a good singing voice, having joined the church choir as a boy. Later, as a *"pleasing baritone,"* he took leading parts in Lymington Music and Dramatic productions. He is seen here on the near left performing in HMS PINNAFORE. He was a popular man, being both Captain and Hon. Secretary of the Lymington Lawn Tennis Club.

PHOTO GEOFF & MAVIS ISTED

He married Vera Willis, of Brackenfields, Lymington, in September 1939 at the Church of St John in Boldre. During the war his brother, Bob, served as a Sergeant in the Royal Tank Regiment.

George joined the Royal Navy and was commissioned Sub-Lieutenant on 24th July 1942. He joined BRONTESAURUS, a training school for RNVR personnel near Dunoon in Scotland, as an acting Lieutenant.

LANDING CRAFT (GUN) 2

Five months later he was promoted to Lieutenant and was posted to DINOSAUR, a gunnery training school, in lieu of a specialist gunner officer. April 1943 found him on the staff of Combined Operations in Troon Golf Club as the pay and drafting secretary for HQ Tank Landing Craft and the associated Landing Craft Gunnery School.

He then moved to the staff of Combined Operations in the Mediterranean theatre of war. Just before he was killed he had been recommended for accelerated promotion to Lieutenant Commander.

He was aboard Landing Craft (Gun) 12 when he was killed in action in the eve of the Salerno landings, on 8th September 1943.

He was buried at sea. His name is therefore recorded on the **Chatham Naval Memorial,** on:

Panel 73, 3.

ROBERT KITCHENER COLLINS

Able Seaman, Royal Navy
P/J 45987
H.M.S. PENELOPE
Who died on
Friday, 18th February 1944, aged 43.

Bob Collins was a native of Lymington, being a son of Fred and Mary Collins, who later moved to Eling Lane, Totton. Another brother and a sister, Daisy, completed the family. Bob later married Nora, and they lived at 1, Helsby Villas, Middle Road, Lymington. Nora, sadly, died suddenly on 15th February 1943, when Bob was away at sea.

He joined the navy as a Boy Seaman in 1915. He had an adventurous war, being in the cruiser CASSANDRA when she was sunk by a mine in the Gulf of Finland on 5th December 1918, with the loss of 11 men.

Being a career sailor he served between the wars. He was among the crew of the battleship RENOWN in 1927 when King George VI and Queen Elizabeth, then the Duke and Duchess of York, made their voyage to Australia.

Bob retired from the Royal Navy just before the Second World War, but in September 1939 was called up as a Reservist. He was drafted to MOHAWK, a modern "Tribal" class destroyer completed in 1938. In November 1940, in the Straits of Otranto, she sank an Italian Motor Torpedo Boat that was part of a convoy escort. In the New Year she joined the 14th Flotilla in the Aegean Sea and was again successful in convoy marauding operations.

On 10th April the Flotilla was transferred to Malta to harass enemy convoys supplying the North African Campaign. On 15th April 1941 the Flotilla left Malta to intercept a convoy off the Tunisian coast. This was successfully done, with the three enemy destroyers and five merchantmen being sunk. In the course of the action, however, MOHAWK was torpedoed twice and sunk. Commander J Eaton and a large portion of her crew were saved - although Bob had been in the sea for about six hours before he was rescued.

In early 1943 Bob was then drafted to PENELOPE, a fast small fleet cruiser of 5,270 tons standard completed in 1936. She had been in the Mediterranean since 1941 as part of Force K - along with her sister ship AURORA and the destroyers LANCE and LIVELY. Whilst in Malta PENELOPE was subject to a severe bombing attack and received so many bomb splinters that she became known as

"THE PEPPER POT"

During 1943 her guns supported the invasions of Sicily and Italy and she operated with distinction in the Aegean. PENELOPE was finally hit at 7.35 a.m. on 18th February 1944 off Anzio by torpedoes fired by the U-410. A major explosion on the PENELOPE of, probably, the after magazine, caused her to sink in under ten minutes. Robert was one of the 415 sailors lost in the sinking.

His name therefore appears on the **Portsmouth Naval Memorial** on:

Panel 82 Column 1

THE SECOND WORLD WAR

EUROPE
1944-1945

EUROPE

The landings in North Africa, Sicily and Italy all proved the practicality of an amphibious invasion of Europe through France.

Stalin continuously pressed for this second front to be opened in Europe. This was not practical in 1942 or 1943, but arms and equipment were given to the Soviet Union to help them in their fight against the Germans.

Convoys were sent, in the course of which **Harry Lewis, George Huddard** and **John Jeans** were to lose their lives helping Russia.

Meanwhile forces were being built up for the invasion in 1944. The Atlantic convoys were an essential part of this, delivering men, material and food to Britain. **George Plumridge, Peter Todd, Ernest Haywood, Thomas Stratton,** and **Frederick Cassey** all died keeping this lifeline open at this crucial time. **Robert Isted** was to die on the same duty later in the war.

These convoys were augmented by smaller coastal and channel convoys around Britain. These essential movements of ships were conducted close to enemy air and naval bases along the "Atlantic Wall," which exposed them to constant day and night attacks. Keeping these routes open cost the lives of **Frederick Young, Cyril Hurst, Frederick Walsh** and **John Gregory**.

As part of the preparation for the invasion of France an offensive bombing campaign was conducted against Germany and the occupied countries of Europe. Whilst the Americans attacked by day the RAF bombed at night. This cost the lives of **William Clarke, Arthur Cole, Terence Frogley** and **Herbert Berger.**

Coastal Command operated with increasing effectiveness against Axis shipping, in the course of which **Robert Lowen** lost his life.

The flying training programme for all aircrew was inherently not without risk, as proved by the deaths of **Phillip Isted** and **Henry Foster.**

As Germany appreciated the imminence of invasion so she stepped up her air attacks on Britain, augmenting bombing with attacks by the new V1s and V2s. **Henry Hall** was killed in such an attack on his searchlight unit in Sussex.

THE BATTLESHIP WARSPITE SUPPORTING THE D-DAY LANDINGS

D-Day, on 6th June 1944, was the start of the advance through France and Germany that was to lead, within ten months, to the defeat of Nazi Germany. **Victor Hobby** died in the Normandy landings.

Reginald Maxted, William Evans and **John Rhodes** all died in the subsequent advance into Germany.

Eric Thompson, however, died from natural causes, whilst **Anthony Crosthwait** died two years after the war was over, from wounds received whilst forcing a crossing over the River Rhine.

HARRY LEWIS

Petty Officer Telegraphist, Royal Navy
D/JX 133115
H.M.S. MATABELE
who died on
Saturday 17th January 1942, aged 28.

Harry was born in April 1913 and was the only son of Mr and Mrs H Lewis of "Wivenhoe," Western Road, Lymington. There were also two daughters, Victoria and Isabel (Edie). His father, Harry, had joined the Royal Navy at the age of eighteen in 1899 and served his 12 years in destroyers - including the FOX - and the battleship GOOD HOPE. He achieved the rank of Petty Officer, but on marriage he transferred to the Coastguard Service. Harry (junior) therefore had a nomadic upbringing as his father was posted to Whitby and Faversham, before settling in Lymington, where he retired to work for the Post Office.

Harry went to the Church of England school and joined the Royal Navy as a Boy Seaman in 1929, when he was sixteen. After training at ST VINCENT he served in the aircraft carrier GLORIOUS and in 1937 was posted to help man the signals station at Seletar naval base in Singapore, where amongst other activities he rode a Harley Davidson motor bike.

At the beginning of the war he returned to the United Kingdom as a "PO Tel" and helped to fit modern signals equipment into the destroyer ECHO. In February 1940 Harry married Miss Freda Bottomer of "Vermosa," Middle Road, Lymington. He then stood by MATABELE as it was nearing completion.

HMS MATEBELE   IWM A6647

MATABELE was laid down in 1939 at Scotts Ship Builders. These "Tribal" destroyers were the first to have their main armament of 4.7-inch guns twin-mounted in the four turrets. They were therefore very heavily armed for their 1,870 tons displacement. The 16 ships of the class had a very active war, with only four surviving it. MATABELE was the sixth of the class to be lost.

In January 1942 the Russian convoys had been operating for six months. PQ 8 sailed for Russia in the middle of the month knowing that German U-boats were waiting South of Bear Island. On 17th January MATABELE was torpedoed by U-454, commanded by Hacklander, off the North Cape, and almost immediately sank. Despite having only two minutes grace many sailors managed to abandon ship, but could not survive in the icy water. Only two men were finally rescued, out of a crew of nearly 200 sailors.

Harry was one of those lost. His name therefore appears on the **Plymouth Naval Memorial**, Devon, on:

Panel 68, Column 1.

Harry's son, Andrew, was born a month later in February 1942.

GEORGE PEPYS HUDDART

Lieutenant Commander, Royal Navy
H.M.S. FORESTER
who died on
Saturday 2nd May 1942, aged 33.

George was the son of Mr and Mrs R Huddart, who lived in Wimbledon. Their country house was The Copse in Pennington. George's mother was formally Frederica Lucy Pepys-Cockrell, of the well-known architectural family. His brother, Bill Huddart, was a solicitor in Lymington before he joined the Royal Artillery. He was posted to Malaya and in February 1942 was captured by the Japanese at the fall of Singapore. He was to survive nearly four years imprisonment and died at Colchester in April 2003.

A career Naval officer, George joined the Royal Navy as a 13-year-old entrant to Dartmouth Naval College in September 1922.

In May 1926 he joined the Mediterranean Fleet as a cadet - and later midshipman - serving on BARHAM and later WARSPITE. Promoted to sub-lieutenant on 1st January 1930, George went to the Persian Gulf on the sloop FOLKESTONE moving, on promotion in October 1931, to FOWEY. He later served on the cruiser COVENTRY, flagship of the destroyer flotillas in the Mediterranean.

George began the war in command of WINDSOR, an old First World War ship completed in 1918, which shot down an enemy aircraft early in the war. He then moved to BROCKLESBY, a new "Hunt" class destroyer completed in 1941, and then was briefly First Lieutenant to MAORI, a powerful "Tribal" class ship, which sank as a result of an air attack off Malta on 12th February 1942.

In October 1941 George married Amy Stansmore, younger daughter of the late John Leslie of Ranchi, India, and of Mrs WS Coutts of Dollar, Scotland.

HMS FORESTER   NMM N6296

In 1942 George took command of FORESTER, an "F" Class destroyer built by White's shipyard in 1935. Equipped with standard destroyer's armament she could steam at 15 knots for 6000 miles and was, essentially, an anti-submarine vessel. FORESTER was deployed on guarding Russian convoys. Conditions were such that the Ship's log records, on one occasion, a roll of 45 degrees in a 6-hour gale off Iceland - and in another entry that the Captain's beard was frozen stiff! She had also, by this stage of the war, steamed 200,000 miles - the equivalent of nine times round the world.

On 28th April convoy QP11, with 13 ships, set sail from Murmansk for Iceland. It shared an escorting force of 45 warships with an incoming convoy PQ15. QP11's close escort, however, was the cruiser EDINBURGH and the destroyers FORESIGHT and FORESTER. EDINBURGH was also carrying a small cargo of Russian state gold. Two days out the EDINBURGH lost her steering gear to an enemy bombing attack. With great skill in the difficult icy conditions FORESTER, under command of George Huddart, took her in tow but after 16 hours this had to be given up to allow FORESTER to search for submarines. At 6.30 a.m. on 2nd May three German Destroyers attacked the EDINBURGH. Twenty minutes later, as FORESTER fired her torpedoes at the enemy, she was hit by three shells that destroyed both X and B-guns and devastated the bridge and boiler room - causing her to stop. FORESTER continued to fire A-gun but before she could get under way again she was repeatedly hit by enemy gunfire. The shell that hit B- gun killed George Huddart.

David Thomas reports, in "*With Ensigns Flying,*"

> ***"As he (George Huddart) lay dying on the bridge his First Lieutenant, Lieutenant J Bitmead, assumed command and carried on the excellent work which his dying captain had so gallantly executed."***

FORESTER regained steerageway after 40 minutes. A torpedo then hit the cruiser EDINBURGH, which was immediately abandoned and later sunk by FORESIGHT.

His Obituary in THE TIMES of 13th May 1942 stated:

> ***"George was one of those lovable characters who would have never grown up, but who was inevitably destined for high rank in the Navy. His buoyancy of spirit allied with a detestation of inefficiency and slackness in any form formed a combination of qualities, which endeared him to officers and men alike. At the same time when dealing with the occasional "bad hat" his essential humanity would come to the surface in time to prevent the offender meeting with the severity he possibly deserved. George would have loved to have been given the opportunity that was given to his great friend Sam Beattie in the CAMPBELTOWN. He can never have that now, but his wife, parents and friends will know that he went out in the same spirit that animated the crusaders of old."***

George Huddart was buried at sea. His name is therefore recorded on the **Portsmouth Naval Memorial** on:

Panel 61, Column 3

JOHN DOUGLAS FRANK JEANS

Apprentice Merchant Navy
S.S. Chumleigh (London)
who died on
Monday 9th November 1942, aged 19.

John Jeans was the only son of Major and Mrs F Jeans of 2, North Street, Pennington. Major Jeans served in the Indian Army towards the end of the First World War. Between the wars he was in business in Brockenhurst and Lymington, but rejoined the army in 1940 and served in Persia.

John was a Brockenhurst County School boy and a member of the 9th Lymington Sea Scouts. When he left school at 17 years of age he become an apprentice in the Merchant Navy. In his first year he made several journeys to South America in meat ships. He was then transferred to Russian convoys, at one time spending eight months in Russia when his ship became iced-in. Joan Staples recalls that he wrote the following letter to a Russian newspaper:

"I am John Jeans, an apprentice in the Merchant Service, 21 years of age. I have been twice across the Atlantic, the second time we were directed to Archangel carrying tanks, high explosives and aircraft. U-boats seized the opportunity to attack. We had some losses but calculated that 6 U-boats were sunk. It grew bitterly cold as we steamed into the Arctic, ice lay 2 ft. thick everywhere. Archangel at last. Red Army soldiers unloaded 24 hours a day. They are wonderful workers. The women too worked for more than 12 hours a day. One of them in control of a winch. In an amazing short time the war materials were unloaded and on their way to the front. The thermometer stood at 42" below zero. I am trying to learn Russian."

John came home on leave in July 1942 and then returned to Russian convoy duty, serving on *S S Chumleigh*, a modern 5,445 ton steamer, built in 1938. Convoy losses had become so severe that on 29th October 1942 an experiment was tried of sending 13 ships – including the *Chumleigh* - from Iceland for Archangel unescorted, at twelve-hour intervals. Three ships turned back to Iceland from this special convoy, five reached Russia and five were sunk.

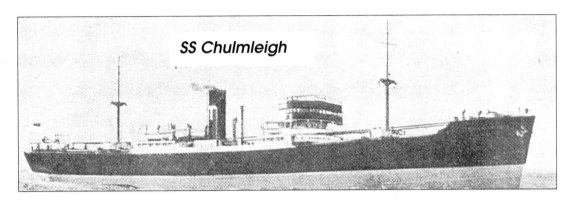

SS Chulmleigh

The *Chumleigh*, loaded with government stores, was attacked and damaged by a Ju-88 on 5th November. The Master, Captain D. Williams, then beached the ship at South Cape, Spitzbergen. Re-floated, she continued her voyage, but was again attacked by a Ju-88 and finally torpedoed by U-625.

John is recorded, by the CWGC as dying on 9th November, aged 19. But when the *Chumleigh* sank on 16th November two boats were successfully launched. One boat, under the Captain, landed at a remote part of Spitzbergen. It was found by the local garrison on 4th January 1943. By this time many of the men had died from frostbite. The Master, 3 crew and 9 gunners were finally saved. When they landed at Thurso on 16th May 1943 the Master reported that on 22nd November 1942 he had seen the other boat, containing John Jeans. He went on to say that John had done valuable service in rescuing one man out of the sea at the time of the sinking and had also tried to rescue a second member of the crew. Nothing more, however, was heard of this second boat. In all 36 crew and 9 gunners were lost in this tragedy.

Having no known grave, John's name is recorded on the **Tower Hill Monument** on:

Panel 28

GEORGE PLUMRIDGE

Lance Bombardier
1556466
Royal Artillery
Who died on
Saturday 20th September 1941, aged 26.

THE LYMINGTON TIMES of 25th October 1941 reported:

LANCE BOMBARDIER GEORGE PLUMRIDGE

"George, aged 25, a brother of Eric, has been reported missing at sea since 20th September. He was employed in a Lymington Works before voluntarily joining the anti-aircraft section of the Royal Artillery. He later volunteered for anti-aircraft action with the Merchant Navy.

He used to play centre-half for Lymington Rovers Football Club, being one of the club's most talented players, and was also a cricketer. His father, who is a retired police officer, is now in Lymington Civil Defence Force. The family have lived in Lymington for nearly twenty years and kept the Solent Inn for thirteen years. Mr and Mrs Plumridge had a daughter who died when 11 years of age."

George lived at home with his parents at 36 Gosport Street, before he joined the army at the outbreak of war. By 1941 he was a member of 7/4th Maritime Regiment, Royal Artillery, whose task was to serve afloat as gunners on Defensively Equipped Merchant Ships (DEMS). George would have manned the close-defence light anti-aircraft

GEORGE
LYMINGTON ROVERS 1936

weapons, assisted by some of the ship's crew whom he would have trained for the task.

THE SOLENT INN ON LEFT

The *Cingalese Prince* was built in 1929 by Blythswood Shipbuilding Co. at Glasgow. With a tonnage of 8474grt, a length of 441ft 6in, a beam of 60ft 4in and a service speed of 14 knots, she was crewed by 73 men. In April 1941, during the Greek campaign, she was bombed and badly damaged when off Piraeus. She was repaired and left Port Said in May 1941 for Bombay.

With her fast speed *Cingalese Prince* sailed independently on her return trip to Liverpool via Trinidad with a cargo of Manganese, pig iron and general cargo. She called in at Cape Town, South Africa, where George and eight other DEMS gunners signed on as a deckhands. Although in the army, this practise brought the DEMS gunners under the command of the Master of the ship.

George was lost at sea on 20th September 1941, on route to Trinidad, when his ship was torpedoed by U-111. He is recorded in the ship's replacement log as:

'missing presumed drowned.'

There were 19 survivors, however, including three of George's DEMS colleagues.

His name appears on the **Plymouth Naval Memorial**, Devon on:

Panel 62, Column 3.

315

PETER CORYDON TODD

Second Radio Officer, Merchant Navy
M.V. British Dominion (London)
who died on
Thursday 14th January 1943, aged 21.

Peter was the eldest son of Herbert and Selina Todd, who lived at Casa Mia, Middle Road, Lymington. He was educated at Westend School in Lymington (run by Miss Annie Banks) and then at Norwich High School, where his sister Gillian later taught. In 1942 his brother Hugh, aged 18, volunteered for pilot training in the RAF.

According to THE LYMINGTON TIMES of 6th February 1943, Peter was reported as being one of nature's gentlemen. Although he held cruelty, pain and the affliction of death on man or beast in abhorrence, he also possessed that quiet courage that led him to join the Merchant Navy. His physique prohibited him from becoming a deckhand, but at the beginning of the war he took a course in wireless operation and joined the Merchant navy in 1940 as a wireless operator.

Peter saw action on his very first voyage, when his ship was sunk by bombing. He then joined the Tanker Service and made numerous voyages.

The *British Dominion* was a tanker of 6,983 tons built in 1928 and operated as part of their fleet by the British Tanker Co. Ltd, of London. In January 1943 it was part of a nine-tanker Convoy, TM 1, carrying aviation fuel from Trinidad to Gibraltar. It carried a crew of 44 men, augmented by a DEMS detachment of 9 gunners.

On 11th January (10th January, according to Volume 1 of LLoyds War Losses) she was torpedoed by U-522 in the Atlantic North West of the Canaries. Given the damage and inferno of burning aviation spirit the Master, Captain Miller, ordered the crew to abandon ship. The hulk was later torpedoed and sunk by U-620. HMS GODETIA rescued the boat containing the master 10 crew and 5 gunners. The remainder of the crew and DEMS detachment, thirty-eight men in total, were not seen again. U-620 was, in turn, sunk a month later by a Catalina aircraft of 202 Squadron flying out of Gibraltar.

Peter had, in fact, been rescued, but had died from the after-effects of his burns three days later, when he was buried at sea.

When his mother was informed of the loss of Peter's ship she took comfort that it was symbolic of Peter's character to remain at his post to the last, sending out his SOS signals, to bring aid to his fellow shipmates.

She also wrote a dignified letter (right), correcting an "erroneous impression" about her son.

THE LATE RADIO OFFICER PETER TODD
To the Editor

Sir,—I am writing to tell you that after reading the paragraph about my son Peter in the "Lymington Times" of February 6th, in which it is stated "his delicate physique would not permit him to undertake the more arduous duties of able seaman," a great many people have inferred from it that Peter tried to become an able seaman, but was rejected as medically unfit.

This was not the case. Peter never tried to become an able seaman, nor was his physique delicate. He had to have a medical examination before he could be accepted as a radio officer, and was passed as first class.

Please do not think I am unmindful of the tribute you paid to Peter, but as I know that he would have hated the stigma of being thought physically unfit more than anything else, I feel that something should be done to correct this erroneous impression.

Casa Mia, Middle Road, Lymington.
MADGE TODD

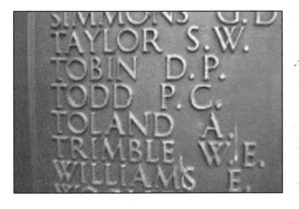

Peter Todd is commemorated on the **Tower Hill Memorial to the Merchant Navy** on:

Panel 19

317

ERNEST HARRY HAYWARD

Able Seaman, Royal Navy
D/JX 208315
HMS PRESIDENT III
who died on
Thursday 18th March 1943, aged 27.

Ernie was the son of William and May Hayward, of Fawcett Road, New Milton. After leaving school Ernie served his time as an apprentice to a printer in New Milton and then worked on the staff of the "Advertiser & Times". He then went to work as a linotype operator on Kelly's Directories in Andover, where he settled with his wife, Lily and two children.

He joined the Royal Navy in 1940 and, after training, was held on strength of PRESIDENT before being posted to a merchant ship as a DEMS gun layer.

Ernie remained part of such a detachment for three years, sailing mainly in convoys all over the world. In 1942 his ship called at an Egyptian port where he was able to meet up with his younger brother Ted. Ted had been serving as a Sapper in Egypt since 1940 (see photograph left). Before the war he had worked for the local electricity company.

Another brother, John, had worked for the Post Office in Bournemouth before joining the army and serving as a Gunner in India. A fourth brother worked at Caslake's in Lymington Road, New Milton.

By 1943 Ernie was part of the Naval detachment of gunners on the *Canadian Star*. This was a modern ship, built in 1938 and operated by the Blue Star Line of London. This refrigeration ship of 8,293 tons was carrying 7806 tons of refrigerated cargo from Sydney, New South Wales. It had called at New York, where it had joined up with 39 other ships to form convoy HX 229 en route to Liverpool. The ship was commanded by its Master, Captain Robert Miller, and was crewed by 55 crew and 8 gunners. It also carried, on this voyage, 24 passengers.

MV Canadian Star

On 18th March the *Canadian Star* was torpedoed and sunk by U-221 in the Atlantic south east of Cape Farewell. A fellow RN gunner, Eynon Hawkins, was awarded the George Cross for saving men trapped in a burning oil slick and Captain Miller was posthumously awarded the LLoyds War Medal for bravery at sea. Twenty-one crew, two gunners (including Ernie) and nine passengers were lost in the attack.

Ernie's name therefore appears on the **Plymouth Naval Memorial** on:

Panel 78, Column 3.

Six months later U-221 was sunk by a Halifax bomber, operating out of RAF Holmsley South, in the New Forest. The Halifax, however, was damaged during the attack and had to ditch. Two crewmen were lost, but the other six were rescued after being adrift for eleven days.

THOMAS PERCY STRATTON

Pantry Boy, Merchant Navy
S.S. Lancastrian Prince (London)
who died on
Sunday 11th April 1943, aged 17.

Tom Stratton was the son of Percy and Kate Stratton of Waterford Lane, Lymington. He was born on 30th December 1925. According to his sister, Phoebe, Tom almost immediately contracted her whooping cough and was not expected to live, so he was hastily christened in the bedroom.

TOM, HIS STEPMOTHER FREDA, HALF SISTER FREDA   SISTER PHOEBE

Survive he did, and went to the Church of England School in Lymington, being in "Puffer" May's class. Many years later Phoebe visited another of his teachers, Miss Shephard, who remembered Tom well. Yet another of his teachers was "Honky" Hoare and Billy Taylor was his headmaster.

As Tom came towards leaving school his thoughts turned to joining the Royal Navy, in which his Uncle Tom was a CPO. He was, however, too young and so, at the age of sixteen, he joined the Merchant Navy and went to sea as a Pantry Boy on S.S. *Lancastrian*

Prince. This was a modern British registered Steam Freighter of 1914 tons built in 1940 and operated by the Prince Line.

Tom made at least one trip on Russian convoys, but it is not known how many trips he made across the Atlantic. On his last visit home from America he brought a doll called "Barbara" as a present for his youngest half-sister, Dophine. On the way back to UK his ship had been involved, between 16th and 20th March, in the largest convoy battle of the war. Over 40 U-boats were deployed against two convoys as they slowly coalesced in the mid-Atlantic air gap, until there were 100 ships plus their escorts. Twenty U-boats sank 21 merchantmen. Of the 23 ships in Tom's convoy only the *Lancastrian Prince* and two other ships made it to Liverpool. The doll was damaged in the pounding the *Lancastrian Prince* took from torpedo and depth charge explosions. As the photo shows, "Barbara" is still in the possession of his half-sister, Freda.

Convoy ON 176 formed up at Liverpool and sailed, via Bermuda, for New York on 31st March 1943. Of the 44 ships in this convoy the *Lancastrian Prince* was the only merchantman to go down, being sunk at 11.30 p.m. by U-404 within sight of its destination – Boston - on 11th April 1943, with the loss of all 45 crew. Tom was an excellent underwater swimmer and his step-mother, Freda, always believed that he would have survived the sinking. Three months later U-404 was sunk by a Liberator in the Atlantic.

Tom Stratton is commemorated on **The Tower Hill Memorial** to the Merchant Navy on:

Panel 63

FREDERICK SYDNEY CASSEY

Able Seaman, Royal Navy
C/JX 580443
H.M.S. CASSANDRA
who died on
Monday 11th December 1944, aged 19.

Fred was born on 6th July 1925 to Alf and Flora Cassey of Lymington. The family, including daughter Betty, lived at 69 Flushards Estate. At this time his father, who had served in the army in the First World War, was employed by Mr Rowland Hill. He had previously worked in the grocery trade in Salisbury and Wilton.

Fred went to the Church of England School in Lymington and left, when he was 14 years old, to work at Mr Bran's butcher's shop in the High Street - where he delivered the meat to customers on his bicycle.

His sister, Betty, has kindly provided the photograph of Fred. She recalls that he loved swimming and was frequently to be seen in the outdoor swimming pool, diving off the top board. She also remembers that his handwriting was excellent.

When he was 16 years old Fred went to work at Wellworthy's. He also, at this time, enlisted in the Home Guard. Two days after his eighteenth birthday in 1943, he joined the Royal Navy and did his basic training as an Ordinary Seaman at Chatham. He was then drafted as an Able Seaman to CASSANDRA.

HMS CASSANDRA   IWM A25018

CASSANDRA was a "C" class destroyer laid down at Yarrow in 1943 to War Emergency design. Of all-welded construction she was completed in 1944 and displaced 2,560 tons in full load. Armed with 4 x 4.5-inch guns, eight torpedo tubes and four depth charge throwers, she was a state-of-the-art well-armed ship capable of steaming at 36 knots. She carried a complement of 235 men.

These modern destroyers had a strong anti-submarine capability and were much in demand at this phase of the war, being used in a variety of roles. At the end of 1944 CASSANDRA found herself escorting convoys to Russia. Convoy RA 62, comprising 29 Merchant ships, left Kola Inlet on 10th December 1944, bound on a 9-day voyage to Loch Ewe in Scotland. Only a day out from Kola, the convoy was attacked by German aircraft and CASSANDRA was hit.

Within a week the Cassey family was informed that Fred had been

"Reported missing, presumably killed, on war service whilst serving in Northern waters."

Although his ship survived Fred was, indeed, killed during the attack. His name therefore appears on the **Chatham Naval Memorial**, in Kent, on:

Panel 75, 1.

ROBERT CLIMPSON ISTED

Able Seaman, Royal Navy
P/JX 183910
H.M.S. VERVAIN
who died on
Tuesday 20th February 1945, aged 24.

Bob was the second son of Violet and Charles Isted of 62, High Street, Lymington and the late Charles Isted. Whilst at school Bob had joined the Rover Sea Scouts and with his interests it was natural that he should join the Royal Navy. He had three brothers; Geoff joined the RAF, Alan the army, whilst Cliff was at school. His two sisters both served - Betty in the WAAF and Mary in the WRNS.

Bob attended local schools and worshipped at St Thomas' Church. When he left school he worked as a professional gardener and was working in London before he went to war.

PHOTO GEOFF AND MAVIS ISTED

At the beginning of the war Bob joined the Royal Navy and was on active service throughout it. At some stage he joined the crew of VERVAIN, a "Flower" class corvette, originally named BROOM, built by Harland and Wolf in 1941. Of 1170 tons displacement it could steam at 17 knots and was armed with a 4-inch gun, six 20 mm cannon and 40 depth charges. An escort maid-of-all-work she was commanded by Lieutenant Commander R A Howell RNVR. On 6 June 1944 she had taken part in the the Normandy landings.

A FLOWER CLASS CORVETTE   PHOTO NICK SAUNDERS

On 11ᵗʰ February 1945 VERVAIN Left St John's, Newfoundland, as part of escort for convoy HX337, consisting of 69 merchant ships. Nine days later - at 11.55 a.m. – she was torpedoed by a German submarine, U1276, 20 miles south of Waterford. The torpedo blew off the bows of the corvette, which sank in twenty minutes. The U-Boat herself was sunk with the loss of all hands shortly afterwards, by a joint attack by the frigates AMETHYST and PEACOCK.

Out of a complement of 109 men, 37 of the VERVAIN's ratings survived, being picked up by the rescue ship *Bury*, although one died later from injuries sustained in the attack. Until then, VERVAIN had shared with her sister-ship CLEMATIS the record for most Atlantic crossings (thirty-two in under two years). Robert was amongst those lost.

PHOTO NICK SAUNDERS

His name is therefore recorded on the **Portsmouth Naval Memorial** on:

Panel 89, Column 1

FREDERICK ALEXANDER YOUNG

Donkeyman
S.S. *Glen Tilt* (Bristol)
Merchant Navy
who died on
Saturday 12th December 1942, aged 35.

Fred Young was born on 27th May 1907 at 9, South Terrace, South Road, St Denys, Portswood, South Stoneham, Southampton. His parents, Eliza (nee Porter) and James Young, later lived at 29 Flushards Estate, Lymington. His father is recorded as being a ship's fireman.

Fred followed his father, James, into the Merchant Navy and was a professional seaman who served in a variety of roles. His CR 1 showed, that he was a tall man with a fair complexion, and distinguished by a tattoo of roses on his right arm inscribed

"Mother"
"Good Luck"

In February 1937 he left the White Star liner *Berengania* and signed on to the *Empress of Britain*, a similar vessel.

He then joined *Northumberland*, on 6th October 1938 - and was on her at the start of the war.

On 29th February 1940 he signed on as a member of the crew of the *Gloucester Castle*, a small and rather old steamer, originally registered in 1911. This vessel was later to be sunk by one of the German surface raiders in July 1942.

By June 1940, however, Fred was one of the crew of the *Beverdale*, a 9957-ton coaster registered in 1928. The *Beverdale* was later to be sunk by a U-boat in early April 1941

After three months aboard *Beverdale*, Fred transferred to the *Glen Tilt* as a donkeyman and worked in the engine-room. The *Glen Tilt* was a coaster of 871 tons carrying whatever cargo was available. The Master and his crew of eleven were augmented by the addition of two DEMS gunners, who manned an anti-aircraft gun. This small coaster spent the early part of the war carrying cargo up and down the east coast of England dodging the threats posed by enemy E-boats, U-boats and aircraft.

In December 1942 *Glen Tilt* was sailing in convoy from London to Middlesborough loaded with a cargo of cement. Three miles from No 4 Buoy, off Lowestoft, she was torpedoed during the night by an E-boat.

In the darkness the *Glen Tilt* sank rapidly and all on board were lost.

As Fred's body was never recovered his CR1 (seaman's record) is annotated

"Supposed drowned."

Fred's name is recorded on the **Tower Hill Memorial:**

Panel 52

WILLIAM GEORGE CYRIL HURST

Petty Officer Stoker, Royal Navy
P/KX 81593
H.M.S. LIMBOURNE
who died on
Saturday 23rd October 1943, aged 30.

William, or **Cyril** as he preferred to be called, came from a military family. His grandfather had been a career soldier and four of his six sons were each born in a different Indian garrison town. After his discharge he settled briefly in Lymington, where Cyril's father, George, was born. George subsequently moved to Wales and became a miner, married a Welsh girl, Margaret Davies and settled in Blaengwyfi, South Wales. Here they raised their family comprising Cyril, born in 1913, and his two sisters May and Margaret. Cyril started work as a miner,

but after many mining disasters the family moved to Rose Cottage, Tithe Barn, Lymington in 1926, with George getting a job with Wellworthy's.

When he became 18 years old in November 1931, Cyril joined the Royal Navy and made it his career. This involved service in all parts of the world including a two-and-a-half year commission in the Mediterranean.

In 1935 Cyril married Freda Bran at Pennington Church. They moved into a house in Portsmouth and in 1938 started a family with the birth of their son David. Freda had her own war, being bombed out of her home in Portsmouth – and then losing her furniture when the repository was itself bombed. Homeless, she and David moved back to Rose Cottage in September 1943 to stay with their family.

Cyril served on all types of ship, from the battleships RESOLUTION and MALAYA to small ships. By 1942 he had qualified for promotion to Chief Petty Officer. His war service included a year with Russian convoys to Murmansk in the "Flower" class corvette SWEET BRIAR. He was also at the successful Battle of Matapan in March 1941 and later took part in the bombardment of Genoa.

HMS LIMBOURNE
NMM N22168

By 1943 Cyril was part of the crew of LIMBOURNE, one of the 72 "Hunt" class destroyers commissioned by the Royal Navy during the war. LIMBOURNE was a Type 3, laid down at Stephen's yard in 1941 and completed a year later. She was designed as a convoy escort, with a range of 3,700 miles at 14 knots - although she could steam at 28 knots when required. This class had a good anti-aircraft capability and also carried an anti-submarine armament of 60 depth charges. LIMBOURNE had a busy war escorting convoys.

LIMBOURNE was torpedoed in the English Channel by an enemy E-boat, T 22, at 1.52 a.m. on 23rd October 1943. Her bows were blown off and whilst an attempt was made to tow her back to port the damage was so great that the attempt failed and she was later sunk at 6.40 a.m. by a torpedo from HMS TALLYBONT and 4.7 inch gunfire from HMS ROCKET. A hundred and three of her crew were saved, but forty-two sailors were lost in the attack.

THE LYMINGTON TIMES of 18th December 1943 reported that:

Some weeks ago Mrs Freda Hurst, who is now living with her widowed mother, Mrs J Bran, at Rose Cottage, The Square, in Pennington, received two telegrams from the Admiralty within a short while of each other, the first telling her that her husband was "MISSING, PRESUMED KILLED," and the second just stating that he was "MISSING".

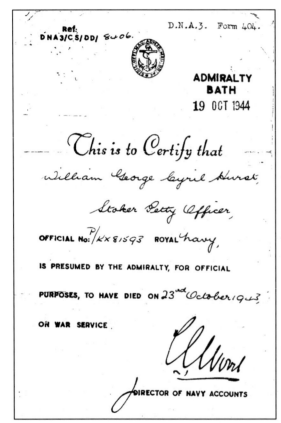

Ref:
DNA3/CS/DD/ 8006.

D.N.A.3. Form 404.

ADMIRALTY
BATH
19 OCT 1944

This is to Certify that

William George Cyril Hurst,

Stoker Petty Officer,

OFFICIAL No: P/KX 81593 ROYAL Navy,

IS PRESUMED BY THE ADMIRALTY, FOR OFFICIAL

PURPOSES, TO HAVE DIED ON 23rd October 1943

ON WAR SERVICE.

DIRECTOR OF NAVY ACCOUNTS

It was here that she received news of her husband's death. Two survivors of the action later called on Freda and told her that Cyril had received severe head injuries from which he never regained consciousness. A mate removed his wedding ring and ditty-box key and gave both items to her. They regretted leaving his body, but had to get the wounded off the ship before it could be hit again.

Three months later Freda learnt that her brother, Sid, (see page 282) was missing in action in Italy. A second son, Nicky, was born in March 1944.

After the war she married an American serviceman and went to live in the United States. Nicky now lives in Florida and David, who has kindly provided the photographs, lives in New York.

Cyril has his name recorded on the **Portsmouth Naval Memorial** on:

Panel 77, Column 3.

FREDERICK JOHN ROBERT WALSH

Engineman
KX 116075
Royal Naval Patrol Service
who died on
Thursday 16th November 1944, aged 32.

Frederick, always known as **John,** was the son of William and Ada Walsh, of Peartree Cottage, Bridge Road, Lymington. The family was a large one, comprising four sons and six daughters. John's father was a career sailor in the Royal Navy and served in the Boer War, the Boxer Rebellion and the First World War. He then went on to become a member of the Coastguard Service. At the time of the outbreak of the Second World War he was 65 years old. His wife is reported as saying that:

"Now, at 65, he would like to go back to
sea again - but he is too old!"

Despite father's age the family certainly could be said to have done their bit for the country. The eldest boy, **Arthur,** had been killed in Mesopotamia in World War 1, but is not recorded on the Lymington War Memorial. **Roy** went to Greenwich Royal Naval School and then joined the Navy. He

was on BULLDOG and helped to save Mountbatten's ship, KELLY, when it was bombed in 1940. His verses were published in the Lymington Times and led him to be dubbed "Lymington's Naval Poet." In 1943 twenty-four of his poems were published locally in book form and sold for a shilling.

John, pictured here, worked as an engineer for Wellworthy's but following family tradition he joined the Royal Navy as an Engineman in 1940. Before the war he married Corona.

By 1943 John was in the Mediterranean. Here he served on HM Patrol Vessel 2013 - a wooden two-masted vessel of 260 tons, armed with a 3-inch gun and two 20mm anti-aircraft cannon, employed on inshore duties. His brother, Roy, who has kindly provided information for this memorial, was serving on the minesweeper ACUTE at the time and sighted a Petty Officer among some Arabs on the jetty at Bone. It was his brother, John. Roy was granted three hours leave and visited his brother's ship, which was employed on covert operations. Disguised as a fishing vessel, the crew wore civvies - their task being to covertly survey harbours, beaches and cliff features. It was the last time the two brothers were to meet.

Both John and Corona were long time friends of the Hursts (see page 328). When Cyril was killed John wrote the following letter to Freda, Cyril's wife, not knowing that her brother, Sid (Bran), was also missing:

> P/o. F.J.R. Walsh Kx 116075.
> No: 1. Special Force
> Central Mediterranean Forces.
>
> Friday Jan: 7th 1944.
>
> Dear Freda,
>
> No doubt lots of things have happened since I last saw you, but as you can imagine, I never dreamed of having to write to you, under the circumstances of the last few weeks.
>
> Corona wrote & told me about Cyril, although I don't know yet if you know any different than the fact that he is missing, well Freda, in any case you may hear good news yet, I know its usual to try to bolster up any remaining hopes. I don't wish to do that, but please accept my sincerest feelings. That I'm afraid is all I can offer, together with the hope that all may yet turn out well.
>
> Give my kind regards to your mother, I should like to see you both again, and have a talk, that opportunity may, or may not present itself in the near future, as I don't know how long we shall be out here.

How is Sid going on these days, should you care to write will you please send me his address.

I met one of Cyrils shipmates out here, but did not know about anything at the time as sometimes my mail is perhaps 3 months adrift, and sometimes I get mail only 2 weeks from posting, so I did not know until about 2 or 3 weeks ago.

I will finish now Vrede, I hope that the new year may bring good news & a brighter outlook for you, I'm sorry I haven't managed to say all I wanted to in the correct way in this letter, but I know you understand.

So for now, again remember me to your mother, I would love to hear how you are both keeping and Dave, and now cheerio, and good news & good luck

Your old friend

John returned to England on leave, but drowned in a boating accident at Falmouth, along with a fellow shipmate Gerald de la Rue. John is buried in **Falmouth Cemetery**, Cornwall, in:

Section K. Row A. Grave 24.

PHOTO CLARE CHURCH

TO A DARLING HUSBAND
AND FATHER
FROM HIS LOVING WIFE AND SON
"TILL WE MEET"

Corona never remarried. She died in 1996 at the age of eighty-four. Their son, Derek lives in New Milton.

JOHN FAIRFAX GREGORY

Able Seaman, Royal Navy
P/JX 307542
H.M.S. PRESIDENT
who died on
Thursday 19th April 1945, aged 41.

John was born on 2nd March 1904 at Liverpool. He was the son of William and Helen Gregory, of Lymington. He married Amy Adelaide (Dolly), who later lived in Bitterne, Southampton.

At some stage he joined the Royal Navy and by 1945 was serving, as a DEMS gunner, aboard the *Gold Shell.*

PHOTO EDDY VAN DRIEL

This was a motorised tanker of 8208 gross tons, which hit a mine and sank on 16th April 1945 – three weeks before the end of the war - off the coast of Zeebrugge in Belgium.

John is buried in **Bergan-op Zoom War Cemetery**, Holland in:

Grave D. 5. 3.

His wife had inscribed on his gravestone:

**"GOD BLESS, SWEETHEART,
TILL WE MEET AGAIN,
LOVING WIFE DOLLY
AND CHILDREN"**

WILLIAM CLARKE

Squadron Leader
Royal Air Force Volunteer Reserve
who died on
Wednesday 3rd February 1943, aged 32.

Bill was the son of George and Tallulah Clarke, the family

being involved with Clarke's Tobacco. He had two brothers who also served in the war – Tom, a Commander in the Royal Navy, who gained the DSO and Lee, who was in the Intelligence Corps.

Bill later married Winifred Mary (nee Harrison of Hindley, in Lancashire) in Letchworth on 8th September 1939 and had two sons - Michael and Bill. The latter, who was born only five weeks before his father's death, has kindly provided information for this memorial.

Bill Clarke was born in Liverpool on 31st May 1910 and went to school at Cheltenham. In 1927 he went up to St Johns Oxford, reading Politics, Philosophy and Economics. He also joined the University Air Squadron and gained his wings. Whilst an undergraduate he had also acquired a triangular-framed Vincent motorbike and raced in all the major trials of the 1930's. His search for spares for the bike led to his meeting Mr Vincent - subsequently joining the Company and becoming a Director.

Bill reported for duty as a Pilot Officer RAFVR when war was declared, becoming a flying instructor at the Central Flying School at RAF LITTLE RISSINGTON. He was promoted Flight Lieutenant on the 13th November 1940.

After a conversion course to Stirlings at 1657 OCU, Bill was posted 214 Squadron, 3 Group, Bomber Command on 13th November 1942 as a Squadron Leader. For such a large aircraft, the Stirling was highly manoeuvrable as a result of its comparatively short wingspan. This meant, however, that it was restricted to operating below 16,000 feet and therefore was more exposed to the flak and night-fighter defences. Bill's first operation, on 28th/29th November, was to Turin. Bad weather prevented further operational flying for two months.

At the start of the year, Air Chief Marshall Harris had been instructed by the War Cabinet to concentrate on targets involving U-boat manufacture and operation, including the Bay of Biscay and the French ports of Lorient and St. Nazaire.

On the night of 2nd/3rd February 1943, therefore, a force of 263 aircraft gathered from fifteen different squadrons to attack the shipyards engaged in U-boat construction in Hamburg. Bomber Command had by now improved the accuracy of attacks with the use of the blind bombing aid OBOE and the air-to-ground radar H2S. However, reasonable visibility was still needed for the main force aircraft to see the target markers that had been dropped by the pathfinder Mosquitoes. On this night cloud cover resulted in the bombs being scattered over a wide area.

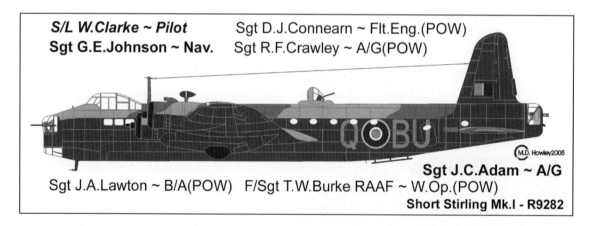

S/L W.Clarke ~ Pilot   Sgt D.J.Connearn ~ Flt.Eng.(POW)
Sgt G.E.Johnson ~ Nav.   Sgt R.F.Crawley ~ A/G(POW)

M.D. Howley 2005

Sgt J.C.Adam ~ A/G
Sgt J.A.Lawton ~ B/A(POW)   F/Sgt T.W.Burke RAAF ~ W.Op.(POW)
Short Stirling Mk.I - R9282

Squadron Leader Clarke and his crew were shot down by a night-fighter from III/NJG1 piloted by Uffz. C Koltringer. The Stirling crashed at Benschop, 14 km. SW of Utrecht in Holland.

PHOTO EDDY VAN DRIEL

As four of the crew survived to become POWs, it is probable they were able to parachute to safety before the crash. The three who died, including Bill, are appropriately buried together in the **Benschop General Cemetery,** Holland, in

a Collective Grave.

The west door of St John's Church, Boldre, is dedicated by his wife and mother to the memory of William and his crew.

When Winifed died in 1994, her ashes were very appropriately scattered over the grave in Benschop.

Her son Bill wryly recalls the apparent paradox of scattering ashes in such an immaculately kept cemetery.

ARTHUR GEORGE COLE

Sergeant
Royal Air Force Volunteer Reserve
who died on
Thursday 2nd December 1943, aged 21.

Jim, as he was always called, was the only Son of Arthur and Annie Cole of South Street, Pennington.

He had always been very air-minded, so when war broke out he volunteered for flying duties with the RAF. This photograph shows him wearing the brevet of an Air Gunner. By 1943 he was a wireless operator flying in Lancasters with 460 Squadron, Royal Australian Air Force (RAAF), out of RAF BINBROOK, in Lincolnshire. This photograph was taken in August 1943.

Jim was an experienced Wireless Operator with twenty-eight missions to his credit. Thirty missions constituted a "Tour" - which relatively few air-crew reached. Those who did were then rested before beginning a second tour. Jim had flown all his missions with a 22-year-old ex- schoolteacher Australian pilot - Pilot Officer JHA English DFC- as captain. It was, therefore, a very experienced crew.

Probably as a result of such classification they were given an extra member, Norman Stockton, a reporter for Australian Associated Newspapers. He was, in fact, one of the four reporters who were allowed to fly on this raid. Captain Grieg, a Norwegian War Correspondent, also failed to return. Ed Morrow, the famous American journalist, survived the mission. He broadcast regularly to the American people even before they entered the war, always starting with the words

"This is London...."

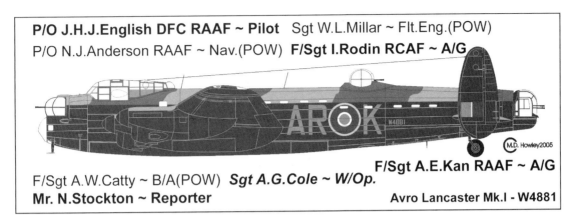

P/O J.H.J.English DFC RAAF ~ Pilot   Sgt W.L.Millar ~ Flt.Eng.(POW)
P/O N.J.Anderson RAAF ~ Nav.(POW)   **F/Sgt I.Rodin RCAF ~ A/G**

AR⊙K   N4881   M.D. Howley2005

F/Sgt A.E.Kan RAAF ~ A/G
F/Sgt A.W.Catty ~ B/A(POW)   *Sgt A.G.Cole ~ W/Op.*
Mr. N.Stockton ~ Reporter   **Avro Lancaster Mk.I - W4881**

The target that night was Berlin, being the fifth of a series of raids on the German capital that had started on 18th November and which became known as the Battle of Berlin. Ed Morrow began his broadcast of this raid by saying:

"Last night, some of the young gentlemen of the RAF took me to Berlin...."

The Germans were able to predict likely routes and deploy night fighters accordingly. Out of a bomber force of 450 aircraft, 40 were lost. 460 Squadron lost five of its twenty-four aircraft. Ed Morrow went on to describe vividly the operation of the crew and the sights they saw as they flew in moonlight above cloud - the searchlights, flak and the colours of the bombs, incendiaries and markers. They saw other aircraft being shot down by the flak and night fighters and even had a battle to evade the attention of two such aircraft. He remembers his friend, Norman Stockton, and ends:

"Berlin was a thing of orchestrated hell - a terrible symphony of light and flames."

Arthur's aircraft was shot down on this raid and all the crew killed.

He is buried in **Berlin 1939-1945 War Cemetery** in:

Grave 8. K. 9.

His mother visited the grave in the 1980s.

TERENCE FREDERICK FROGLEY DFM

Sergeant
1609273
Royal Air Force Volunteer Reserve
who died on
Wednesday 19th July 1944, aged 20.

Terry was born in Northampton 1924, the son of Police Constable Cecil and Mrs Anne Frogley. Cecil was later stationed in Lymington, living at 93, High Street. During the war he was a War Reserve Constable, with the family living at Orchard Cottage, Efford Park, Pennington

On leaving school Terry worked as a printer for Messrs CT King in Lymington. He was, however, one of the original members of the Lymington Flight of the Air Training Corps and it was therefore no surprise when he volunteered for the RAF as soon as he was old enough. He was called up in May 1943 and after basic training specialised as an Air Gunner. He was then posted, as a sergeant, to 619 Squadron. This Squadron was equipped with Lancaster IIIs and by July 1944 was operating out of RAF DUNHOLME LODGE, Lincolnshire.

For Bomber Command, the months of June and July saw them concentrating on targets in France in support of the D-Day invasion and subsequent land battles. Apart from some raids on German synthetic oil plants, there were a series of raids against communications, ammunition dumps and naval targets. The other target that required Bomber Command's attention were the V-1 sites that Hitler had ordered into action as part of his response to the invasion. Terence had involvement in many of these raids, indeed his actions during the operation against a V-1 site at Creil on 4th July earned him an immediate award of the Distinguished Flying Medal.

This was reported in the LONDON GAZETTE on 29th August, as follows:

> *"In July 1944, this airman was a rear gunner of an aircraft detailed to attack a target near Paris. Whilst over the target area, the aircraft was engaged by an enemy fighter. Early in the fight, the bomber was struck by the enemy's bullets. The inter-communication system was rendered useless and the mid-upper turret was hit and its occupant was wounded; the rear turret was also damaged and could only be operated manually. Despite this, Sergeant Frogley used his guns to excellent effect, causing the enemy aircraft to break away with smoke pouring from it. After the target had been bombed, the aircraft was twice engaged by enemy aircraft but Sergeant Frogley drove them off. This airman displayed high skill and great resolution, qualities which contributed materially to the safe return of his aircraft."*

His Lancaster made it back across the channel and crash-landed at Ford in Sussex.

On 7th July, 619 Squadron participated in a raid against the tunnels housing a flying-bomb storage depot at St. Leu-d'Esserent. It was a successful attack, although it was intercepted by night-fighters and 31 of the 221 bombers failed to return. They were in action on 12th July against a rail junction at Culmont-Chalindrey and on the 14th, when Villeneuvre was the target.

The squadron was airborne again in the early hours of 18th July when Bomber Command acted in direct support of Operation GOODWOOD. The ground troops advanced southeast of Caen, with the bombers attacking fortified positions ahead of the advancing forces. This involved the use of over 1,000 Bomber Command aircraft and some 860 bombers of the American Army Air Force over a period of three days. It was the biggest of the eight attacks that Bomber Command was to make in close support of the Allied Armies' ground campaign in Normandy.

Terry was airborne again at 22:58 on 18th July, when thirteen 619 Squadron aircraft took off for a raid on an important rail junction at Revigny. All such targets were heavily defended by anti-aircraft artillery and by night fighters and Bomber Command suffered some high loss rates.

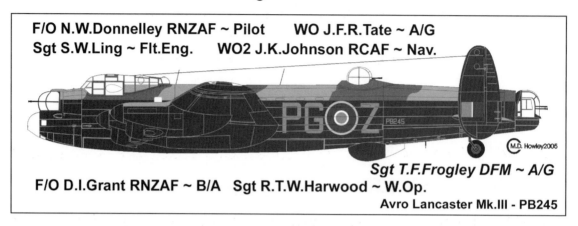

F/O N.W.Donnelley RNZAF ~ Pilot   WO J.F.R.Tate ~ A/G
Sgt S.W.Ling ~ Flt.Eng.   WO2 J.K.Johnson RCAF ~ Nav.

Sgt T.F.Frogley DFM ~ A/G
F/O D.I.Grant RNZAF ~ B/A   Sgt R.T.W.Harwood ~ W.Op.
Avro Lancaster Mk.III - PB245

Five aircraft from this one squadron failed to return, including Terence's Lancaster. It was shot down, probably by a night fighter, and crashed near Ussy-sur-Marne. Terry was identified by his identity disc as one of the three airmen whose bodies had been found near wreckage. The local villagers took his body to the church and started to bury him in the early hours of the morning, when they were interrupted by the arrival of a German officer. The villagers later informed Terry's sister that the officer was the fighter pilot who had shot the Lancaster down. Apparently he walked to the grave, saluted and said to the villagers

"Him today – maybe me tomorrow."

A week after Terence's parents learnt of his failure to return they received a letter from the Air Ministry stating that the King had approved the immediate award of the DFM to him

"As a result of some outstanding performance on a recent operational sortie."

His parents later received his medal at Buckingham Palace.

The seven members of the crew, including two New Zealanders and a Canadian, illustrating the mix of nationalities that was common in Bomber Command squadrons, are buried in the only military grave in **Ussy-sur-Marne Communal Cemetery**, France.

HERBERT OTTO BERGER DFM

Flying Officer
169506
Royal Air Force Volunteer Reserve
who died on
Tuesday 16th January 1945.

Whilst his background is unknown, the Electoral Roll in 1940 lists **Herbert** as living with his wife, Bridie, at 1 Preston Place, Lower Buckland,

By 1945, Herbert was an experienced and decorated member of a Bomber Command aircrew. As Sergeant, No.1455027, he had already completed a very successful tour of operational flights with No. 101 Squadron, between April 1943 and January 1944. During this time his crew had attacked most of the enemy's major targets in Germany.

No. 101 Squadron took on a unique role amongst the Lancaster-equipped Bomber squadrons, when its aircraft were fitted with secret communications jamming equipment. Such aircraft also carried an eighth crewmember whom, as a German speaker, had the job to find and then jam the German radio frequencies being used to control their night-fighter defences. Even today, the exact nature of these secret operations is largely unknown.

In May 1943, following a sortie against Bochum, his skill and cooperation were of great assistance in enabling his captain to fly the badly damaged aircraft back to base. At the end of the tour he was awarded the Distinguished Flying Medal, notice of which appeared in the LONDON GAZETTE on 21st April 1944. The citation added that

> *"in times of stress this airman has invariably shown great fortitude and skill, setting a fine example of courage and devotion to duty."*

Herbert was then posted to No.1656 Heavy Conversion Unit at RAF LINDHOLME in Yorkshire.

In January 1945 he was commissioned and with his new rank of Flying Officer he was posted to No. 100 Squadron, again flying Lancasters with Bomber Command. This squadron was based at WALTHAM, Grimsby, having been re-formed there in 1943.

By this stage of the war, Bomber command main force squadrons were increasing their attacks on oil production, with 24 raids in January - representing twice that achieved the previous month. The targets too, were at greater range as new navigational equipment became available. Herbert flew on the operation to the oil plant at Mersburg/Leuna, on 14th January, but the raid was inconclusive because of solid cloud.

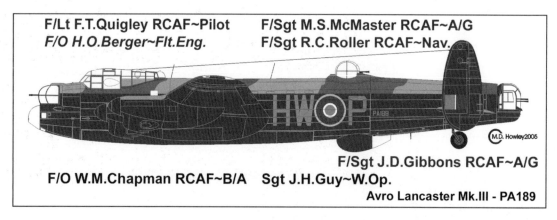

F/Lt F.T.Quigley RCAF~Pilot   F/Sgt M.S.McMaster RCAF~A/G
F/O H.O.Berger~Flt.Eng.   F/Sgt R.C.Roller RCAF~Nav.

F/Sgt J.D.Gibbons RCAF~A/G
F/O W.M.Chapman RCAF~B/A   Sgt J.H.Guy~W.Op.
Avro Lancaster Mk.III - PA189

The target for the 16th January 1945 was to the Braunkohle-Benzin synthetic oil complex at Zeitz, near Leipzig. Herbert's aircraft was one of seventeen employed from 100 Squadron. The operational records report that five aircraft were detailed to act as Path Finder Force supporters, bombing blind using H2S radar, ahead of the main force. Several crews reported identifying the target and saw the plant in snow before it was obscured by smoke and flames from continuous direct hits, resulting in a series of most promising explosions. They described the raid, in which a total of 328 aircraft took part, as well controlled by the Master Bomber. Herbert's Lancaster B, Mk I, was the only one lost from 100 Squadron. It crashed near Questenberg, where all the members of the crew were originally buried.

They were later re-interred in **Berlin 1939-1945 War Cemetery**, in:

Collective Grave 14. Z. 2-7.

ROBERT GEORGE LOWEN

Flying Officer
Royal Air Force Volunteer Reserve
who died on
Wednesday 11th April 1945, aged 22.

Bob was born in Ramsgate on 27th April 1922 to Lillian and George Lowen. The family, which also included sisters Irene and Joan, moved to the New Forest in 1933. When Bob left his School in East Boldre he became a shipwright, working at Berthon Boatyard in Lymington. In 1940, the family moved again, this time to settle in Spring Road, Lymington.

Although Bob was in a reserved occupation he volunteered for the RAF in 1941. After initial training he was selected and sent to Canada for flying training and graduated as a navigator.

Commissioned as a Flying Officer, he initially flew in Mosquito fighter/bombers.

By 1945, Bob had joined 144 Squadron, of Coastal Command, stationed at RAF DALLACHY near Lossiemouth in Scotland. Bob's squadron was part of the "Dallachy Wing" which operated against enemy shipping off the Norwegian coast. On average, the wing normally did nine full sorties a month, interspersed with aircraft flying reconnaissance missions.

On 11th April, Bob's Mark X Beaufighter was one of eight aircraft from 144 Squadron, armed with rockets and cannon that took off for Eeidfjord on an anti-shipping strike. The Dallachy Wing, that day, also consisted of six aircraft each from 489 RNZAF and 455 RAAF Squadrons, armed with bombs and torpedoes respectively, twelve Mustang fighters for escort and two Warwicks - whose task was to drop lifeboats to any crew that ditched in the North Sea.

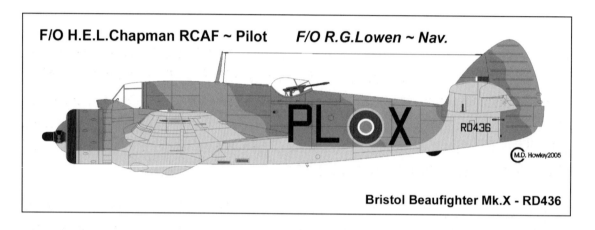

F/O H.E.L.Chapman RCAF ~ Pilot   F/O R.G.Lowen ~ Nav.

PL ○ X   RD436

M.D. Howley2005

Bristol Beaufighter Mk.X - RD436

Bob was flying in aircraft "**PL-X**," which was tasked as one of two "outriders" for the mission. As they approached the target area, his Beaufighter reported enemy aircraft in sight. Eight Mustangs promptly attacked the ten aircraft in question. The main force then attacked shipping in Eeidfjord, with 144 Squadron reporting 15 rocket hits on a 2,500-ton merchantman. This ship was observed to be on fire both amidships and abaft the bridge.

The other "outrider" saw a Messerschmitt Bf 109 heading towards Bob's aircraft before being, in turn, attacked by it. There was also heavy enemy anti-aircraft fire from naval vessels and coastal batteries during the attack. Shortly afterwards, the formation leader noted Bob's Beaufighter climbing away to the South West with its port engine smoking. The aircraft was not seen again and both crewmembers were reported as missing.

Robert's name is therefore recorded on the **Runnymede Memorial**, Surrey, on:

Panel 267

PHILIP HASTINGS ISTED

Pilot Officer
89823
Royal Air Force Volunteer Reserve
who died on
Sunday 28th December 1941, aged 24.

Philip Isted, known to his family as **"Peter"** was born in Emsworth Road, Lymington, in June 1917. His parents, Alfred and Violet Grace Isted had two other sons, John and Kenneth, and two daughters, Edna and Patricia. Peter was educated at Lymington Junior School and, from 1927-1932, at Brockenhurst County High School.

From 1934-1938 Peter was apprenticed to the furnishing trade in Oxford and then joined the family firm at Lymington. This was Ford & Co. house fitters and furnishers, who traded in Lymington for over 150 years. Robert Climpson Isted (see page 324) was also part of this family. At this time Peter's younger brother, Kenneth, held a commission in the Royal Navy and his sister worked for Lloyds Bank in Lymington.

The 1939 Electoral Roll shows Peter living with his mother at Southway, Kings Park Road, Lymington.

Peter joined the RAFVR in 1938 at the age of 22. He learnt to fly during six months training in Canada and gained his wings in 1941. He was then posted to RAF CHIVENOR on 19th July 1941 and started training on Beauforts with No 5 Coastal Operational Training Unit shortly afterwards. These courses were designed to convert the Pilots, Observers and Wireless Operator/Air Gunners onto the Beaufort and form them into crews.

The Bristol Beaufort was a twin-engined torpedo-bomber that was used for attacks on surface shipping as well as general maritime reconnaissance missions. But the Beaufort Mk.1 was beset with engine problems and No. 5 Coastal OTU had eight crashes in August; their first month of operations.

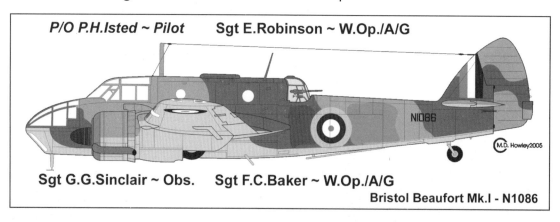

P/O P.H.Isted ~ Pilot   Sgt E.Robinson ~ W.Op./A/G

Sgt G.G.Sinclair ~ Obs.   Sgt F.C.Baker ~ W.Op./A/G

Bristol Beaufort Mk.I - N1086

On Sunday 28th December 1941 Peter was returning from a training sortie over the western English Channel with his port engine out of action. Over Plymouth his starboard engine also failed. As the hilly landscape offered no suitable terrain for a forced landing the crew were obliged to crash-land at Stoke Climsford. They successfully avoided the tower of the village church in which an evening service was being held. This

came to an abrupt close as the congregation rushed out to render assistance, but Peter and his three crew members had been killed instantly.

Peter's funeral took place at the parish church of St Thomas on 1st January 1942. Conducted by the vicar, the Reverend K Lamplugh, a large number of friends attended the service. He is buried in **Lymington Cemetery** in

Consolidated Plot Grave 1905

Amongst the many beautiful flowers was a wreath, in the form of RAF wings, from the Officers and Men of his RAF station.

HENRY ORLANDO FOSTER

Sergeant
1318113
Royal Air Force Volunteer Reserve
who died on
Tuesday 27th April 1943, aged 34.

Harry, as he was known, was the son of James and Alice Foster of 25, Duke Street, Southampton. He married a local girl - Irene Ida Johnson ("Sunny") and they later moved to a house near The Borough Arms in Lymington, where a daughter, Jean, was born. Eventually they lived at Sapphire Villa in Brook Road, Lymington. Harry worked at Wellworthy Piston Rings Limited, where he secured promotion to the Inspection Department. He was always very interested in music and had joined the band of the Territorial Hampshire Heavy Brigade RA. He is 1st from right in the middle row below.

He also played the double bass in Charlie Case's works' band.

Harry volunteered for the Royal Air Force and was called up in November 1941. After completing his Basic Training, he went to South Africa for Pilot Training. Here he showed considerable keenness and efficiency. He returned, having trained as an observer and was promoted to Sergeant. On the way back to England in October 1942, however, his troopship – the 20,000-ton *Dutchess of Atholl* - was torpedoed in the Atlantic Ocean:

At Sea.

My Darling Sunny.

Well Darling, such a lot has happened since last I wrote to you. The cheif thing is that we were torpedoed on Sat. 10th Oct and so my dear all the nice presents I had for you and Jean are gone. I lost everything Kit, books and my notes gathered and rewritten so carefully, since I've been in the R.A.F. I spent nearly all my money on presents and I enclose a list of them. Please break the news to Jean & Allen that Munby has no toys for them not even her doll. I shall hate Jerry more than ever about that Doll.

Now I suppose you will want to know what happened I was in that happy state half asleep and half awake at 6.20 in the morning when the first one struck. You'll never imagine how

the ship shudders Reve ? just as if
a big hand shook it – then all
the lights went out and we were
scrambling and trying to dress in
the dark and a job it was to
find everything – then out on deck
and stand by the boats. We were
standing there when along came No 2.
then we were ordered into the boats
we had about 25 in ours and
just as we were trying to get
away from the ships side No 3 came
one boat was blown over by the
explosion but no one was hurt.

About an hour after this
we were about a mile from the
ship, when she started to list and
went down about quarter of an hour
after. It's a heart rending sight
to see your boat slipp down into
the water Sunny and suddenly you
realise that the Ocean is all
yours. – and that theirs a hell of
a lot of it. We found out after
that we were 800 miles from Africa
and 200 from the Ascension Isles.

The life boats were then
gathered together a Roll call and
was found that only 4 poor devils were
missing believed killed by the tin
fish and there were 821 of us in
boats. – including 100 women & 50 kiddies
– in about 24 lifeboats. all that day
we hung together but in the night
about 5 boats lost touch and
what with rain and the rough sea

351

it was very unpleasant. Everyone was gloriously sick. When dawn came, the waves were a bit quieter and a ship was sighted about 10% — a very welcome sight — after 31 hrs on the lifeboat. We were all on board by 1.30 and had a nice cup of tea + free issue of cigarettes

Then our troubles started as she was only a small ship and over 800 people was not room or food for them so we had to sleep on the decks — and steel is very hard — with a sandwich every meal time and a cup of weak soup they had no more food and it was 3 days to Freetown where we were put on this boat. Well Rene thats all there is to it — imagine me with a pr trousers a coat a topee and a pr of plimsols and nothing else. Also a beard (1 week) as we

werent allowed to wash or shave on the rescue ship. Taking it all in we were very lucky only to lose 4 and to be picked up so quickly

And now I can say I love you more than ever Dear I thought of you during that night and also while we were having a thanksgiving service the hymn was "Eternal Father strong to save" — Ive never been so near crying —

The remainder of his letter is, understandably, personal.

While undergoing training as operational aircrew, Harry was attached to No. 13 Operational Training Unit operating from Bicester, Oxfordshire. This training was designed to provide aircrew for the Squadrons of No. 2 Group Bomber Command, engaged on short-range raids on specific targets within occupied Europe. The training was split into four Flights, A to D. The first three each provided training for the three different operational roles: Pilot, Observer and Wireless operator/Air Gunner. On D Flight, the pupils met and formed themselves into individual crews and trained together to form an efficient fighting team. Henry had obviously reached this last stage as he is listed as the second member (observer) of the crew.

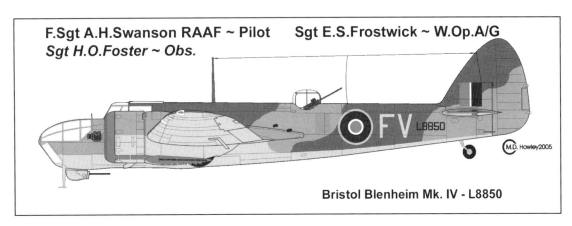

F.Sgt A.H.Swanson RAAF ~ Pilot   Sgt E.S.Frostwick ~ W.Op.A/G
Sgt H.O.Foster ~ Obs.

FV L8850

M.D. Howley 2005

Bristol Blenheim Mk. IV - L8850

On the night of 27th April, he took off at 1 a.m. in Blenheim Mk. IV, L8850, on a night cross-country training flight. At 3.15 a.m. the Blenheim blew up and crashed near Stewkley, 10 miles ESE

of Buckingham, killing all the crew. The cause of the accident was not known, but flying at night was always hazardous, especially for a trainee aircrew. The weather, disorientation, or mechanical failure, could each affect a flight, with fatal consequences.

Harry is buried in **Southampton (South Stoneham) Cemetery**, Hampshire, in:

Section L. 4. Grave 115.

HENRY LONG CLIFFORD HALL

Lieutenant Colonel
18483
Royal Artillery
who died on
Tuesday 29th August 1944, aged 43.

Henry was born on 2nd December 1901, the son of Lieutenant Colonel George Clifford Miller Hall CMG CBE DSO late of the Royal Engineers. The family lived at Grove House, Lymington.

Educated at Repton (1915-19) Henry joined the army as a Gentleman Cadet at the Royal Military Academy at Woolwich. He was commissioned on 13th July 1921 into the Royal Regiment of Artillery and was promoted to Lieutenant two years later. By 1934 he was a Battery Captain with 1 Field Regiment and was with them when war was declared.

The 38th Searchlight Regiment had been established before the war from the 6th Battalion the Kings Regiment (Liverpool). Initially, in 1936, this TA unit had belonged to the Royal Engineers, but in 1939 it became a Royal Artillery unit. In March 1944 its headquarters was located at Lingfield, where the task of its outlying batteries was to illuminate – with 150 cm searchlights - enemy night bombers as they tried to disrupt supplies heading across Kent for the Normandy beachhead.

PHOTO NICK SAUNDERS

On 29th August 1944 Henry was visiting 352 Battery at Coleman's Hatch Camp. At 1.50 p.m., just as lunch was finishing, a V1 Flying bomb exploded outside the Officers' Mess, where all the battery officers had been lunching with their Commanding Officer. The camp was extensively damaged and the Mess completely destroyed.

Henry Hall was the only immediate fatality, but six officers and a Lance Bombardier were wounded and admitted to hospital. Junior Commander E Phelp, OC of E Company and Private

Davies, Assistant Cook, both of the ATS, were both discharged from the unit Casualty Reception Station after treatment. Major HR Stirling later died from his wounds and is buried beside him.

The War Diary records that

"**No disturbance was caused to Search Light operations.**"

Henry was buried by his regiment, at 3.00 p.m. on 2nd September, in

Edenbridge Cemetery Extension, Kent, in

Grave 11.

VICTOR REGINALD HOBBY

Private
5494206
1st Battalion The Hampshire Regiment
Who died on
Tuesday 6th June 1944, aged 37.

Victor and Eric were the two sons of Jack and Hannah Hobby, who lived in Ropewalk Cottages, Lymington. Jack worked on Normandy Farm.

In 1932 Victor and Dorothy were married in the Lymington Congregational Church, and their son Eric was born in 1938. Dorothy and Eric later moved to live in the Old Alarm on Quay Hill.

The family believe that Victor's brother Eric served in the RAF during the war. He returned to live in Lymington until his death in 1997.

Victor joined the 1st Battalion the Hampshire Regiment. This regular unit had gone to India in 1925 and remained there until 1938, when they had been posted to Palestine. Since 1939 it had seen action in the Middle East, Malta and Sicily.

The 1st Battalion returned to England in November 1943 to prepare for D-Day. In February 1944 it moved to Cadlands Camp at Fawley for invasion training. The battalion trained intensively with tanks and specialist armoured vehicles and practiced assault landings at Studland Bay and on Hayling Island.

At 6.30 p.m. on the evening of 5th June 1944 Force G, carrying 50th (Northumbrian Division), sailed past the Isle of Wight bound for the Arromanches beaches. 1 Hampshires were part of its 231 Brigade, along with 1 Dorsets and 2 Devons. Their task was to assault the beach at JIG GREEN and secure a lodgement, which could then be secured and exploited, thus allowing the vital Mulberry Harbour to be built.

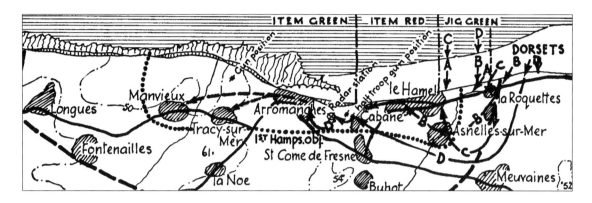

The battalion embarked into their assault craft at 6.0 a.m. and began the beach approach. In the aftermath of the worst gales for 70 years the sea was very choppy, and most men were cold, wet and seasick. Whilst they were "shot in" by the 6-inch guns of the cruiser AJAX, enemy mortar and artillery fire caused casualties, as did the beach defences and their associated mines and explosive charges - not all of which had been defused by allied frogmen. The assault craft beached 30 yards offshore and the Hampshires waded in under intense small-arms fire. On shore, the specialist tanks had failed to clear any breaches through the minefields and the enemy were offering determined resistance.

By the end of the day the Hampshires had been successful as one of the spearhead battalions leading the invasion of Europe. The cost, however, was high with 182 men being killed or wounded

Victor was one of those killed on the beaches. He is buried in **Bayeux War Cemetery**, France, in

Grave X1. C. 14.

REGINALD HENRY MAXTED

Private
14204941
4th Battalion, The Wiltshire Regiment
Who died on
19th November 1944, aged 21.

Reg was the youngest son of Thomas and Ethel Maxted of 90, Queen Katherine Road, Lymington. He had an older brother, Alf and two sisters – Dorrie, and Nellie (who was married to Norm). Reg was a member of the Congregational Church and took a keen interest in young people's organisations. Reggie's two pals were Fred and Mick.

On leaving school Reg worked in the Post Office, initially as a Telegraph boy. A few months before he joined up he had worked as a postman. In 1941 he enlisted into the 4th Battalion, The Wiltshire Regiment. This was part of 129 Infantry Brigade in the 43rd Wessex Division. His brother, Alf, was already in the army serving in the same division.

The Brigade landed at Normandy on 25th June. The next day they moved forward to take part in OPERATION EPSOM, the battle that was intended to breakout of the Normandy beachhead. The battle continued until 23rd August, when Reg's division captured and held Hill 112.

All was now cleared for the advance northwards into Belgium and Holland to take place. By November 1944 4 Wiltshires was operating in the Groesbeek border area of Holland/Germany, with the 4th Somerset Light Infantry on their right and the US 82nd Airborne Division on the left. The situation was quiet as it was easy to observe each other during the day. At night, however, it was a different matter with intensive patrolling by both sides.

The Wiltshires were relieved on 7th November and moved back to Maastricht. They then, on 12th November, took over a long stretch of the front at Hatterath from the 102nd US Division. Here the enemy showed no sign of offensive action, except for intermittent shelling all along the front. Reggie's battalion was heavily involved in patrolling and supporting the four Observation Posts in their area, in preparation for the forthcoming attack by 130 and 214 Brigades. The enemy were very careless and made no attempt at concealment.

The pioneers searched for and cleared many mines buried in the ground over which the attack was planned to cross. The attack by 214 Brigade on 18th November was successful and removed the threat from the right flank. The following day Reg and another soldier were killed by one of the uncleared mines, just four days before his twenty-second birthday.

THE LYMINGTON TIMES reported:

> *"Reg Maxted was a fine upstanding young man, his generous nature and happy smile endeared him to a large circle of friends. He will be greatly missed by all who knew him."*

PHOTO CWGC

Reg is buried in the **Reichswald Forest War Cemetery** in:

Grave 47. F. 1.

WILLIAM PERCY EVANS

Private
4269805
8th Battalion, The Middlesex Regiment,
who died on
Wednesday 21st February 1945, aged 25.

Bill was the son of William and Margaret Evans of Oakwood, Manor Road, Milton. In 1941 he married Iris Watson, of Highfield, Milford Road, Pennington. She later lived at Cowplain, Hampshire, where her father was the Headmaster of the Junior School.

Bill was an all-round athlete and held several trophies. He joined the army before the war and reached the final of the Army bantamweight championship in Palestine. The 1/8th Territorial battalion of the Middlesex Regiment mobilised at Hounslow on 1st September 1939. It moved to France in February 1940 and what was left of it – including Bill - returned, via Dunkirk, in June. Early in 1943 the battalion changed its name to 8th battalion the Middlesex Regiment and in 1944 it reverted to being a machine gun battalion, with three machine-guns and one 4.2-inch mortar companies.

The battalion landed in France on D+14 in support of the 43rd Wessex Division. Its role was to provide machine gun and heavy mortar support for its three brigades in specific operations such as river crossings. Its first action was on 26th June, when it supported the extension of the Normandy beachhead by the crossing of the River Odon. This new bridgehead was expanded during July by five weeks of incessant fighting. In August Bill's battalion supported a breakout by XXX and VIII Corps through Villers Bocage and over the rivers Orne and Noireau, thus driving the fifteen German divisions facing them into the Falaise-Argentan pocket and capture. The battalion next supported a breakout operation over the River Seine at Vernon - which, ten days later, led to the capture of Antwerp.

In mid September it moved forward to the Meuse-Escaut bridgehead to support the airborne operation at Arnhem. This began on 17th September. October was a comparatively quiet month as the Scheldt was cleared and the port of Antwerp brought back into service. In November the battalion moved into the Geilenkirchen area and supported the advance into Germany. On 19th December Bill and his unit were withdrawn and spent Christmas at Hasselt in Holland. On 4th January 1945 the battalion moved back to the Geilenkirchen front.

Here conditions were severe, with extreme cold. As can be seen from this photograph of the 8th Battalion, white camouflage suits were issued because of the snow. Bill's unit developed a new form of "saturation fire" that used all available weapons to cover the ground like sprinkling pepper from a pot. These "pepperpot" fire-plans demoralised the enemy, many of whom surrendered.

In late January Bill got leave in England with his family. He returned to his unit on 7th February, in time to take part in the crossing of the River Maas. This operation was successfully completed with the battalion's pepperpot fire consuming 850,000 rounds of machine gun ammunition and 8,000 4.2-inch mortar bombs. With Cleve being captured on the 10th the advance into the Reichwald headed for Goch, which was taken on 17th February. The next few days were quiet ones for the battalion, but by this stage Bill had been wounded, being one of the 22 casualties incurred by his unit in this week of operations. Despite being evacuated he died in hospital on 21st February.

Bill is buried in **Reichswald Forest War Cemetery**, Germany, in:

Grave 57. H. 19

JOHN OSWALD VICTOR RHODES

Second Lieutenant
342543
Royal Armoured Corps
who died on
Monday 16th April 1945, aged 26.

John was the only son of Lieutenant Commander Sydney Gerald Rhodes RNVR and his wife Edith, of Olinda, Lymington, and Brazil. The family had lived in Lymington since 1933, although John was in business in London.

John joined the army in 1938 as a Trooper in the Royal Armoured Corps, serving in the 3rd County of London Yeomanry (Sharpshooters). He served in the 8th Army throughout the Libyan campaign, the defence of Egypt, the invasions of both Sicily and Italy and took part in the battles of Sangro and Moro before returning to England for D-Day.

This territorial regiment was equipped with Sherman tanks when it landed in France on 7th June 1944. It was immediately thrown into the battle to expand the Normandy bridgehead and suffered heavy casualties. John was awarded the Croix de Guerre

"for gallant and distinguished services in Normandy."

On 31st July John's regiment amalgamated with its sister regiment to become the 3/4th County of London Yeomanry (Sharpshooters). The new regiment then fought its way north through Antwerp and up to the River Maas. John, by this stage, was a Squadron Sergeant Major in A Squadron.

On 8th January 1945 he received a direct commission in the field and took over a troop of tanks in "B" Squadron. They crossed the Mass at the end of January 1945 as part of 11 Armoured Brigade and continued to advance northwards up the German/Dutch border.

Resistance stiffened on German soil as the fighting recorded in the regimental War Diary for 28th March 1945 shows:

0200 - Regiment continued along its centre line, B Sqn in the lead still, with inf of 4th RWF riding on the tanks. Bad going held up the Regt at 240562 and bazooka attacks from a field on the right, covered by Spandau fire, brewed two tanks and caused casualties. Buildings at 238574 were reached with arty support. B Sqn, though subjected to considerable SA and later AP fire, reached their objective, woods at 237568, for the loss of one tank to A/Tk fire. There the Sqn engaged enemy inf in the area of the wood, inflicting cas and taking 60 POWs. Claims:- 100 POWs Casualties:- 5 ORs killed, 2 ORs wounded

Two days later they were pulled out and sent back to Nijmegan. The regiment then came under command of the 4th Armoured Brigade in 79th Division. This was the largest division in the army, with nearly 2,400 armoured vehicles and 20,369 men. By the middle of March John's unit had been moved to Venlo. It crossed the Dortmund-Ems canal on 6th April and then faced north as left flank protection to 52 (L) Division. Over the next few days it fought with 53 Division through Hopsten and Voltlage towards Munster.

On 15th April A Squadron took part in a formal assault on a wooded area. During the early afternoon, John's Squadron, which had remained uncommitted in the adjoining area to RHQ, was suddenly shelled. The OC, 2i/c and 6 ORs were wounded and 1 OR killed. Among the nine casualties were no fewer than 6 tank commanders.

In the early afternoon of the following day, moving again with 1st E Lancs, B Squadron reached its objective on high ground against light opposition. John's tank, however, was hit and set on fire by a bazooka and he and two of his crew were killed.

John is buried in **Becklingen War Cemetery,** Germany, in:

Grave 6. F. 4.

According to THE LYMINGTON TIMES of 2nd June 1945

His Commanding Officer, the second in command and his captain speak of the love and respect all had for him ": for his absolute fairness to the men and his known courage in action. One officer wrote: " A finer soldier and a more lovable personality I never met."

ERIC VINCENT THOMPSON

Leading Aircraftman
1313426
Royal Air Force Volunteer Reserve
who died on
Friday 4th May 1945, aged 33.

Eric was a local boy, whose mother, Edith, died aged 76 on 28th March 1958. He married Lilian Mary and the couple lived at Broadmead Copse, Sway.

Regrettably, nothing further has been discovered about his life, or his service in the RAF.

PHOTO NICK SAUNDERS

His Death Certificate records that he died of acute Myoloid leukaemia at the RAF Hospital at Wroughton. In 1946 his mother sent this entry for the ROLL OF HONOUR

Thompson.—In loving memory of my dear son, Eric Vincent, who died on active service on May 4th, 1945. "He was a nature generous and loving; He left us with his duty fully done; And time shall never take from us who love him: The memory of so excellent a son."—Mum.

He is buried in the family grave in **Lymington Cemetery**, in Consolidated Plot:

1055

ANTHONY EDWARD LELAND CROSTHWAIT MBE

**Major
50838
Royal Engineers,**
Who died on
Saturday 12th April 1947, aged 35.

Anthony was one of the sons of Colonel Leland George Crosthwait and of Catherine Rosa Crosthwait (nee Man) of Leelands, Pennington. The Colonel had served for thirty-two years in India, being with the 6th Jats Light Infantry and then the Survey of India. One of Anthony's brothers, Timothy Leland Crosthwait CMG MBE, was to have a distinguished career in H M Diplomatic Service with a final appointment, in 1975, as Ambassador to the Malagasy Republic. A younger brother, Temporary Major Michael Crosthwait BA RE was appointed MBE. (Military Division) for his distinguished service in North West Europe during the war.

Anthony was educated at Wellington, attending Picton House from 1925 to 1930. He passed high into the Royal Military Academy, Woolwich, being subsequently commissioned into the Royal Engineers. He then went on to take a BA degree at Cambridge On 27th November 1943 he married Amy Burdett Morony, of Alverstoke, Gosport, Hampshire. In 1944 a daughter, Katherine, was born. In the family Amy was always called Molly and after the war she lived in a cottage in Pennington Lane. Katherine went to Ridgeway School, that used to be at the top of the lane. She now lives in Devon.

In 1941, Anthony was in Persia. At this stage of the war, oil was of great strategic importance to the Allies and a German attack on the Persian oilfields was considered a strong possibility.

Anthony was therefore tasked with drawing up a scorched earth plan that would ensure the denial of the Persian oil facilities to the Axis powers in the face of the assumed German advance. Although the attack did not take place Anthony's oilfield denial plan won him both the MBE and a Mention in Despatches. From the Middle East he attended the Indian Army's Staff College at Quetta and then returned to England to take part in the liberation of Europe.

In March 1945, Anthony was in command of the 91st Field Company of the Royal Engineers. As part of the Second Army he took part in the assault crossing of the Rhine, and it was whilst he was directing the building of a bridge across the river that he was hit in the head by a shell splinter. As he was still conscious it was apparently hard to persuade him to be evacuated back to hospital.

THE LYMINGTON TIMES of 7th July 1945 reported that Acting Major A. E. L. Crosthwait had been severely wounded whilst

PHOTO NICK SAUNDERS

building a bridge over the river during the assault crossing of the Rhine and was still in hospital. Whilst in hospital in Oxford it seemed likely that he would recover. However, after more than two years hospitalisation, he died from the effects of the wound he had received

He is buried in **Oxford (Botley) Cemetery**, Oxfordshire, in:

Plot I/1. Grave 227.

In 1951 his mother presented the cross and candle sticks for the Memorial Chapel in St Mark's Church at Pennington in memory of Anthony.

THE SECOND WORLD WAR

THE FAR EAST

THE FAR EAST

The Far East was not to prove a happy posting for many Lymingtonians. Before the Japanese attacked our Far Eastern interests in Malaya, Singapore and Hong Kong, a number of local men were already serving in Singapore as part of the garrison. Such troops were reinforced in anticipation of a Japanese attack. When it came on 7th December 1941, down the Malay Peninsula, the attack was both rapid and ruthless. Allied troops tumbled back into Singapore in disarray and the "fortress" fell on 15th February 1942.

The Japanese then moved their sights towards India and the Indian Ocean. They attacked our maritime assets in Ceylon in April 1942 and in the course of this **Garfield Thomas** lost his life.

Of the POWs, **John Gunnell** was sent in a party to Kranji, where he died in September. By October more parties had left for upcountry. **George Hayter** and **Victor Jones** were sent to work on the railway, where they both died. **Ron Dimmick** died from malaria a year later whilst in transit for Java. **Spencer Cresswell** survived his captivity, but the experience contributed to his death in 1973.

THE SINGAPORE MEMORIAL PHOTO CHRIS ROGERS

Once the Japanese advance on India had been stopped in 1944 at Kohima, the war in the Far East turned in our favour. **Charles Young, Leslie Croucher** and **William Lewington** were all to die, however, before the Japanese surrendered in August 1945.

GARFIELD THOMAS

Air Mechanic 2nd Class, Royal Navy
FAA/FX. 86270
H.M.S. HERMES
who died on
Sunday 9th April 1942, aged 20.

Garfield was a son of Mrs A E Thomas of Pennington.

He joined the Royal Navy in 1941 and underwent an initial six-week basic training course at a Naval establishment. This comprised the usual routine of drilling, marching and learning to lash up a hammock with the correct seven turns of cordage. Garfield was then selected for training as an Air Mechanic and sent to RAF LOCKING for five months. At the end of this he passed out as an Air Mechanic 2nd Class and was sent to HERMES to help maintain its Swordfish aircraft.

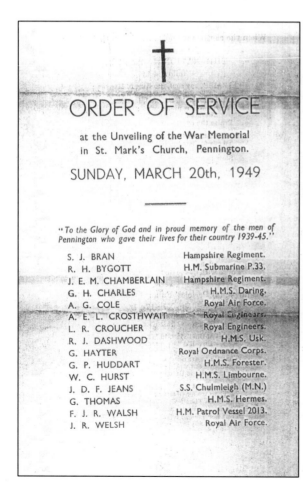

HERMES was launched in 1919 and was the world's first purpose built aircraft carrier. On 8th July 1940, her Swordfish aircraft attacked the Vichy French battleship *Richelieu* at Dakar and scored one torpedo hit. But she was unsuitable for operations in European waters as she only carried a small aircraft complement, had little anti-aircraft armament and limited high-speed endurance. The large starboard island also caused stability problems, so fuel had to be carefully distributed to balance the ship.

HERMES was consequently employed in trade protection in the South Atlantic and Indian Oceans where her Walrus aircraft of 710 Squadron could be of use.

Once Japan had consolidated her hold on the southwest Pacific she turned her attention to the Indian Ocean and at the end of March 1942 sent the Task group that had attacked Pearl Harbour against Ceylon. This they did on 5th April by targetting Columbo. The fleet had, however, left the port six days earlier. They then conducted raiding operations against our merchant shipping in the Indian Ocean.

On 9th April 1942, the Japanese launched another raid from their 1st Carrier Fleet, this time on Trincomalee, the main Royal Naval base, hoping to repeat their earlier Pearl Harbour success.

HERMES SINKING

Following normal procedure in the case of attack against a harbour Admiral Somerville ordered all ships to put to sea. The destroyer VAMPIRE, the corvette HOLLYHOCK, two tankers and HERMES – with no fighters embarked - headed southwards along the coast, but were sighted and all five ships sunk by eighty-five Japanese dive-bombers.

Garfield was one of the 700 men lost on the HERMES that day. His name is recorded on the **Lee-on-the-Solent Memorial** on:

Bay 3, Panel 6

JOHN JORDAN HENRY GUNNELL

Lance Corporal
1867067
Royal Engineers
who died on
Monday 14th September 1942, aged 31.

Jack was born on 31st January 1911 at 25, Dyer Road, Freemantle, Southampton. He was the elder son of John William Gunnell - a chef - and his wife, Edith Emily (nee Starks). His younger brother, George (known as "Jim") was born a year later. The family moved to Lymington when Jack was very young and three of his five sisters were born there. He attended the Council School, near to where the library is today.

Jack was a career soldier and joined the Royal Engineers as a boy soldier, probably in late 1925. Jim joined the Hampshires as a bugle boy in 1926, when he was virtually fifteen. The photograph above shows both brothers (Jack on right) with their mother. Edith died in 1932.

Jack married Mollie Towers in St Marks Church on 25th January, 1938. In the photograph Jack's sister, Nora, is the bridesmaid, Jim is best man and Mollie's father –who kept the Quay Stores on the quay at Lymington - is behind his daughter. Jack's widow and Nora, later kept the shop, until it was sold when they reached retirement age. Jack's niece, Rosemary Gunnell, (who has provided the photographs) is in the foreground.

Jack continued his career in the Royal Engineers and was posted to Singapore, probably to one of the Fortress Companies, in 1940. This photograph shows him in tropical rig in Singapore.

POSTALE

Adresse

N

How's this for Hiking.

among "The Gentlemen"

Jack became a prisoner when the Fortress surrendered. They were

initially all herded into Changi barracks, but the Japanese soon began to organise working parties. Jack was sent in one such party to Kranji, on Singapore Island. Here the prisoners were subjected to forced labour and insufficient food.

According to his Death Certificate, Jack died from dysentery whilst a Prisoner of War. He is buried in **Kranji War Cemetery**, Singapore, in:

PHOTO CHRIS ROGERS

Grave 10. C. 8

His name is also on the family grave in Lymington Cemetery.

GEORGE HAYTER

Private
7648481
Royal Army Ordnance Corps
who died on
Sunday 11th July 1943, aged 32.

George was the son of William and Nellie Hayter of *Sunnyside*, Ramley Road, Pennington. His wife, Phyllis, was a nurse at Lymington Hospital and lived with her in-laws. George was a well-known local sportsman, being the Hon Secretary of Pennington Football Club for 5 years and a popular member of Walhampton Cricket Club. He also belonged to the Lymington Brotherhood.

When Singapore fell in February 1942 George was reported as "missing." The family were not to know, until May 1943, that he was a Prisoner of War.

George was sent to work on the notorious Burma-Siam railway, built by Commonwealth, Dutch and American prisoners of war, to supply the large Japanese army in Burma. George worked on the Burma end of the railway from Bangkok to Nieke and was one of the approximately 13,000 prisoners of war who died during its construction. The line, 424 kilometres long, was completed by December 1943.

Before this George had died and been buried in a camp burial ground by the railway. His body was recovered after the war and reburied in **Kanchanaburi War Cemetery**, Thailand, in:

Grave 6. B. 44.

VICTOR HAROLD JONES

Sapper
5496607
Royal Engineers
who died on
Friday 2nd November 1943, aged 29.

Victor was a son of Mr and Mrs George Chaffey Jones. At the beginning of the war he married Ivy Jones and lived at Moorlands, Dudley Road, Hordle.

Victor was posted to 41 Fortress Company, one of the four Fortress Companies in Singapore. These static companies were tasked with building coastal and harbour defences. Nothing was done, however, to improve the defences on the northern side of the island of Singapore until after the Japanese had invaded Malaya. Just before capture, the Fortress Squadrons were used to repair bomb damage to essential services as well to fight the invaders.

Victor was captured when Singapore surrendered and was transported to Thailand for work on the Burma/Thailand railway. According to his Japanese Card he died in 1943. His death certificate confirms this and records that he died of avitaminosis - the result of prolonged malnutrition.

PHOTO CWGC

He is buried in **Chungkai War Cemetery**, Thailand, in:

Grave 6. K. 7.

DOUGLAS RONALD JOHN ELTON DIMMICK

Leading Aircraftman
Royal Air Force Volunteer Reserve
who died on
Saturday 4th November 1944, aged 27.

Ron was the only son of Mrs Dimmick, who ran the Newsagents in the High Street in Lymington. There was also a daughter, Doris. Before the war Ron worked at Messrs W. and R. Fletcher Ltd, in Lymington. He was a member of the 9th Rover Sea Scouts and was a popular local dance band drummer.

Ron joined the RAFVR at the beginning of 1940 and was stationed at RAF BOSCOMBE DOWN, in Wiltshire, before leaving for the Far East at the end of 1941. He was one of the airmen captured in Java on 8th March 1942, who were then transported to the Mollucan islands of Haruku and Ambon.

At the end of 1943, his mother received two cards from Ron in Java, stating he was well. She actually learnt of his death from the only survivor of six young RAF men who were hutted together in a Japanese Prisoner of War camp.

In a letter to Mrs Dimmick, LAC Yates said that Ron, known as "Jock" to his POW friends, had died from malaria whilst in transit returning to Java from the Moluccas on the dreadful *Maros Maru*. LAC Yates had been present at Ron's burial at sea in the South Celebes. He later visited Ron's mother and told her how her son and four other Hampshire men - three from Southampton and one from Andover - had spent their time in captivity. All of them, except for Yates, had died from the effects of malaria.

PHOTO CHRIS ROGERS

Ron Dimmick's name is recorded on the **Singapore Memorial,**

Column 438

376

SPENCER JACK CRESSWELL

Lance/Sergeant
Royal Artillery
who died on
8ᵗʰ January 1973, aged 65.

Jack was born on 23ʳᵈ December 1907 in Campbellpore, India the only son of Mr and Mrs W J Cresswell - His father, John, a Boer War veteran, being Sergeant Farrier to the 69ᵗʰ Battery RFA there. John finally retired from the Royal Artillery as a Warrant Officer after twenty-seven years service. He then became the steward of the National Reserve Club in Bournemouth for thirteen years before moving to take on the Dorset Arms Hotel, Lymington.

After leaving school Jack worked for seventeen years in the stereo department of the **Bournemouth Daily Echo.** On 27ᵗʰ May 1931 he married Ida Lavinia Bryant in Bournemouth. In 1935 their daughter, Margaret, was born, followed in 1939 by son John. The family lived at 1, Newcombe Road, Southbourne.

Shortly before the war Jack joined the Hampshire Territorial and served in Malta, India and Malaya. In the 14ᵗʰ April 1942 edition of the LYMINGTON TIMES he is reported as being amongst those missing in the surrender of Singapore. He was captured there on 15ᵗʰ February 1942 and transported to Japan. Jack survived this experience and was released on the Japanese island of Kyushu, returning to England to resume his printing job. He died in 1973 in the Queen Mary Hospital, Roehampton, London. His prison camp experiences would not have helped his body resist the long-term effects attributed to hepatitis – to which he would have been exposed and susceptible as a Prisoner of War in the Far East.

It is not known where he is buried.

CHARLES EDWARD YOUNG

Private
14511051
West Yorkshire Regiment (Prince of Wales's Own)
who died on
Monday 28th February 1944, aged 22.

Charles was the eldest son of Charles and Edith Maud Young of 67, Flushards Estate, Lymington. His father, also named Charles, served with the old Lymington Fire Brigade which - during the war - became the National Fire Service. A second son, Sapper W. E. A. Young, joined the Pioneer Corps and was wounded in October 1943. He then transferred to the Royal Engineers and in February 1944 was serving in Italy, aged 19.

Charles worked for a Lymington firm before joining the army in January 1943. A year later he was with the 2nd Battalion, the West Yorkshire Regiment, part of the 14th Army, serving on the Arakan Front in Burma.

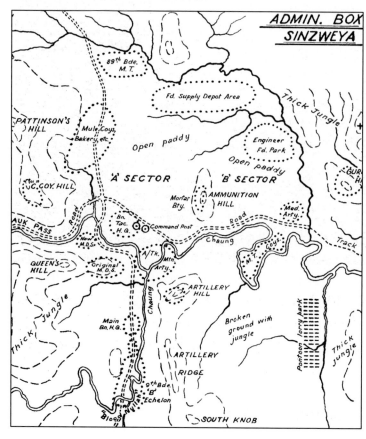

In January 1944 the battalion captured Maungdaw. This cost the battalion 136 casualties.

By the beginning of February Charles' unit had been switched to defend the Admin Box at Sinzweya, northwest of Maungdaw.

The Box consisted of 8000 admin troops, with very few other fighting units.

The Japanese attacked the Box on the night of 7th/8th February including the Medical dressing Station, killing doctors, orderlies and patients. The Japanese continued to attack for the next two weeks, culminating on 21st/22nd February with an assault on the "Blood Nullah" area, which was decisively repulsed. The Box was relieved the following day. Whilst this defeat meant that the Battle for the Arakan had been won with the deaths of 4,500 Japanese, it had also cost the West Yorkshires a further 142 battle casualties.

Charles' battalion then switched from defence to offensive patrolling, with the aim of pushing the enemy back from the area. In a brush with the enemy on Sunday 27th February Charles received severe machine-gun wounds and died the following day. His parents learnt of his death in a letter from his Commanding Officer, which described their son as

"A brave and determined soldier."

TAUKKYAN WAR CEMETERY   PHOTO CWGC

He was buried with military honours at the foot of a hill east of the Mayu Range. After the war his grave could not be properly maintained, so his body was reburied in **Taukkyan War Cemetery**, Myanmar, in:

Grave 11. G. 6.

379

LESLIE ROY CROUCHER

Corporal
2158427
Royal Engineers
who died on
Monday 30th October 1944, aged 23.

Roy was born in 1921, the third son of Herbert and Lydia Croucher of Burton, Christchurch, Hampshire. Five sons were in the armed forces during the war. Before the war Roy worked for a Lymington firm. In 1940, he married Marjorie Shepherd, of Pennington, who was employed as a conductress on the Hants and Dorset buses based at Lymington Depot. She also worked as an usherette at the Lyric Cinema. In 1943 a son, Anthony Leslie Croucher, was born. Marjorie later lived at Highfield.

Roy joined the army in 1941and went to India in March 1944. He died eight months later. In a letter of sympathy to his widow Roy's Commanding Officer wrote:

"He was much admired and respected by all of us and he was a fine type of Englishman of whom you must have been very proud. He did his duty with a competence which was good to see and I was sure he had a successful future career in front of him. But disease struck him down – appendicitis and malaria – though he appeared to be pulling round when some of us saw him only a few hours before the end. The shock to us in consequence was all the greater. It may be some consolation to you to know that he had the finest medical and nursing attention this area can provide. All ranks in this unit send you their deepest sympathy in your sad bereavement."

Roy was buried with full military honours in **Kohima War Cemetery**, India, in

Grave 6. C. 3.

WILLIAM CLIVE LEWINGTON

Flying Officer
Royal Air Force Volunteer Reserve
who died on
Tuesday 12ᵗʰ June 1945, aged 20.

"**Curly,**" as he was called, was the elder son of Albert and Nellie Lewington, of Sidney Villa, Brook Road, Lymington. He went to the Church of England School and was one of the most popular members of the Lymington Sea Scouts. After leaving school at the age of 14 years he went to work in

the Buying Office at Wellworthy in Lymington. Being a talented artist he drew the Springbok sketch, above, for one of the Wellworthy Simplex Piston Ring advertisements.

In 1943 his younger brother Jeffery, aged 16, enlisted in the Royal Navy as a Boy and trained at St Georges in the Isle of Man as a telegraphist.

Curly was also one of the original members of the Lymington Air Training Corps, in which he became a Flight Sergeant. He volunteered for the RAF in 1943 and went to Canada for training. He passed out from the course as a bomb-aimer and was commissioned in August 1944, a month in which (on the 15ᵗʰ) he also celebrated his twentieth birthday.

One of his letters from Canada patriotically retails:

> There is a good
> time in the mess this evening. a
> Yank was getting a strip torn off
> by the briefing officer for bombing
> too low, and was told to fly at 30,000ft.
> Yank. "What happens if I bomb at 25000
> Officer" "You'll get the such & such medal"
> Yank "And what if I bomb at 20,000"
> Off. "You'll get such & such medal
> Yank "And what about 15000
> Officer" again giving medals to be won
>   until the Yank says" and
> what if I bomb at 5,000ft."
> Officer. "Dont be a damn fool, you
> bump into the RAF at that height".

Curly returned from Canada in February 1945 and, a month later, was on his way to the Far East. Here he joined 358 Squadron - a bomber unit which had retrained for a special duties role which involved dropping agents and supplies behind Japanese lines. In June 1945 alone, it flew 49 sorties, dropping 18 agents, 276 containers and 204 packages at various locations in Burma, Siam, French Indo-China and Malaya. In this period three aircraft crashed or were listed as missing. Part of a letter, dated 10th May 1945, reads:

> I'm just about getting used to
> this mysterious (and smelly) East. its
> not too bad when you get acclimatized
> the creepy things come part and parcel
> of every day life, the sun is a bit
> trying at times, but that is easily got
> over by staying out of it as much
> as poss and wearing a shady hat(see note)
> I know they look a bit dippy
> but all the same they serve their
> purpose well.   The natives are a queer

382

In May, Curly's aircraft is logged as being on a training flight.

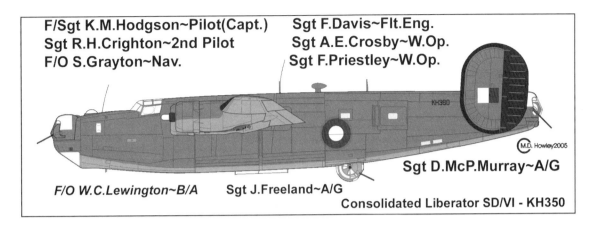

F/Sgt K.M.Hodgson~Pilot(Capt.)
Sgt R.H.Crighton~2nd Pilot
F/O S.Grayton~Nav.

Sgt F.Davis~Flt.Eng.
Sgt A.E.Crosby~W.Op.
Sgt F.Priestley~W.Op.

Sgt D.McP.Murray~A/G

F/O W.C.Lewington~B/A   Sgt J.Freeland~A/G

Consolidated Liberator SD/VI - KH350

On 12th June 1945, his Liberator, SD/VI took off at 0205 hours from RAF JESSORE on the crew's first operation. One and a half minutes later it crashed into paddy fields 3 miles North West of the runway, killing all the crew. Curiously, Curly's uncle, George Lewington (see page 156) died shortly before the end of the First World War, aged 20.

They were all buried in the European Cemetery, Jessore, that

evening, the service being taken by a padre who had flown from HQ 231 to officiate. The bodies were later reburied in **Chittagong War Cemetery**, Bangladesh. Curly is buried in:

Grave 3. C. 11.

His young sister, Gwynneth, has kindly provided much of the information in this article. She also writes

> *"I have no relatives living in Lymington now, but friends tell me that there is always a little cross planted in the Garden of Remembrance with his name on it each Armistice day. Who puts it there is not known, but I thank them for doing so."*

Qwen has now discovered that Peggy James has been planting the cross each year and the two ladies have discovered a new friendship.

LATER CONFLICTS

BOSNIA 1997

MISSING

INDEX OF NAMES

BOSNIA 1997

Since the Second World War there has only been one year when a member of the Armed Forces has not been killed on active service.

Bosnia. A bloody war had raged in Bosnia since 1992, but by 1995 the Bosnian Serb superiority in the conflict was under threat. The balance of power was shifting in favour of the Croatian and Muslim forces. This placed the Serbs under pressure to consolidate their gains in eastern Bosnia, where Gorazde lies, and to seek an end to the war. Meanwhile, however, the US Clinton administration, NATO, the UN, and the EU in Brussels, not to mention the various European governments, were struggling to rein in the Serb President Milosevich, and the Bosnian Serb leader, Radovan Karadjic.

In 1994, John Major's government and Whitehall defence chiefs sent hundreds of British peacekeepers to the UN-declared 'safe area' of Gorazde. The UN had established six of these areas in Bosnia in 1993, but the Security Council resolutions 819, 824 and 836, which governed them, were ambiguous. The peacekeepers were to 'deter' attacks on the town (the UN avoided the more explicit terms 'defend' or 'protect') and the use of force was authorised but linked to 'self-defence'. British officers and their troops had to translate this unclear language into decisive action on the ground, in the face of Serb hostilities, their front line just 3km outside Gorazde.

As it happened the outcome at Gorazde was a relative success story. In contrast to the terrible fate that befell Srebrenica and Zepa, the other Bosnian 'safe areas', the Bosnian army ultimately held the town. And crucially, Gorazde proved a turning point from the point of view of UN peacekeeping: it provides a rare and generally neglected example of effective, robust peacekeeping.

Sadly **_Stuart Wilson_** was to lose his life whilst serving in this peacekeeping operation at Kupres in Northern Bosnia.

STUART BRIAN WILSON

Driver
25036951
Royal Logistics Corps
who died on
Monday 7th July 1997, aged 20.

Stuart was born on 9th July 1976 at Boscombe to Ian Wilson and his wife, Sally Anne. The Wilsons were living at New Milton at the time and Ian was to join the Royal Engineers in 1982 as a combat Sapper, following the family tradition of service in the army.

Stuart went to school at the Lymington Catholic Junior School, progressing to Priestlands and finished his education at Brockenhurst College. His oldest brother, Ian, had tried for the Royal Navy, but was let down by his hearing. An older brother, Bob, was already in the Royal Corps of Transport and another brother, James, joined the Royal Marines.

Stuart was an active young man with many interests. At various times he was in the Scouts, St John Ambulance, Army Cadet Corps, New Milton Rugby Club, and enjoyed weight training and sailing. This photograph was taken when he was helping to sail the regimental yacht from Cyprus to Split in 1997.

As an adventurous young man and with his family background it was natural for him to join the army. He therefore joined the Royal Logistical Corps, doing his basic training at Pirbright and his driver training at Leaconfield, in Yorkshire. His father nicknamed him "Diesel" at this time, as he was adept in acquiring anything in short supply.

Stuart was then posted to Dalton Barracks at Abingdon in Oxfordshire and took part in exercises in Gibraltar, Canada, Germany and Greenland.

His first operational tour was to Bosnia in April 1997. His squadron, heavily reinforced with reservists, was based at Kupres in Northern Bosnia, and tasked with delivering fuel, food and other supplies to the Household Cavalry, Engineers and other British units in the area. He died two days before his twenty-first birthday, when he was driving a 40-ton fuel tanker to Sanskimois. On a mountain route he was approached by a minibus. Stuart swerved to avoid it. According to his father, a heavy transport controller, the gearbox blew off the tanker and Stuart drove off the road to avoid hitting the civilian vehicle. Both Stuart and his co-driver, Marc Symonds – a nineteen year old from Colesford in Gloucestershire – were killed in the accident.

The local Bosnians created a shrine at the scene of the incident and still lay flowers there, in recognition of Stuarts sacrifice to save others. His name is recorded on a memorial in the Peace Park in Serajevo, to those who died – and continue to die - in Bosnia.

Stuart was buried with full military honours at **St John's Church, Boldre,** on 16th July 1997.

MISSING

Of the 158 names on the memorial we have been unable to establish beyond doubt the identity of four men as their Lymington or military connections have not been confirmed.

HENRY JACK LEONARD
Kings Own Yorkshire Light Infantry

Of the One Hundred and ninety-six **Leonards** who were killed in the First War, none have any recorded connection of birth, residence or enlistment with Lymington. The three Leonards in the KOYLI (Frederick, George and Richard) have clear connections in the north of England.

On 13th March 1912 William Ronald Leonard was born. His father, Robert, was a fish salesman and his mother, Beatrice (nee Yeatman), lived at the Solent Inn. The following year a daughter, Ivy Leonard, was born. George William Leonard, a milkman journeyman, lived in Arnewood Row, Hordle – dying there in 1921 aged thirty-four. Despite these leads no trace of Herbert Jack has been found.

We researched intensively **Henry Francis Dujardin Leonard**, of the Kings Liverpool Regiment, who was wounded at Cambrai and died on 25th November 1917, aged thirty-nine. But no connection with Lymington could be established.

R KITCHENER

Of the twelve **Kitcheners** who died in the Second World War, none have recorded local connections.

Of the four men with an initial of "**R**" only one is from Hampshire. **Reginald James Kitchener** went down with HOOD when she sank. His brother has affirmed, however, that he came from Alton and had no connection with Lymington.

R MARSHALL

Five hundred and eighty-five **Marshalls** died in World War 2, of whom fifty-three had "**R**" in their initials. None of these, however, have a recorded connection with Lymington.

An RG Marshall was "not out 8," when playing for Lymington Cricket team in 1935. Norman Gannaway believes that a Dick Marshall may well have been a Prisoner of War, but nothing further has been discovered in this matter.

K RENYARD

Renyard is a strong local name, so it is not surprising that of the four Renyards who died in the Second World War three had links with Portsmouth, Southampton or Eastleigh.

None, however, possessed an initial "**K**."

 The most local was Petty Officer **Arthur Renyard**, son of Mr and Mrs Renyard of Blackfield, Fawley. He was top boy at Fareham Senior School and left to join the Royal Navy as soon as he could. In August 1941 he married Doris, of Eastleigh, but was soon drafted to the Mediterranean. When he died on 7th January 1943 he was part of the crew of HM Trawler JURA operating in support of the North African campaign. He was 23 years old.

There is, however, no proof that Arthur is our man, but it is possible that his widow may have moved to Lymington.

"And some there be, which have no memorial,
Who are perished,
as though they had never been,"

Ecclesiasticus Chapter 44 Verse 9.

INDEX OF NAMES

Names recorded are to be seen on the War Memorial. Personal photographs are shown in **bold**.